# THE COMPLETE BOOK OF HOME INSPECTION

## FOR THE BUYER OR OWNER

# Norman Becker, P.E.

McGRAW-HILL BOOK COMPANY

New York  St. Louis  San Francisco  Auckland  Bogotá  Düsseldorf
Johannesburg  London  Madrid  Mexico  Montreal  New Delhi
Panama  Paris  São Paulo  Singapore  Sydney  Tokyo  Toronto

**ACKNOWLEDGMENTS**

I would like to thank the staff of Universal Home Inspection for their helpful suggestions and comments. In particular, a special thanks is due Herbert P. Klaus, P.E., for reviewing the manuscript and for his overall help and support in bringing this book to a timely finish.

For Renée, Jeffrey, Piper, and Ginger

Copyright © 1980 by McGraw-Hill, Inc.

3 4 5 6 7 8 9 S M S M 8 7 6 5 4 3

LIBRARY OF CONGRESS CATALOGING IN
PUBLICATION DATA

Becker, Norman.
   The complete book of home inspection.
   Includes index.
   1. Dwellings—Inspection.    I.  Title.
TH4817.5.B43      643      79-23444
ISBN 0-07-004180-6

Book design by Marsha Picker.

# CONTENTS

# 1. INSPECTING THE HOUSE—WHY AND HOW

No house is perfect, even a brand-new one. I've inspected thousands of homes and have yet to see one in flawless condition. This doesn't mean that you won't find the house of your dreams. It does mean that when you find a house that's just what you want, you should go one step further and find out what problems or potential problems exist in it. Problems can be the result of deficiencies in construction, deterioration due to aging, or safety and fire hazards. Very often the problems are quite minor and can be corrected at little or no cost. However, at times there are major problems that are quite costly to correct. It's very important to know the house's true condition so that you can determine the true cost of buying it. Don't walk away from a house just because there are major problems—you may be getting a good buy, since every house has its market value. The true cost of buying a house is its purchase price plus the costs for upgrading substandard, deteriorated, or malfunctioning components.

The chart in Figure 1-1 illustrates various types of problems that have been found in homes and their probability of occurrence. It is based on a survey of the homes that I have personally inspected. The types of problems encountered for each category are defined in the chapters that follow and are summarized at the end of each chapter.

The purpose of this book is to provide you with the know-how with which you can inspect the house that you are interested in buying and determine its true condition. If you are already living in a house, the book will also be helpful to you. The condition of the various components of your home has been changing with age. Knowing the true condition will enable you to repair or correct minor problems before they become major ones.

The inspection procedure outlined in this book is similar to the one that I use when inspecting residential structures. Because the various components of homes are basically the same, this procedure is valid regardless of the geographic location of the structure. It has been used on homes of all ages, from newly constructed to pre-Revolutionary, from vacation homes to stately mansions.

Usually when people decide to buy a home, the decision is based on a superficial inspection of the house. They are "walked through" the house by a

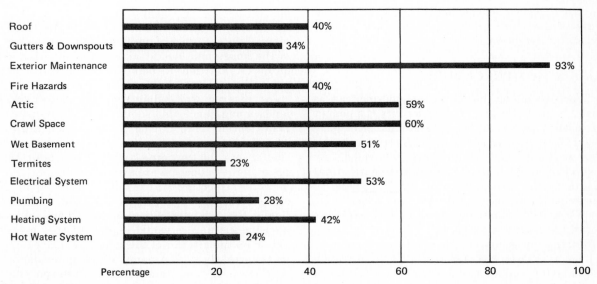

FIGURE 1-1   Percentage of homes inspected that have the above-listed problems.

salesperson or owner who points out the number of bathrooms and tells them how lovely the flowering shrubs are in the spring. This provides the buyer with enough information to make an emotional decision that can, in the long run, be quite costly. The emotional decision may be correct; however, it should be based on an understanding of the true condition of the house and not on its cosmetic condition. By following the procedures in this book, you will get a different perspective of your house.

## TOOLS NEEDED

In order to properly inspect the house, you will need the following tools: a flashlight to see in dark places (and you'll be surprised what you may find); a magnet to determine whether or not there are iron plumbing pipes; a marble to note if the floors are relatively level; an ice pick or screwdriver to aid in looking for wood rot and termite infestation; a six-foot step ladder for those houses that do not provide direct access (built-in or pull-down steps) to the attic; an electrical tester for checking the electrical ground connection, particularly in the kitchen and bathroom outlet receptacles; a pair of binoculars to get a closer look at the roof and roof-mounted structures; and finally, a compass to determine the building's exposure. Knowledge of the exposure is helpful in evaluating the condition of various structural elements and components of the house.

When performing the inspection, you should wear old clothes. Such areas as unfinished attics, basements, and crawl spaces are often quite dusty. The last items you will need for inspection are a pencil and inspection worksheets. The worksheets are provided in the back of this book and should be completed as you perform the inspection. Later, you can use these worksheets to evaluate the true condition of the house and base your decision on facts rather than emotion.

## INSPECTION PROCEDURE

A house, no matter how large or imposing, can be easily inspected if it is divided into its component parts, such as the exterior, interior, and electromechanical systems. In addition, the exterior and interior portions can be further subdivided. By approaching the inspection in a systematic order and using the worksheets provided as a guide, all the items of any consequence will be checked.

When driving up to the house, take a moment to notice the overall topography or shape of the land. Often, the topography in the immediate vicinity of the house is level; however, the overall topography might be inclined. Consequently, there is the possi-bility of subsurface water movement in the direction of the house. When you see inclined topography in the general area of the house, you should be alerted to the possibility of some degree of water seepage into the lower level of the structure.

The exterior of the building should be inspected before the interior. This is important because it provides you with an overall view of the structure that, in turn, can reveal the cause for some interior problems. Specifically, water seepage into a lower level can be the result of faulty gutters or downspouts, or improper grading (when the ground immediately adjacent to the house slopes toward the house rather than away). A faulty roof can manifest itself in the form of water stains one or two levels below the roof. Cracked and open exterior joints can allow the entry of water, which will be noted as cosmetic damage to interior portions of the structure.

## EXTERIOR INSPECTION

Before you actually start the exterior inspection, stand in front of the house and take a compass reading. The exposure for all four sides of the building should be marked on the worksheet (i.e., Front exposure—Southerly; Right exposure—Easterly, etc.). The exterior inspection is performed while walking around the house twice. The first time you walk around the house, you should look at the roof, gutters, chimney, vent stack, and anything else that is roof-mounted. The details of what to look for and how to inspect the various components of the house are discussed in the chapters that follow. During this first pass around the house, use binoculars so that you can get a closer view of the items on the upper portion of the structure. After the first pass, the condition of those items inspected should be noted on the worksheet.

During the second pass, you will be looking for many different types of problems. Start at the front of the house and look at all of the items that are either on the front of the structure or in the front yard. Examples of these items are paths, entry steps, exterior wall siding, windows, doors, decks, landscaping, fence, and so on. All of the items normally encountered during an inspection are discussed in detail in the following chapters. You should only be concerned with those items that apply to the house you are inspecting.

After inspecting the front of the house, apply the same technique to the left side, the rear, and, finally, the right side of the building. If any items of a suspicious nature would require further investigation on the interior of the structure, make a note on the worksheet as a reminder. As an example, if an elbow is missing from one of the downspouts and there is no splash plate on the ground to deflect the effluent from the downspout away from the building, you should suspect and check for water seepage from that area into the lower level of the structure. By noting this fact on your worksheet, it will help you to remember to check the interior wall opposite the downspout for signs of water seepage.

After going around the building the second time, you should be finished with the exterior inspection. Double check your worksheet to see if you've recorded the condition of all of the items inspected. At this point, you should inspect the garage. After the garage inspection, you are ready for the inside of the house.

## INTERIOR INSPECTION

Enter the house through the front door. Try the doorbell to make sure it is operational. It's important to remember that you are looking at a house that you are interested in buying. If all goes well, this will be your home; so don't be shy or feel embarrassed about doing things that any homeowner would do. As part of the inspection, you should open and close faucets on sinks, tubs, and shower; flush toilets; open and shut doors and windows; turn on the heating system and/or air-conditioning system by means of the thermostats; feel the air flow from heat/cooling registers; see if radiators get warm; and turn on and shut off switches controlling lights and fans.

Start the interior inspection at the uppermost portion of the building. If there is an attic, that's where you start. To inspect the attic, you may need your ladder to get up into it—check with the owner. Some homes don't have an attic, so begin this portion of the inspection with the rooms directly below the roof.

After the attic inspection, check all of the rooms on the level directly below. In some large homes you can easily miss a room. To avoid overlooking any rooms or items, begin your inspection at the entry to that level. If you start at the entry and walk either clockwise or counterclockwise looking at each room in order, you will return to your starting point and will have inspected all of the rooms. However, if you jump around from one side to another, you could easily overlook a room or two. Again, there is no substitute for good procedure.

After all of the rooms on one level have been checked, proceed to the next lower level, inspecting the connecting staircase along the way. Check all of the rooms on this level in the same manner. After all of the finished rooms have been checked, inspect any unfinished areas such as the basement and/or crawl space. This is the end of the interior inspec-

tion. At this point, all of the rooms, halls, and staircases throughout the house have been checked. In order to complete the home inspection, you must now check the electromechanical systems.

## ELECTROMECHANICAL SYSTEMS

The systems and associated equipment included in this category are electrical, plumbing, domestic water heater, heating and air conditioning. The condition, operation, and adequacy of each system that applies to your house must be checked as described in its respective chapter and recorded on the worksheet.

This will conclude your home inspection. You have now looked at every item in the house of any consequence and should have recorded on the worksheets all problems and deficiencies. Some of the problems you uncover might require the services of a professional for further investigation. All situations requiring the services of a professional are indicated in the chapters that follow.

Look at your worksheets and try to evaluate the major problems. Do *not* expect a perfect house. There will always be minor problems, and the costs for correcting these problems should not be of any concern. However, if there are many minor problems, the costs for correction can be significant.

Of main concern, from a cost point of view, are major problems some of which are defined as follows:

1. The need for structural rehabilitation to the foundation
2. The need for re-siding the exterior walls
3. Water penetration into the basement or lower level
4. A malfunctioning or obsolete heating system
5. The need for repiping the plumbing system
6. The need for a new roof
7. A malfunctioning air-conditioning system
8. Inadequate electrical service
9. Termite infestation
10. The need for complete rehabilitation to
    a. paved areas
    b. deck
    c. detached garage
    d. retaining walls

If you found a major problem, have a contractor look at it and give you a written estimate on the cost for correction. At this point, you should be able to determine the true cost of buying the house—the purchase price plus the costs for upgrading substandard, deteriorated, or malfunctioning components.

## FINAL INSPECTION

On the day of, but prior to, the contract closing, you should take one final walk through the house and look at the walls, windows, doors, and plumbing fixtures for cracked and broken sections. Sometimes damage occurs when the seller's furniture is being moved out or through vandalism when the house is left vacant for a period of time. Specifically look for physical changes that occurred between the time of the contract signing and the closing.

During your "walk-through," check the operation of the electrical, plumbing, and heating systems. The central air-conditioning system should also be checked if the weather permits. In addition, check the operation of all of the appliances that are considered part of the purchase. If there are any appliances or electromechanical systems that are malfunctioning, list them on a sheet of paper along with any items that were badly damaged since the contract signing. This list should be taken to the closing and discussed with the seller. Very often, dollar adjustments are made to compensate for the cost of repair.

**E**very roof has two basic elements—the deck and the weather-resistant covering. The deck (also called "roof sheathing") serves as a base for supporting the roof covering that, in turn, protects the structure from the weather. A proper roof inspection includes an evaluation of both the roof covering and the deck. Even though a roof covering may be in good condition, it is possible that the deck underneath may be soft and spongy and structurally unsound. This condition can be caused by rot and/or delamination and would not necessarily be noticeable from an exterior inspection.

## PITCHED ROOFS

The technique used for inspecting the roof will differ depending on whether the roof is pitched or flat. Pitched roofs are checked during your initial pass around the house. Because of the hazards involved, it is normally not recommended that you climb onto a pitched roof. Begin your inspection by stepping far enough away from the house so that you are able to see all exposed sections of the roof as you circle the structure. The use of binoculars is recommended for this inspection so that you are able to get a close-up view of the roof.

As you walk around the structure looking at the roof, make note of any uneven, sagging, or damaged sections. Unevenness in the roof may be the result of warped sections of roof deck or, possibly, a less-than-quality installation of a second layer of shingles. This is usually not a problem condition. However, shingles in uneven areas are more vulnerable to damage and water intrusion. Make a note on your worksheet of the approximate location(s) of the uneven area(s). During the attic inspection, these areas should be checked for signs of leakage and to verify the cause of the unevenness.

Sagging sections in the roof, on the other hand, may be symptomatic of an existing structural problem or may reflect a past problem that has been corrected. A sagging ridge beam or roof deck could indicate a structural failure, inadequate bracing and/or spacing of wood-frame support members. The possibility also exists that the condition causing the sagging has stabilized, so that no further corrective action is necessary. If you see a sagging ridge beam or sagging section of the roof deck during your first pass around the house, have this condition evaluated by a professional.

Damaged sections of the roof can occur from falling tree limbs or, possibly, from swaying tree branches that overhang the roof. If you see a damaged section, record its location on your worksheet, as it must be repaired. Usually, patching the damaged area is all that is required.

Ventilation of the area directly below the roof deck is very important, especially in newer buildings where the roof deck is constructed of plywood sheets rather than of tongue-and-groove boards. If the area is inadequately ventilated, a moisture buildup could occur that would eventually cause the plywood sheathing to delaminate. This moisture problem is particularly acute in those homes that have cathedral ceilings constructed in the following manner: The ceiling is gypsum board or an equivalent type of panel and is nailed directly to the roof rafters. Above the ceiling is insulation and above this is the roof deck. Often, there is a small air space between the insulation and the roof deck. When the moisture that is normally generated in the house due to cooking, bathing, and so on reaches the area of the roof deck, there must be vent openings through which it can escape. Otherwise, rot and/or delamination may occur. A high percentage of the homes built with this type of cathedral ceiling have inadequately ventilated roof structures. Vent openings are needed near the top of each channel that is formed by the roof rafters and the ceiling and are also needed around the soffit. Often, only the soffit vents are installed. Vent openings for the top portion of the rafter channel can be provided either through individual roof vents or a ridge vent. (See Figure 2-1.) When the cathedral ceiling is the exposed roof deck planks or panels, there is usually a rigid insulation on the top side between the roof deck and covering. This type of construction will not result in a roof deck having a problem with moisture accumulation and, therefore, venting is not necessary.

FIGURE 2-1  Ridge vent. Note the ridge vent along the top of the roof. This low-profile ventilator will help circulate air through the area below the roof deck.

If your house has the type of cathedral ceiling with no vent openings near the ridge, then problems with the roof deck should be anticipated. You can tell if you have an existing deck problem by walking on the roof. If sections of the roof deck yield with each step and feel soft and spongy beneath your feet, there are problems. Note that you should not attempt to walk on the roof if the pitch is steep or if the shingles are of a type that can easily be damaged, such as tile or slate. Also, if the roof is not readily accessible from a deck or an intermediate level area, then it is best to leave this part of the inspection to a professional. Even if the roof deck shows no signs of a problem, if the area is not adequately ventilated near the top of the roof, then the installation of a ridge vent should be considered to prevent future problems.

### Shingles

Pitched roofs are usually covered with shingles that are applied in an overlapping fashion. The shingles are not intended to be watertight; rather they protect the structure from rain intrusion by shedding water. The more common types of shingles are made of asphaltic material, wood, asbestos-cement, slate, and clay tiles. When inspecting the roof, pay particular attention to a slope that has a southerly or southwesterly exposure. These slopes receive a maximum amount of sun exposure, and it is the sun's rays that cause the shingles to become brittle and age prematurely. Consequently, the shingles on these exposures will deteriorate more rapidly than the shingles on the other exposures. (See Figure 2-2.)

Since shingles are intended to shed water rather than be watertight, any water that gets under them

will leak into the interior of the structure. Shingles that are lifting, cracked, or broken are vulnerable to this type of water leakage. If you see this problem with the shingles, it is an indication that some maintenance is needed. In areas where the winter temperature drops below freezing, roof leakage may also occur as a result of an ice dam. Because of heat loss through the roof and heat from the sun, snow on a roof may start melting, even in freezing weather. As the water reaches the roof overhang, it often refreezes, forming an ice dam and blocking the melting snow from draining. As the snow continues to melt, the water backs up under the shingles and leaks into the interior. (See Figure 2-3.)

Water leakage from this type of problem is not an indication of a faulty roof and should not be interpreted that roof repairs are necessary. It is an indication, however, that adequate precautionary measures were not taken during the installation of the roof covering to eliminate or minimize the effects of the ice dam. The condition could have been avoided by the installation of eaves flashing. On existing roofs, the condition can be avoided by installing de-icing cables along the edge of the roof and in the gutters and downspouts.

When looking at a roof after all the snow has melted off, you would never know whether there had been an ice dam and water leakage. Sometimes, however, there are indications of a past problem, as noted by stained or warped sections of soffit trim or by water stains on the ceiling of the rooms below the roof near the exterior walls. I have seen water stains on the ceiling of rooms two levels below the roof that were the result of water leakage because of an ice dam. Ice dam problems will not necessarily

FIGURE 2-2  The orientation of the house can affect the projected life of the roof shingles. The deteriorated shingles on the right slope have a southerly exposure, whereas the shingles on the left slope have a northerly exposure.

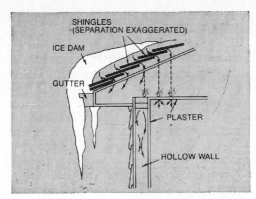

FIGURE 2-3 Ice dam at roof eave. Because of the ice dam, water from melting snow backs up under the shingles and leaks into the house.

occur every year; they depend on the severity of winter weather conditions.

Portions of the roof that are particularly vulnerable to leakage are the joints between the roof and roof-mounted structures such as the chimney, the joint between the roof and a vertical sidewall, and the joint where two sloping sections of the roof intersect. The latter joint is commonly referred to as a "valley." In order to protect the joints from water intrusion, they are normally covered with strips of a thin, impervious material called "flashing." Sheetmetal is usually used as a flashing material, with copper flashing as the top of the line; however, roll roofing strips are also used. Valley or sidewall flashing may or may not be visible depending on the type of joint construction.

When inspecting the roof, check the condition of the exposed flashing at the various joints. Loose, cracked, and deteriorated sections must be repaired. If there is leakage through any of these joints, it will usually be noted by water stains on the wood-framing or roof sheathing in the attic or by stains in the ceiling of the interior room(s) below the roof. Faulty joints are often resealed with an asphaltic cement rather than reflashed. The cement, however, is not as durable a seal as sheetmetal flashing and the joint will often require periodic resealing.

### Asphalt Shingles

The most common type of roof shingle used in this country is asphalt shingle. This shingle is made by impregnating mats of either an organic felt material or fiberglass with asphalt and covering one surface with mineral granules. The mat is the vehicle for supporting the asphalt, which is a water-resistant material. The granules protect the shingle from damaging sun rays and also provide color. When inspecting asphalt shingles, look for loss of granules, missing, and torn sections with erosion of

the mat. (See Figure 2-4.) A particularly vulnerable location on the shingles for leakage is the area between the shingle tabs. The granules in this area tend to come loose before those in other sections, thus exposing the mat to the weather. Although most roofs have a double and triple layer of shingles for protection, a small section of the area between the shingles has only one shingle coverage. Thus, an eroded mat in this area is very vulnerable to water leakage through the roof. Loss of granules and erosion of the mat between shingle tabs is a deficiency that usually occurs on the roof slope with the southerly or southwesterly exposure before occurring on other slopes. The condition is usually visible from the ground and can be clearly seen with the aid of your binoculars. When you see such a problem, you should anticipate early replacement of the roof shingles.

Most homes are designed to take three separate layers of shingles, although in some communities

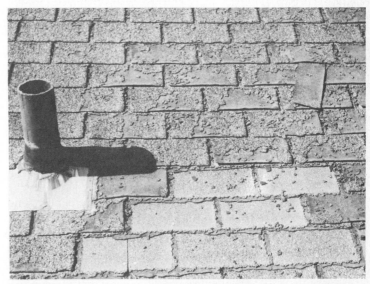

FIGURE 2-4 Deteriorating asphalt roof shingles. Note torn, missing, and brittle shingles with a loss of the granule covering, exposing the roofing mat.

only two are allowed. When a new roof covering is needed on a structure that already has the maximum layers allowed, it is necessary to remove all the layers before installing the new shingles. When reroofing, it is more costly to first remove existing layers of shingles than to install a new layer over already existing shingles. Therefore, you should try to determine the number of layers of shingles on the roof. When the roof has an exposed edge, as in the case of a gable roof, look at the thickness of the layers. If you see two to three overlapping shingles, then the roof covering is the first layer. In a hip type of roof, since there are no exposed edges, this type of determination cannot be made. In this case, try to find out the age of the house. Asphalt shingles have a projected life of seventeen to twenty-two years. The actual life span of the shingles will depend on the weight of the shingles, the type of mat, and the exposure. Asphalt shingles are classified by weight (pounds per roofing square). A roofing square is 100 square feet. Lightweight shingles, the least costly, weigh about 215 pounds per roofing square. Heavyweight shingles weigh about 350 pounds per square and have a longer life expectancy than lightweight ones. Also, shingles made with an organic-type mat will deteriorate more rapidly than those made with a fiberglass mat.

If the roof covering is over seventeen years old, extended life for the shingles should not be anticipated. Even though the shingles may look all right (i.e., laying flat with no noticeable loss of granules or erosion), they are becoming brittle and vulnerable to wind damage. Also, these shingles will be more vulnerable to damage from someone walking on the roof when cleaning the gutters, installing a TV antenna, and so on. Often, these shingles will show signs of aging such as curling, cupping, and cracking. (See Figure 2-5.) Such shingles are vulnerable to damage and will deteriorate rapidly. An exact estimate of the usable years or months remaining for the shingles is difficult, if not impossible, to give. Some people do not replace an aging roof until there is a leakage problem into the interior. Others will replace it before any leakage occurs and will thus avoid the cosmetic damage caused by leakage. The life span of an aging roof can be extended by patching and coating exposed cracks and eroded areas. If more than approximately one third of the roof shingles show signs of advanced aging, I recommend reroofing. At this point,

FIGURE 2-5  Aging asphalt roof shingles. Note the curling and cupping of the edges with some pitting.

attempts to extend the life of the shingles are usually not economically justifiable.

### Wood Shingles and Shakes

In many parts of the country, wood shingles and wood shakes are used as a roof covering. The basic difference between the two is their appearance and thickness. During the manufacturing process, shingles are sawed and shakes are split. Consequently, wood shingles have a relatively smooth surface and shakes have a textured surface.

Because of the need for resistance to decay, most of the wood shingles and shakes (hereafter referred to as shingles) are made from cedar. They are also made from redwood and southern cypress. The shingles, although resistant to decay, are not *immune* to decay and will rot after prolonged exposure to moisture. (Rot-producing fungi are discussed in Chapter 8.) The projected life expectancy for a wood-shingle roof is about twenty-five to thirty years. As a wood-shingle roof ages, the shingles dry, crack, curl, and rot. As you walk around the house looking at the roof, be aware of aging shingles. Rotting shingles should be replaced. If there are loose, damaged, or missing sections, repair to these sections is needed, even if there are no signs of water leakage through the roof. When approximately one third of the shingles on a slope shows signs of excessive aging (rotting, chipped, cracked, loose, missing or curling), all of the shingles on that slope should be replaced.

On the northern slope or on portions of the roof that are usually shaded, you may see moss growing in clusters between the joints of the shingles. If there is moss, it should be removed. The moss will function like a wick, as the root system will provide a direct path for water entry. In addition, as the moss cluster builds up, it may lift the shingles slightly, making them more vulnerable to water penetration, particularly during a driving rain.

When wood shingles are installed, they are spaced between ⅛ and ¼ of an inch apart to allow for swelling during damp weather. Because of this space and the irregularities of some of the shingles (due to thickness and texture), daylight may be visible through portions of the roof from inside the attic. If, during your inspection of the attic, you indeed see daylight through a wood-shingle roof, don't misinterpret it and think that roof maintenance is necessary. If daylight is visible through the roof by means of an *indirect path*, then maintenance is not required. On the other hand, if daylight is visible via a *direct path* such as a crack, then some maintenance is needed. Depending on the pitch of the roof, the shingles are either two-, three-, or four-ply and are installed so that the joints between the shingles for the various plies do not line up. When daylight is visible via a direct path, there are cracks in the shingles that line up with the joints. In this case, water can penetrate the roof and maintenance is needed.

### Asbestos-Cement Shingles

Asbestos-cement shingles, currently called "mineral fiber shingles," are manufactured essentially by combining asbestos fibers with Portland cement under high pressure. The shingles thus formed possess properties that make them highly suitable for exterior use. They are immune to rot, are unaffected by exposure to salt air, and are fireproof. One drawback, however, is that they are weak in their resistance to impact and, thus, are vulnerable to cracking and chipping.

As you walk around the exterior of the building during the roof inspection, look for cracked, loose, chipped, and missing shingles. Note on your worksheet the areas that will require maintenance. Although asbestos-cement shingles individually last many years, an asbestos-cement shingle roof should not be considered maintenance-free, and periodic repairs should be anticipated. Occasionally, as with a wood-shingle roof, clusters of moss may be found growing on the northern slope or on slopes usually shaded by trees. If you see this condition, note it on your worksheet. The moss is a potential problem and should be removed.

### Slate Shingles

Of all the roof coverings, slate shingles are the most durable. If they are of good quality, they may last indefinitely (at least in excess of one hundred years). The slate roof over the Saxon Chapel at Stratford-on-Avon in England is over eleven hundred years old and, according to the Vermont Structural Slate Company, is in good condition. A slate roof will not, however, remain maintenance-free, even though the slates are of good quality. I have seen very few slate roofs that did not have some cracked, loose, chipped, or missing slates, a condition that requires some repair. These repairs are considered to be minor roof maintenance and should be anticipated on a periodic basis. Slate roofs are often patched with asphalt cement, which has a tendency to dry and crack and requires periodic application. When inspecting this type of roof from the exterior, look for cracked, loose, chipped, or missing shingles. If you find any, make a note on your worksheet.

Repairs to a slate roof, even minor ones, can be somewhat costly. Several roofers have told me that their fee reflects additional work above and beyond the required repair because they always anticipate accidental cracking of some of the slates during the actual repair. One difficulty of which you should be

FIGURE 2-6   Slate roof shingles. The "ribbon" slate shown above is of inferior quality. Often, cracking occurs along the ribbon after only ten years.

aware is that, when replacing a slate shingle, the roofer may not be able to match the color of the new slate to the existing weathered shingles.

Sometimes a poor quality slate, called "ribbon slate," is used as a roof covering. (See Figure 2-6.) The ribbons within the individual shingles are softer than the normal slate and will cause the shingles to crack along the ribbon. Often, cracking occurs along the ribbon after only 10 years. Repairs to these shingles must then be made on an as-needed basis.

When inspecting the roof, flaking slates may also be noted. Surface flaking is of no concern as the shingles are at least 3/16 of an inch thick and are basically impervious to water. However, if any of the shingles are deteriorating as a result of excessive splitting and flaking (a condition brought about by winter freeze-and-thaw cycles), then they should be replaced.

If the house that you are inspecting is in the northern part of the country where snow may accumulate, look for snow guards on the lower portion of the roof. In particular, they should be located above doorways, sidewalks, or other areas where people will pass or gather. Snow guards are needed to prevent sliding masses of snow and ice from falling off the roof and damaging the gutters. It may interest you to know that the slate roofs on the buildings of the Harriman Estate in New York had 35,000 copper wire snow guards.

### Clay Tiles

Clay tiles are available in many different patterns. The most common ones are Spanish and Mission. These tiles are made by shaping moist clay in molds and firing the various shapes. They are hard, durable, and fireproof. However, they are also brittle and can be easily damaged by falling tree limbs or when climbing on the roof to make repairs. As with slate shingles, repair or replacement of individual tiles is more difficult and more costly than that of asphalt shingles. Also, matching new tiles to the older, weathered tiles that are on the roof is usually a problem. When inspecting this type of roof, look for loose, broken, chipped, cracked, or missing tiles. If any of these conditions are found, they should be noted on the worksheet, as repairs are needed. Tiles may also deteriorate as a result of freeze-thaw cycles. You may find some cracked areas that have been sealed with asphalt cement. This is usually an indication of past problems. Since asphalt cement does dry and crack, periodic reapplication should be anticipated.

## FLAT ROOFS

A roof that is perfectly level or slightly pitched is referred to as a flat roof. Since this type of roof is not visible from the ground, the inspection must be made from the roof itself. As with a pitched roof, a flat roof should be the first item inspected. Safe access to the roof is of prime importance. If the building is higher than one story, the roof should be accessible from the interior. Anything other than an interior means of access is a potential hazard and is considered a deficiency in the structure's design. If the roof on the house that you are inspecting is flat and is more than one story high with no interior access, then it is best to have it inspected by a professional roofer.

Ventilation of the area directly below the roof deck is needed in order to minimize the moisture buildup in this area. An excessive moisture condition can result in deterioration of the roof deck, a lowering of the thermal resistance of the insulation, and, eventually, damage to the interior of the structure. During the cooler months, the moisture that is trapped in the area between the roof and the upper-level ceiling will condense, drip onto the insulation, and cause random water stains on the ceiling. Adequate ventilation of this area is also important in reducing the summer heat load on the rooms located immediately below the roof.

All too often, you will find that provisions for ventilation have been omitted by the builder. Therefore, when inspecting a flat roof, be sure to look for ventilation openings. The openings may be in the form of roof vents (vertical pipes protruding through the roof deck) or open areas in the side of the building just below the roof. The roof vents are often shielded from the rain by a cover and should not be confused with the plumbing vent stacks, which also protrude through the roof deck. The plumbing vent stack is connected to the house sewer line and is easily identified by the odor of the discharging gases. If no ventilation openings are noted, that fact should be marked on your worksheet. Installation of ventilation openings should then be considered.

A flat roof must have a watertight covering, rather than one that sheds water, in order to protect the area below the roof from water intrusion. The most common types of flat roof coverings are built-up, roll roofing, and metal. When inspecting a flat roof, look for ponded water. In the past, it was considered desirable to have a roof that was perpetually flooded. The thinking was that the standing water would reduce the heat load during the summer.

Today, ponded water on a roof is no longer thought of as desirable, as the disadvantages far outweigh the advantages. Ponded water can become a breeding place for insects and may promote the growth of vegetation and fungi. The roots of plants growing on the roof can puncture an asphalt covering. The freezing of ponded water that has penetrated into the layers of a built-up roof can delaminate the roof covering. The temperature difference of the wet and dry areas on a randomly ponded roof will result in differential expansion that may cause warping and cracking of the roof cover. If you do see ponded water or signs of past ponding on the roof during your inspection, note the location on your worksheet as an area that should be drained.

A properly designed roof should have provisions for drainage. There are two basic drainage designs used in conjunction with a flat roof, the perimeter system and the interior drainage system. In the perimeter system, water that drains from the interior portions of the roof collects in gutters or scuppers (openings in a parapet wall) located along the perimeter and then flows into downspouts or merely drips off the roof. In the interior drainage system, drains are located in the roof itself and are connected to downspouts that run through the interior portion of the structure. Look for one of these drainage provisions as you walk around the roof. The interior roof drains are often clogged with debris and are sometimes set higher than the surrounding area, a condition that will result in ponding. Look for cracks around the joints between the roof drain and the roof covering.

When inspecting a flat roof, you should also inspect all roof-mounted structures and projections such as skylights, hatch covers, chimneys, vent stacks, and so on. These items are discussed in Chapter 3.

## Built-up Roof

This type of roof consists of bitumen (asphalt or coal tar pitch) sandwiched between two to five layers of roofing felts, and is usually covered with a mineral aggregate imbedded in the top surface. The bitumen is the waterproofing agent that is stabilized and reinforced by the roofing felts. The felts restrain the bitumen from flowing in hot weather and they help resist cracking in cold weather. The aggregate surfacing generally consists of gravel, slag, or crushed rock. Its purpose is to protect the bitumen from the damaging effects of the sun's infrared and ultraviolet rays. These rays, through a combination of heat and photochemical oxidation, accelerate the aging of bitumen resulting in premature brittleness and cracking. Depending on the number of layers in the built-up roof and on the quality of construction, the projected life may vary from ten to twenty years.

A built-up roof is difficult to inspect, principally because of the mineral aggregate topping. Nevertheless, look for telltale signs of past, current, and potential problems. Walk around the roof systematically, so you cover the entire roof area. Look for patched areas, cracking, blistering, surface erosion, alligatoring, and wrinkling. In particular, look for cracks at the joints of roof projections and roof-mounted structures.

Usually, this type of roof has a flanged metallic strip along the perimeter called a "gravel stop." It provides a finished edge for the built-up roofing and also prevents loose aggregates from washing off the roof. Look for cracks in the joint between the gravel stop and the roof. All cracks noted in the roof cover should be sealed. Record the location of any cracked and/or patched areas on your worksheet, so that you can check the ceiling of the rooms below these areas for water stains.

Incidentally, when walking on the roof, be careful not to step on any blisters. Blisters are weak spots in the roof covering and are usually the result of air or water vapor being trapped between the layers of roofing felts. Depending on a blister's degree of brittleness, the weight of someone walking on the blister may cause the roofing felt to crack.

## Roll Roofing

This type of roof covering is often found on older structures in urban areas and over porch roofs. Sometimes, it is also found on pitched roofs of low-cost homes and outbuildings. It consists basically of an asphalt-saturated roofing felt that is applied directly over the roof deck and provides only single- or two-ply coverage. Quite often, the outer surface is coated with hot tar to seal joints and small cracks. Roll roofing should be inspected for blistered,

FIGURE 2-7 Cracked and open joint between the roof and the parapet wall.

cracked, eroded, and torn sections. As with a built-up roof, be careful not to walk on blistered sections. Sometimes the lapped joints between the strips curl and lift, making the joints vulnerable to water seepage. Check the joints between the roof and the parapet wall and other roof projections. These joints are vulnerable to cracking and periodically require resealing. (See Figure 2-7.) If any of the above items are noted, they should be recorded on your worksheet, as they indicate the need for some maintenance.

## Metal Roof

Sheetmetal roof coverings are usually made of galvanized iron (sheet iron coated with zinc), terne metal (steel-coated with a mixture of lead and tin), or copper. A galvanized roof with a heavy zinc coating will last many years without painting. However, a lightly galvanized roof will rust and must be kept well painted. A terne metal roof, if kept well painted, may last for over forty years. A copper roof will also last for many years and does not require painting. For the most part, sheetmetal is no longer used to cover the main roof on residential structures. Rather, it is used to cover the roof over porches or other exterior side projections such as sunrooms or garages. Occasionally, a sheetmetal roof covering may be found on the main roof of a Victorian-type structure. When you are inspecting a sheetmetal roof, look for cracks or open joints at the soldered seam. Because of the large amount of expansion that takes place, the seam is a vulnerable joint for leakage. Also, look for exposed corroding sections of metal. If any exist, they must be scraped and coated with paint or a bituminous compound such as asphalt cement. In some cases, problem conditions that have occurred over the years have necessitated coating the entire roof with a bituminous compound as a means of sealing corroded areas. Be aware that this type of roof coating requires periodic maintenance.

## CHECKPOINT SUMMARY

### PITCHED ROOFS

- Visually inspect all portions (slopes) of the roof.
- Note any sagging, uneven, damaged, or patched sections.
- Look for overhanging tree limbs or branches that can cause damage.
- Is the area directly below the roof deck ventilated?

### Asphalt Shingles

- Look for curling, cracked, torn, or missing shingles.
- Are shingles losing their stone granules?
- Look for eroded sections in the slot between the shingle tabs.
- Pay particular attention to slopes with a southerly or southwesterly exposure.
- How old are the roof shingles?
- How many layers of shingles are there?

- If roof has been recently reshingled, is there a guarantee/warranty available?

### Wood Shingles/Shakes

- Look for rotting, loose, cracked, chipped, or missing sections.
- Pay particular attention to the slopes with heavy shade.
- Did you note any signs of moss?

### Slate/Asbestos-Cement/Clay Tiles

- Look for missing, cracked, chipped, flaking, or loose sections.
- Are there sections patched with asphalt cement?

## FLAT ROOFS

- Is safe access available?
- Are there cracked, blistered, eroded, or torn sections?
- Are there areas of ponding water or low points where water will accumulate?
- Is the drainage system functional?
- Is area below the roof deck adequately ventilated?

### Roll Roofing (tar paper)

- Are sections drying, eroding, or blistered?
- Look for open seams.

# 3. ROOF-MOUNTED STRUCTURES AND PROJECTIONS

**W**hen inspecting a roof, you should also inspect all roof-mounted structures and projections. Specifically, look at chimney(s), plumbing vent stack(s), roof vent(s), roof hatch, skylight(s), TV antenna, and gutters and downspouts. For all of the above except the last two items, an area of concern is the joint between the particular item and the roof. This joint, although normally sealed with flashing, is vulnerable to water leakage. With years of weathering, the flashing can develop cracks, pinholes, or breaks, resulting in periodic leaks. To correct this type of water leakage, and rather than reflash the joints, the homeowner may often seal the joints with asphalt cement. While this is an effective correction, the asphalt cement will eventually become brittle and crack and the joints will require periodic resealing.

## CHIMNEYS

Chimneys are used to vent smoke and combustion gases from heating units as well as from fireplaces. If, during your exterior inspection, you do not find a chimney, it does not necessarily mean that the house lacks a heating system. In all probability, the house is heated electrically.

Chimneys are normally constructed of masonry (brick, concrete, stone) or are prefabricated from metal or a cement-asbestos material. Masonry chimneys are usually supported by their own foundations which, in the northern communities, extend below the frost line. These chimneys are not dependent on the main structure for support. When inspecting a masonry chimney that extends up along the side of a building, if you see open joints between the chimney and the sidewall, it is an indication of some settlement and is usually not a concerning factor. (See Figure 3-1.) However, the open areas should be resealed. On the other hand, if the chimney is no longer vertical, it may indicate excessive settlement or the need for rehabilitation and should be checked by a professional. Depending on the amount of settlement, the flashing at the joint between the chimney and the roof may need repair. The movement of the chimney could result in open and loose sections of flashing. (See Figure 3-2.)

If your house has a brick chimney, look at the area above the roof line to see that it is vertical. Over the years, the mortar joints may weaken on one side and cause the chimney to lean. (See Figure 3-3.) A leaning chimney represents a potential safety hazard, and corrective measures are needed. The chimney requires either bracing or rebuilding from the roof line up. If you ask the owner about the chimney, he'll probably say that is has been in that condition for at least fifteen years. That fact does not mean that corrective action is not needed. A leaning chimney is an indication of weakening mortar joints and should be considered of questionable structural integrity.

FIGURE 3-1 Uneven settlement of chimney. Note open joint (arrow) between the chimney and the sidewall.

FIGURE 3-2 Open and loose sections of flashing caused by movement of the chimney.

Sometimes, brick chimneys on relatively new houses may be coated with white mineral deposits called "efflorescence." This condition is often caused by the absorption of water by the porous bricks. The minerals in the bricks dissolve in the water and then surface when the water evaporates. Although efflorescence is quite common in new brick work, it can easily be scrubbed or washed off with a dilute solution of muriatic acid. Recurrence can usually be controlled by covering the bricks with a silicone sealant. When there is efflorescence on a brick chimney that has been up for many years, it usually means that water is getting inside the chimney, either through cracks in the joints on top of the chimney or through cracks in the bricks or mortar joints. If you see heavy efflorescence on an older chimney, make a note on your worksheet. The top of a masonry chimney should have a cement finish that slopes from the flue to the edge of the chimney. The purpose of this finish is to deflect rain and protect the joints between the flue and the chimney. This cement finish is vulnerable to cracking, and periodic resealing of this area should be anticipated.

The top of the chimney must extend above the roof line. This is necessary in order to prevent downdrafts caused by the turbulence of the wind as it sweeps past nearby obstructions or over sloping roofs. The top of the chimney should extend at least 3 feet above a flat roof and 2 feet above the ridge of a pitched roof. When a chimney is 10 feet horizontally beyond a roof ridge, builders often terminate the top of the chimney below the ridge. This is not quality construction, but it satisfies the code. In this case, downdrafts can still occur as a result of air currents that are formed when the wind hits the side of the building. The downdrafts can affect the efficiency of the heating system or may result in backsmoking of the fireplace. This type of problem, if it should occur, can usually be controlled by installing a concrete or stone cap about 8 inches above the top of the flue.

Older homes very often have unlined chimneys. Although these chimneys may operate satisfactorily, they are more of a potential hazard than those with a flue lining. Over the years, the corrosive gases can have a deteriorating effect on the mortar joints. If there is an unlined chimney in your house that is connected to a fireplace that has not been used for many years, it is recommended that the integrity of the chimney joints be verified by a competent chimney contractor. If it turns out that there are leaks in the chimney that cannot be easily sealed, then very often the condition can be corrected by installing a metal liner down the existing flue.

All masonry chimneys should be inspected for cracked, loose, chipped, deteriorating, and missing sections of brick and mortar joints. Some masonry chimneys have a stucco finish. In this case, look for

FIGURE 3-3 The portion of the chimney that extends above the roof is leaning (arrow)—a potentially hazardous condition.

cracked, chipped, and loose sections of stucco. On occasion, brick chimneys on older homes are covered with an asphalt-type coating, especially above the roof line. This technique is often used to prolong the life of the chimney when there are many cracked mortar joints and deteriorating bricks. It is considered a makeshift fix. If you see any of the above items, they should be recorded on your worksheet.

For the most part, very little maintenance is needed to prefabricated chimneys. Metal chimneys have a tendency to rust and should be checked for corrosion holes. If there is no rain cover on a metal chimney, it should be noted on the worksheet, for the installation of a cover is recommended.

## VENT STACKS

The vent stack is part of the plumbing system. Its purpose is to permit adequate circulation of air in all parts of the sanitary drainage system and to allow a means by which sewer gas can vent harmlessly to the atmosphere. All homes should have vent stacks. The absence of a vent stack will usually indicate that the plumbing system is not properly vented, which is almost always a violation of the plumbing code. As you inspect the roof, look for a pipe that projects through the roof and terminates about 8 inches above the roof line. In newer homes, the vent stack is usually fairly obvious. In older homes, however, the vent stack may be missing or, at least, may not be visible when looking at the roof. On occasion, I have found vent stacks that terminate in the attic. This condition is a violation of the plumbing code, as the vent stack must extend above the roof line so that the escaping gases may discharge to the outside.

In some older homes, when kitchens or bathrooms are renovated, vent stacks are often run up along the outside of the building to a point above the roof line. (See Figure 3-4.) If these homes are located in the northern part of the United States, this type of installation is undesirable. Because of the moisture in the escaping gas, the possibility exists that during cold weather, it could freeze over and eventually block the opening within the pipe. Sometimes you may find vent stacks that terminate near a window. (See Figure 3-5.) This installation is also undesirable because of the possibility of the discharging sewer gas seeping into the house when the adjacent window is open.

When looking at vent stacks that terminate above the roof, very often there is a black ring at the base of the stack adjacent to the flashing. This black ring is asphalt cement, which has been used to seal the joint. This joint is vulnerable to leakage and should be periodically checked. On one inspec-

FIGURE 3-4   Exterior-mounted plumbing vent stack.

FIGURE 3-5   Plumbing vent stack terminating near window. Depending on the wind direction, if the window is open, the discharging sewer gases can be blown into the house.

tion, I found water dripping from a ceiling tile in a suspended ceiling located two levels below the roof. When I lifted the tile, water came cascading down. After the initial shock and after all of the water had spilled away, it became obvious that the water was not caused by a leak in the above laundry room, but indeed had collected during the previous day's driving rain when water had leaked into the structure through the small crack between the vent stack and the flashing. This area should be periodically checked and sealed on an as-needed basis.

## ROOF VENTS

These vents can be found on pitched and flat roofs and are available in both round and square hood styles. Normally, there are no problems with these types of vents. However, the joint between the vents and the roof is vulnerable to water leakage. Even though the joints may look okay from the roof side, it is best to periodically check the vent openings from the attic. If there is leakage, it will be noted by water stains on the roof sheathing in those areas. Water leakage around the joints can be easily corrected with asphalt cement or a suitable caulking.

## ROOF HATCH

Access to a flat roof from the interior portion of the structure is provided through a roof hatch. Don't be surprised if you find a roof hatch on a house with a pitched roof. In some older and larger structures, they were installed as a means for easy access. Roof hatch covers should be checked to determine whether or not they are operational; they should be. I have found that in about 30 percent of the cases, the hatch covers could not be opened. In all probability, during reroofing or maintenance, asphalt cement accidentally or intentionally sealed the hatch cover frame. If this condition exists, it should be corrected. Usually, the hatch cover is constructed of wood and is covered with either sheet-metal or asphalt roll roofing. Of particular concern is the integrity of the waterproofing cover. There should not be any cracked or open joints. The wood framing should not have any cracked or broken sections.

## SKYLIGHTS

Skylights are installed on a structure to provide daylighting and, in some cases, ventilation. The newer styles are prefabricated with aluminum frames and plastic or glass panels or domes. Skylights can be found on pitched or flat roofs. These units should be checked for cracked or broken panes and for signs of leakage. The leakage can be checked by inspecting the interior area below the skylight. If there are leaks around the skylight, they will be noted by water stains on the wall or finished ceiling in those areas. The skylights found on older flat-roof homes should be carefully checked for corroding frames and cracked and broken panes. Quite often, the frames have corroded through and provide no support for the panes. If this condition is found, it should be marked on your worksheet because these skylights require complete rehabilitation.

## TV ANTENNA

Quite often, TV antennas are strapped to the chimney for support. This is an undesirable means of bracing the antenna because repeated twisting action on the antenna from strong winds can cause stresses on the chimney that can, in turn, result in cracked mortar joints. When you see a TV antenna strapped to the chimney, look carefully at the joints. Sometimes, the antenna is supported on the roof by means of guy wires that are anchored to the roof deck. When inspecting the roof, check the area around the anchors for deterioration of the roof covering. On some occasions, the guy wires are strapped to vent stacks. This is an undesirable practice because in a strong wind, the movement of the antenna can cause the joint at the base of the vent stack to crack. I have also run into a situation where a homeowner inserted the TV antenna mast down into a vent stack in order to secure the antenna. If you see this situation when you inspect the house, make a note of it so that you can remove the antenna after you take possession of the house. Finally, look for a ground wire that connects the antenna to a metal rod that is imbedded in the ground. According to the National Electrical Code, this wire should not have any intervening splices or connections. The TV ground wire does not protect the house from lightning. Its purpose is to protect the television set in the event of a lightning surge.

## GUTTERS AND DOWNSPOUTS

Gutters and downspouts are installed on a structure to control and direct rain runoff from the roof. The absence of gutters may result in water seepage into the basement, rotting sections of wood trim, damage to foundation plantings, and the washing away of topsoil. Regardless of whether they are masonry constructed or have long overhanging eaves, most residential structures that are not in the snow belt would benefit from gutters. In the snow belt, gutters are considered more of an inconvenience than a help because the snow and ice often tear them from the supports and maintenance is constantly necessary. If you do not see gutters on the structure during your inspection, indicate their absence on your worksheet. There are basically two types of gutters, built-in and exterior-mounted.

### Built-in Gutters

These gutters are essentially extensions of the roof framing with waterways built into the roof surface over the edges. The gutter channel may be lined with asphalt roll roofing or some other type of impermeable material. These channels require periodic maintenance, such as applications of an asphalt-type cement. Leakage through these channels can often be detected by water stains in the soffit below the leaks or possibly by water stains into the interior portion of the structure. Leaks in this type of gutter often result in rotting sections of trim. If stains or rotting sections are noted, they should be indicated on the worksheet. Built-in gutters are seldom used on modern residential structures.

### Exterior-mounted Gutters

These gutters can be made from copper, galvanized iron, wood, plastic, or, most commonly, aluminum. Copper gutters are considered the top of the line. They are expensive, considered virtually corrosion-resistant, and have a projected life in excess of forty years. However, as these gutters age, they will corrode and develop tiny holes in the bottom portion of the gutter channel. Depending on the gutters' height, the holes may not be visible to the naked eye from the ground. However, by standing directly below the gutters and looking straight up, the sky is often visible through any corrosion holes. Sometimes, the gutters are painted, although painting is not required. You can tell whether you have copper gutters by the fact that the joints are soldered rather than clipped together. Sometimes leaks develop around the soldered joints. For the most part, because of their cost, copper gutters and downspouts are no longer used when replacing faulty gutters and downspouts. Several years ago, I inspected a church in Ossining, New York, that had a wet basement. It turned out that most of the copper gutters and downspouts had been stolen from the structure by someone in search of a quick dollar because there was a copper shortage at that time.

Galvanized gutters have been used on many homes because of their low initial cost. However, they rust easily and require periodic maintenance such as patching corrosion holes and repainting. The inside portion of the gutter channel should also be painted. This area is often overlooked by the homeowner.

Aluminum gutters are quite popular as they do not have the corrosion problems of galvanized gutters. Older aluminum gutters will, on occasion, leak around the seam, a condition requiring resealing. Leakage from the seams may be noted by discoloration at the joint or possibly by some water stains or erosion on the area directly below the joint. Techniques have been developed so that aluminum gutters can now be manufactured to almost any length, producing what is called "seamless gutters." Leaks that develop in this type of gutter usually occur at corner joints or at the joint around the downspout.

Wood gutters are usually made of Douglas fir or red cedar and have a tendency to crack and rot at the various end joints and seams along their length. (See Figure 3-6.) The joints around the end sections, particularly those where the connection is made to the downspout, deteriorate more rapidly than other portions and should be checked for rot and cracking. Wood gutters should be painted every few years and the inside channel coated with an asphalt-type roof paint.

Plastic gutters, although relatively maintenance-free, have not received wide acceptance. They are found occasionally, but not necessarily, on those homes that have exterior vinyl siding.

When inspecting the roof with binoculars, the gutters should be checked to see if there are any loose support straps or spikes that should be resecured. In addition, an overall view will show whether any of the gutters are pitched incorrectly or are sagging and should be reset. Sagging is a condition occasionally found on those homes with slate roofs that do not have snow guards. All types of gutters have a tendency to become cluttered with leaves, twigs, seed pods, and mineral granules from roof shingles. They should be cleaned at least twice a year, once in the spring after the trees have bloomed and once in the fall after the leaves have fallen. Gutter screens are available to help prevent

FIGURE 3-6 Wood gutters. Note the cracked and rotting corner joint.

FIGURE 3-7 Gutters must be cleaned periodically in order to be effective. Note the weeds growing out of this gutter.

larger items, such as leaves and twigs, from cluttering the gutter channel. However, often a homeowner installs the screens and then forgets about cleaning the gutters. The gutters still require cleaning, although at less frequent intervals. Sometimes you can tell from the ground whether or not a gutter channel requires cleaning. Figure 3-7 shows weeds growing out of the gutter. Obviously, this gutter has not been cleaned for some time.

### Downspouts

Downspouts are normally constructed of aluminum, copper, or galvanized iron. Copper and galvanized downspouts that have aged often have corrosion holes in the elbow sections. In some cases, the

FIGURE 3-8 Water stains on the exterior siding are the result of a missing downspout.

copper corrodes to a point where there are cracked sections that are paper thin and can be stripped away very easily. If you see this condition, it indicates that those sections should be replaced. Some downspouts have loose and open seams along their length that interfere with their effectiveness.

If you do not specifically look for the downspouts, you may not realize that some of them are missing. Figure 3-8 shows a missing downspout with water stains on the asbestos-cement shingles. In this case, it is obvious that a downspout is missing. However, if the house is inspected during dry weather, there may not be any stains, and this item can be overlooked. Check the assembly of the downspout at the various joints. The lower portion of the downspout should be outside the upper portion. Otherwise, water will leak around the joint. Figure 3-9 shows an incorrect downspout assembly. On occasion, some downspouts come loose from their connection to the gutters and should be resecured. Loose sup-

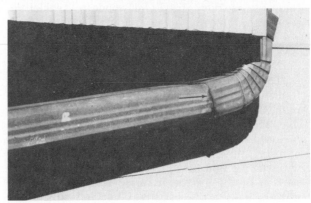

FIGURE 3-9 Incorrectly assembled downspout joint—the lower section is inside the upper section (arrow). It should be reversed. Otherwise, water will leak out of the joint.

port straps around downspouts should be resecured. Water from downspouts must go somewhere; it can be piped away under ground to suitable drainage or discharged onto the ground at the base. Any water discharging from the base of the downspouts must be directed away from the structure. Otherwise, it can accumulate around the foundation and may eventually enter the lower level. To help deflect this water away from the structure, there should be an elbow at the base of the downspout and a splash plate below on the ground. If you see the effluent discharging around the foundation, it should be indicated on your worksheet.

Sometimes the downspouts terminate directly into the ground. It is usually not possible during an inspection to determine whether the downspouts are connected to freeflowing drain tiles or to dry wells. Freeflowing tiles are more desirable since dry wells may become clogged or will become ineffective if the level of the subsurface groundwater (water table) is high. Occasionally, some freeflowing tiles are visible at the street curb. If there are outlets at the curb, they must always be kept clear so that they can be effective.

## CHECKPOINT SUMMARY

### CHIMNEYS

**Masonry Type (Brick, Stone, Concrete Block)**
- Inspect for cracked, loose, chipped, eroding, or missing sections of masonry.
- Check mortar joints for cracked, loose, and deteriorating sections.
- For stucco-finished chimneys, are there cracked, chipped, missing, or loose sections of stucco?
- Is chimney vertical or is it leaning?
- Are there open joints between the chimney and the sidewall?
- If the roof is flat, does the chimney extend 3 feet above the roof line?
- If the roof is pitched, does the chimney extend 2 feet above the roof ridge?
- If possible, check for cracked or missing sections of the chimney cap.
- If possible, check the chimney flashing for holes, tears, or loose sections. Check these vulnerable areas for leakage again during your attic inspection.

**Metal Type (Prefabricated)**
- Check for corrosion holes, rusting, or missing sections.
- Is there a rain cover present?
- Note condition of flashing and seal around the roof joint.

### VENT STACKS
- Are plumbing vent stacks visible? (Their absence can be verified during attic inspection.)
- Are there black rings (asphalt cement) at the base joint of the vent stacks?
- Note any questionable roof joints and check further during attic inspection.
- Note vent stacks that:
    terminate near windows.
    run up an exterior side of the house (in northern climates).
    have TV antennas strapped to them.

### ROOF VENTS, HATCHES, SKYLIGHTS, TV ANTENNA
- Check all roof joints associated with vents, hatches, and skylights.
- Note questionable sections and verify tightness of joints during attic inspection.
- Does structure contain a roof hatch?
- Are you able to open it?
- Are there cracks or open joints in the cover?
- Check skylights for corroding frames and cracked or broken panes.
- Inspect ceiling area below for signs of leakage.
- Check TV antenna mast and guy wire connections to roof.
- Is antenna adequately grounded?

### GUTTERS AND DOWNSPOUTS

**Exterior-mounted Gutters**
- Check for missing sections of gutters.
- Note type of material: copper, aluminum, galvanized iron, wood.
- Note gutter sections that are incorrectly pitched.
- Check metal gutters for corrosion holes, sagging sections, loose support straps or spikes, and leaking sections.
- Check wood gutters for cracked sections and areas of rot, particularly at connections and end sections.

**Built-in Gutters**
- Check for areas with rotting trim.
- Check for signs of leakage.
- Note signs of seepage (stains) in soffit trim below gutters.
- Where possible, check condition of gutter channel.

**Downspouts**
- Note type of material: copper, aluminum, galvanized iron.
- Check for missing sections and improper joining.
- Inspect for loose straps, open seams, and corrosion holes at elbows.
- Do downspouts have elbows at base and extensions and splash plates (where required) to direct roof rain runoff away from the house?
- If downspouts terminate in the ground, try to find out whether they are connected to dry wells or to freeflowing outlets.

# 4. PAVED AREAS AROUND THE STRUCTURE

As you walk around the house on the second pass, inspect the paths, steps, patio, and driveway. The problems normally encountered with these items are usually not the type that require immediate correction. Nevertheless, depending on the problem, there may be a tripping hazard, cosmetic maintenance may be needed, or a condition may exist that makes the lower level of the house vulnerable to water penetration. If you see problems in these areas, they should be recorded on your worksheet for early correction.

## SIDEWALKS

Sidewalks are usually constructed of concrete, asphalt, or stone embedded in the ground. Not all communities have sidewalks. If there is a sidewalk in front of or on the sides of the house that you are inspecting, look for cracked or uneven sections because they are a potential tripping hazard. Even though the sidewalk may be on property that is owned by the town, its maintenance is usually the owner's responsibility. If someone should trip or get hurt as a result of a cracked or uneven section, you would be vulnerable to a lawsuit. Very often, uneven sections are caused by the roots of trees that are growing nearby. Correcting the condition would require chopping that section of root away and resetting the sidewalk. You should be aware of the fact that trees adjacent to the sidewalk are often the property of the local municipality and prior to altering the roots, permission should be obtained.

## STREET-LEVEL/DRIVEWAY-LEVEL STEPS

Depending on the topography, there may be steps leading from the sidewalk or driveway up to the front path. These steps should be inspected for cracked, chipped, broken, or uneven sections. Look specifically for dimensional variations in the step risers. The riser for the top step or the bottom step is often a different size than for the other steps.

This is a tripping hazard. If there are more than two steps (risers), then there should be a handrail as a safety precaution.

## FRONT AND SIDE PATHS

There are two general types of paths that are used with residential structures. One is a ribbon type generally constructed of concrete or asphalt, and the other is a sectional type that is generally inlaid with material such as stones, bricks, sections of tree trunks, or precast concrete blocks. The sectional type normally requires periodic maintenance because of the tendency toward uneven settlement and weed growth between the sections. Sometimes the sections are loose and uneven and present a tripping hazard. Occasionally, the sections are set in mortar. Look for loose, cracked, and chipped mortar joints that require repointing. When inspecting the ribbon-type path, look for cracked, uneven, and broken sections. Very often, this occurs because the base below the path was not properly prepared during construction. Look particularly for settled sections that are sloping toward the house. These areas will direct rain runoff toward the house so that water will accumulate around the foundation. This water can enter the lower level. In this case, the path should either be repositioned so that it slopes away from the structure (if possible) or completely rehabilitated.

While inspecting the paths, look for small, abrupt changes in the elevation. Occasionally, I have found a single step in the middle of a path. This is a potential tripping hazard because it is often unnoticed. A single step in a path, except at an entrance, should be avoided. If a slight elevation change is necessary and there is a step, either it should be converted to a ramp or shrubs should be planted at the step to call attention to the elevation change. An outdoor light should also be placed here. (See Figure 4-1.) You may find a path that is partially blocked by overgrown shrubs and, consequently, is no longer functional. In this case, if a path is needed, the shrubs should be pruned or the path repositioned.

## ENTRY STEPS

These steps can be made of stone, concrete, brick, metal, or wood. As a safety precaution, when there are more than two steps, there should be at least one handrail, especially if the house is located in an area where the temperature drops below freezing. In those areas, the steps will be coated with a layer of ice after a freezing rain. Look specifically for differences in the vertical distance between the steps (risers). (See Figure 4-2.) There should not be any dimensional variations in the risers. If there are, they are potential tripping hazards. Some steps are designed so that the vertical distance between the treads is open (open risers). Although this may be aesthetically pleasing, it is a potential tripping hazard.

If the swing of the entry door is such that it opens onto the entry steps, there should be a landing platform at the doorway. The turnaround area of a single step tread is not considered adequate to operate a door safely.

When inspecting the steps, look specifically for cracked, broken, rotting, chipped, and loose sections. The treads should be level. Uneven sections are a tripping hazard. If the steps are masonry constructed, look at the step foundation walls for cracked, broken, and chipped sections. If there are wood stringers (the side portion of the steps that support the treads), they should be resting on a concrete pad rather than on the soil. Check the base of wooden stringers for rot by probing the area with a screwdriver. If the screwdriver easily penetrates the wood, the stringer should be replaced. Metal handrails are often used with exterior steps. Very often, these handrails are corroding and have deep pockets of rust. In this case, the handrails should be scraped, primed, and repainted.

## PATIO

There are probably as many types and styles of patios as there are of houses. The more common types are concrete slab, stone set in mortar, and brick set in the ground. In all cases, of particular concern is whether any tripping hazards can result from cracked, broken, or uneven sections. Some patios have a grid pattern consisting of wood imbedded in the ground around sections of brick or concrete. This wood should be pressure-treated to protect it from rot. However, and unfortunately so, the wood is normally not pressure-treated so that after a few years, it rots and requires replacement. Concrete slab patios should have expansion joints and control joints for cracking. Very often, these items are omitted, and the patio cracks in a random fashion that is aesthetically undesirable. Look at the patio for signs of uneven settlement. If a patio is adjacent to the house and has settled so that it is sloping toward the house, water will accumulate around the joint between the patio and the foundation wall. This water will eventually accumulate around the foundation and, if there is a basement, may enter the lower level. If this condition exists, it should be indicated on your worksheet for later cor-

FIGURE 4-1 A single step in the middle of a path is a potential hazard. The shrubs on both sides of this path call attention to the step. However, there should also be an outdoor light in the area.

rection and as a reminder for you to check the area of the basement that is adjacent to the patio.

## DRIVEWAY

Driveways are normally constructed of asphalt, concrete, or gravel, or may just be a clearing with no particular covering. The latter is not particularly desirable from both a cosmetic point of view and because of the ease with which ruts can develop. Gravel driveways, on occasion, also develop ruts and will require periodic replacement of the gravel. Concrete and asphalt driveways should be inspected for cracked, broken, or settled areas that require rehabilitation. When there is extensive cracking such as alligator-type cracks, it is usually

FIGURE 4-2 Note that the vertical distances between the steps vary. The top step is less and the bottom is greater than the distance between the two center steps. These steps are considered a potential tripping hazard. Note also that there is no handrail and the bottom riser is in need of masonry repair.

an indication of poor drainage of the subbase or poor construction. In this case, the cracks cannot be sealed effectively. The entire area should be patched. If a large portion of the driveway has this type of cracking, then resurfacing is required.

Sometimes. the driveway is on an incline so that subsurface water flows below the driveway, undermining the subbase. In this case, prior to resurfacing, adequate provision for drainage of the subbase should be made.

When standing at the front of the driveway, look to see if it pitches directly down toward the house. If it does, the garage and any other portion of the lower level will be vulnerable to flooding, unless there is a large operational drain at the base of the driveway to intercept the surface water. Usually a slotted drain that runs across the width of the driveway is needed to control the water runoff in this type of situation. The drain, however, should have a freeflowing outlet. If the drain is connected to a dry well, it may be ineffective during those months when there is a high water table. If this is the case, one corrective procedure would be to connect the drain to a sump pit and remove the water by means of a sump pump.

When a house is located on a street that is inclined, the curb cut for the driveway should not be feathered into the street. Instead there should be a small ridge on the driveway at the joint between the driveway and the street. This ridge will prevent water that normally accumulates around the curb from flowing onto the driveway and onto the property. This is normally not a problem in newer structures. However, in older houses, the ridge tends to deteriorate, allowing water to overflow. If this condition exists, it should be corrected.

In some northern areas, raised and inclined driveways have scratch marks that are caused by studded snow tires. This indicates that those driveways will be difficult to negotiate during some winter months. In those areas, it is recommended that 100 pounds of salt and sand be stored in the garage or near the driveway to help after a freezing rain.

The minimum width for a driveway is 8 feet, although 9 feet is preferred. If the driveway is used both as an areaway for the car and as a walkway in place of a path, then it should be at least 10 feet wide. Anything less will make walking quite difficult when a car is parked in the driveway. Note whether or not the driveway discharges into a heavily trafficked street. If it does, there should be an area in the driveway that functions as a turnaround. This will allow a driver to head onto the street rather than back out onto the street. Also, look for overgrown trees and shrubs at the end of the driveway that might obstruct the driver's view when entering the street.

## CHECKPOINT SUMMARY

### SIDEWALKS—PATHS

- Inspect for cracked, missing, eroding, and uneven sections.
- Check for areas that might present a tripping hazard.
- Check slope of all paved paths adjacent to the house for improperly pitched sections.

### STREET-LEVEL/DRIVEWAY-LEVEL STEPS

- Inspect for cracked, chipped, broken, or uneven sections.
- Check for missing handrails and/or railings.

### ENTRY STEPS (MASONRY, WOOD)

- Inspect for cracked, broken, loose, or deteriorating sections.
- Note potential tripping hazards such as variations in riser heights and narrow treads.
- Check (probe) for rot in wood stringers, step treads, and handrails.
- Are wood stringers supported on concrete pads or are they resting on the earth?
- Check for handrails.
- Inspect metal handrails for rusting, loose, and broken sections.
- Inspect wooden handrails for cracked, broken, loose, and rotting sections.

### PATIO

- Check for cracked, broken, eroding, and uneven areas.
- Inspect for uneven and settled sections adjacent to the house that can allow water to accumulate around the house foundation.
- Check for rot and insect damage to imbedded wood sections.

### DRIVEWAY

- Inspect for cracked, broken, eroding, or settled areas. Note extensively cracked and deteriorated areas for future rehabilitation.
- Check slope of driveway: level, raised, or inclined?
- For an inclined driveway, is there an adequate drain at the base?
- Does drain discharge to a drywell or to a freeflowing outlet?
- Is driveway width adequate? (8-feet minimum, 9-feet preferred)

As you walk around the house inspecting the paved areas, you should also inspect the exterior walls, windows, trim, and doors. Before actually inspecting these items, however, look at the overall wall area for indications of past or current structural problems. Usually there are no problems; nevertheless, the possibility does exist. Are the window and door lines square? Are any portions of the walls sagging or bulging? Are the walls and corner sections vertical? When a problem condition is found, it should be recorded on your worksheet for further investigation. If, by the end of the house inspection, you cannot determine the cause, you should have the condition checked by a professional.

While inspecting the exterior walls, also note, for further investigation, any pipe or hood projecting through a wall or basement window. These items are usually not problem conditions, but it is useful to understand their function. The hood is often covering the discharge end of an exhaust fan or clothes dryer duct, and the pipe may be the discharge line for a sump pump or condensate line from an air-conditioning system. If the pipe is connected to a sump pump, it may indicate a past or, possibly, a current water seepage problem. Sump pumps and water seepage are discussed in detail in Chapter 11.

## EXTERIOR WALLS

The exterior walls in most residential structures will be either wood-frame or masonry constructed or, sometimes, a combination of the two. The latter is commonly called a "veneer wall." The exterior walls rest directly on the foundation and are bearing (load-supporting) walls. They support the roof, floors, and the vertical loads imposed by other building components. The outer covering of the exterior walls provides protection from the weather and, if properly installed, minimizes the flow of air, moisture, and heat into or out of the structure.

When the walls are wood-frame constructed, the vertical framing members (called "studs") support all of the imposed vertical loads, while the outer finish covering (generally called "siding") provides the weather protection. Insulation is normally located in the space between the studs. In masonry walls, the masonry (clay tile, brick, stone, concrete block, etc.) provides both the structural support and the weather barrier. A masonry veneer wall is a wood-frame wall with masonry used in place of the siding. Although the masonry in a veneer wall is not used for supporting the vertical loads, it does support its own weight.

Basically, a wood-frame exterior wall consists of 2 × 4-inch studs covered on the interior side by materials such as plaster, Sheetrock, wood, or hardboard panels (as is described in Chapter 10) and covered on the exterior side by sheathing, sheathing paper, and the finish siding. (See Figure 5-1.) In some parts of the country, where rot and termite activity are problems, metal studs are now being used in place of wood studs.

Sheathing is installed over the studs to provide bracing and to minimize air infiltration. Depending on the type of sheathing, it can also be used to form a surface onto which the exterior finish can be nailed. Wood boards, plywood, fiberboard, and gypsum board are often used for wall sheathing. Fiberboard sheathing will add a small amount of insulation to the overall exterior wall. However, it should *not* be used as a nailing base for the direct attachment of the exterior siding. Rather, the siding should be nailed either to the studding through the sheathing or to wood nailing strips that have been attached to the sheathing. In many communities, when the exterior siding is capable of supplying adequate bracing and weather protection (as with

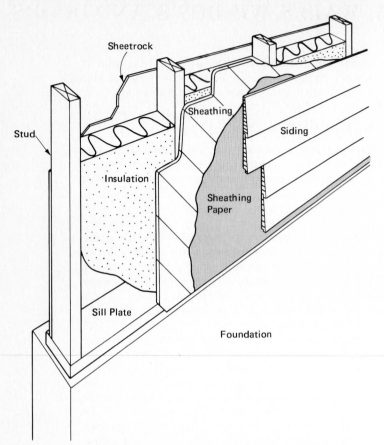

Sheetrock

Sheathing

Siding

Stud

Insulation

Sheathing Paper

Sill Plate

Foundation

FIGURE 5-1 Components of a wood-framed exterior wall.

exterior plywood panels), the sheathing is often omitted.

The purpose of the sheathing paper is to resist the direct entry of water that might occur during a driving rain. Sheathing paper (an asphalt-saturated felt) is water-resistant but not vapor-resistant, and, as such, it allows water vapor (which often builds up in the voids of the frame wall) to escape rather than condense and cause problems. Sheathing paper can also be very effective in reducing air infiltration.

## Exterior Siding

There are many types of exterior siding. If the siding is of good quality and has been maintained, it could last as long as the house. Normally, the type of maintenance required (other than painting) is the repair of cracked, broken, loose, rotting, or missing sections. When maintenance is needed, it is usually required on a small section rather than over

the entire wall. However, some homeowners neglect the siding and allow it to deteriorate to a point where complete re-siding is necessary. Several clients have asked me about the condition of the old siding on a house that had been re-sided. Actually, the degree of deterioration of the old siding does not matter, as long as the new siding is properly installed and provides the needed weather protection.

When inspecting the siding, pay particular attention to the sections that are facing south or southwesterly. These areas receive the maximum exposure to the sun and are more vulnerable to weather deterioration. The bottom of exterior siding should not be close to, or in contact with, the ground. Because of the dampness associated with the ground, the bottom of the siding should be at least 8 inches above the finished grade. Otherwise, the wood siding or the wood nailing boards for non-wood siding will be vulnerable to rot and termite infestation.

On occasion, I have found vines growing up an exterior wall and, in some cases, reaching up to the roof. Although this may be aesthetically pleasing, the vines are actually undesirable. They can cover a multitude of problems and can cause problems themselves. The vines can conceal termite shelter tubes (see Chapter 8) or cracked portions of the siding. They can widen cracks, damage mortar joints, and loosen shingles. In addition, the dampness associated with the vines can promote rot and cause paint to blister and peel. If you find vines growing up an exterior wall, you should consider removing them.

### Wood Siding

Wood siding is a broad classification that includes shingles, shakes, boards (applied vertically and horizontally), plywood panels, and hardboard. When inspecting wood siding, pay particular attention to exterior corner joints and to the joints between the siding and window and door frames. In addition, the area where the siding joins a dissimilar material (such as masonry or metal) is also vulnerable to water penetration during a driving rain. These areas should be checked for weathertightness and rot.

Occasionally, on wood siding you may find dark, blotchy sections. This condition is generally caused by spores of fungi or mildew and often occurs in shaded areas. It is not a concerning factor in that it does not cause the siding to decay. However, it is unsightly. On painted surfaces, it can often be removed by washing with bleach and water. New paint on such areas should contain a mildew-inhibitor additive. On unpainted wood surfaces, this condition can usually be controlled by coating the siding with a penetrating preservative containing pentachlorophenol. You may also find brown and black discolorations on the siding. (See Figure 5-2.) This staining is caused by rusting of the nails that were used to secure the siding. The discolorations could have been avoided if aluminum or galvanized (rust-resistant) nails had been used. Eliminating this condition is somewhat difficult and usually not cost-justified.

**Wood Shingles/Shakes** Most shingles and shakes (hereafter referred to as shingles) used for exterior sidewall application are made from cedar or redwood. They are basically the same ones that are used for roofing (as described in Chapter 2). However, their application is somewhat different. Because vertical walls present fewer water-penetration problems than do roofs, the shingles on walls can be installed with a greater weather exposure than on roofs. In addition, roofs generally have a three-ply layer of shingles, whereas exterior walls only have a two-ply layer. For full weather protection, the butt joints between the wall shingles for the upper ply should not line up with the vertical joints for the lower ply. Otherwise, the possibility does exist that water can penetrate the wall during a driving rain.

Since the shingles are decay-resistant, they do not have to be painted for weather protection. However, new shingles that replace deteriorated unpainted weathered shingles will not match with the remaining shingles. Many shingles are painted to achieve a particular color decor. After a number of years, the paint begins to peel and flake. Consequently, once the shingles are painted, they will require periodic repainting for cosmetic purposes.

When inspecting the shingles, look for cracked, loose, chipped, rotting, and missing sections. Inspect for warped shingles. If there are any, they will generally be on the sidewall with the southerly or southwesterly exposure. Also look at the quality of the shingles. In some cases, you may find that the top portions of some are paper thin and can crack or chip very easily. These shingles are of a lower quality and are intended either for use as an undercourse or for installation with less shingle-length exposure. This type of shingled sidewall has a short projected life and periodic repairs, with eventual residing, should be anticipated. Try to gently lift a few shingles. They should not lift up. If they do, it is an indication that they were improperly nailed. Shingles that are nailed directly to fiberboard sheathing rather than to wooden nailing strips (that are attached to the sheathing) will lift up under gentle pressure. If you find any of the above conditions, they should be recorded on your worksheet for future correction.

**Wood Boards** Wood-board siding can be applied horizontally or vertically. Horizontal siding tends to make a house appear lower and longer; vertical siding tends to make a house appear taller (and is popular on one-story houses). The wood used for board siding should be free of knots. Otherwise, over a period of time, shrinkage can cause the knotty cores to drop out, leaving the siding with holes that are vulnerable to water penetration.

With the exception of redwood and cedar boards, most wood siding is painted for protection against weathering and decay. When inspecting the siding, look at the condition of the paint. Are there any bare spots, peeling, flaking, or blistered sections? If there are, depending on the extent, paint touchup or repainting may be needed. Blistered and peeling paint is often caused by moisture in the painted wood, although it can also be the result of a poor-quality paint job. The determination of the exact cause for blistering and peeling paint cannot be made during a single inspection. Nevertheless, this condition should not affect your thinking about the house. If it is caused by moisture in the wood, it can be corrected after you move in and usually at a minimal expense.

Wood-board siding should be inspected for cracked, loose, and rotting sections. In addition, look for loose and/or missing knots. All holes should be patched with a wood filler. In vertical siding, check the joints between the vertical sections for weathertightness. In both vertical and horizontal siding, pay particular attention to the outside corner joints. These joints are vulnerable to water penetration during a rain, and if any open joints are noted, they must be sealed.

**Plywood Panels** Plywood panels are also used for siding. They are made from exterior-type plywood in which the veneer layers are bonded together with a waterproof glue. The exterior facing

FIGURE 5-2 Discolorations of wood shingles caused by rust stains from iron nails.

of the panel comes in a variety of surface textures and grooves. The panels are 4 feet wide by 8, 9, or 10 feet long. The thickness of the panel will depend on the depth of the grooves and will generally vary between ⅜ and ⅝ of an inch. Plywood panels are usually installed in a vertical position with the vertical joints occurring over studs. This minimizes the number of horizontal joints, which is desirable, since plywood panels are often applied directly to the studs rather than over sheathing. Because of their vulnerability to water penetration, any horizontal joints should be shiplapped (not visible to the inspector) or protected by metal flashing (which is visible). When inspecting plywood siding, look for loose, warped, cracked, delaminated, and rotting sections. Also check for open and nonweathertight joints. If the panel siding is painted, check the finish for peeling and flaking paint and blistered sections.

**Hardboard Siding** Hardboard siding is made by bonding (under heat and pressure) wood fibers that have been ground down almost to a pulp. The siding is dense, tough, and has a fairly good dimensional stability, although not as good as that of plywood. Hardboard, like plywood, is available in a wide range of textures and surface treatments. It is available in 4-foot wide panels and 9- and 12-inch wide planks. When inspecting hardboard siding, look for cracked, chipped, broken, deteriorated, and loose sections. Also check horizontal and vertical joints for weathertightness.

## Aluminum Siding

Aluminum siding is used in new construction and is also often used when re-siding the exterior walls of a house. The siding comes in planks that are either smooth or embossed with a wood-grain texture (to resemble painted wood boards) and also as shingles and vertical panels. Aluminum siding is relatively maintenance-free. It is noncorrosive, termite-proof, and will not rot. The siding surface is generally covered with a baked enamel paint finish that can stand up for many years before it fades, becomes dull, and needs a coat of paint. If the siding is scratched, it will expose bare aluminum. However, since the aluminum will not corrode, the scratch is only of cosmetic concern and can easily be corrected with touchup paint. One problem with the siding is that it can be dented if struck hard enough—as with a baseball or stone thrown from a power mower. In many communities, it is required that aluminum siding be grounded electrically as a precaution against electrical shock hazards.

Aluminum siding is available with or without insulation backer boards. The insulation is generally a rigid-foam type (such as polystyrene) or fiberboard. Although the backer boards are only about ⅜ of an inch thick, they are quite effective as an insu-

lator for a house that has no insulation in the exterior walls. Because of increasing energy costs, even a house with insulation in the exterior walls will benefit from the additional insulation. The backer boards will reduce heat loss in the winter and heat gain in the summer. They will also increase the strength and rigidity of the siding. However, insulation-backed siding (and tight siding jobs) can cause moisture to accumulate within the exterior walls of houses that have no vapor barriers on the inside surface. (Insulation and vapor barriers are discussed in Chapter 18.) You can usually tell whether the aluminum siding has an insulation backer board by pressing on it. If the siding is relatively firm, there is a backer board. But if it yields and bends under the pressure, there is no insulation board. Another method is to tap the siding. If there is no insulation, you will get a hollow sound.

When inspecting aluminum siding, look for loose, missing, and dented sections. Check the exterior joints for open sections and for weathertightness. In those areas where electrical grounding of the siding is required, you should look for an electrical ground connection. This is a wire that runs from the siding to the inlet water pipe or to a rod or pipe that has been driven into the ground. (See Chapter 12.) You can find out whether or not an electrical ground connection is required by checking with the local municipal Building Department.

## Vinyl Siding

Vinyl siding is very much like aluminum siding in size, shape, application procedure, and appearance. Quite often, close examination of the siding is needed to tell the difference between the two. The coloring in vinyl siding is imbedded in the material and is the same throughout its thickness. Since the coloring in aluminum siding is only on the surface, an end cut or scratch in the aluminum will reveal the silvery color of the bare metal. In order to tell whether the siding is vinyl or aluminum, look at an end cut or joint.

Vinyl siding is usually installed with an insulation backer board behind each sheet. In addition to insulation value, the board adds rigidity and strength. Vinyl siding will normally not dent as a result of an impact. It merely flexes and springs back to its original shape. However, during very cold weather, the siding becomes brittle and a hard blow could crack or shatter it. When inspecting vinyl siding, check for cracked and broken sections. In addition, look for loose and sagging sections with open joints.

## Asbestos-Cement Shingles

As with roofing shingles, asbestos-cement siding shingles are manufactured by combining asbestos fibers with Portland cement under pressure. These shingles are currently called "mineral fiber shingles." They are available in a variety of textures and colors, wear well, and are very durable. Since the shingles are unaffected by the weather and are immune to rot and termite activity, they require very little maintenance. However, the shingles are brittle and can be damaged and cracked by an impact. The lower courses of the shingles are the ones most vulnerable to damage. Usually, damaged shingles are replaced rather than repaired. When inspecting asbestos shingle siding, look for cracked, chipped, broken, loose, and missing shingles. If you notice any shingles that have slipped out of place, it is usually because they were improperly nailed or because the nails used were not rust-resistant and deteriorated. If the condition is caused by the latter, then additional shingles will slip out of place in the future and maintenance should be anticipated.

Asbestos-cement shingles are generally installed with sheathing-paper-type backer strips behind the vertical shingle joints. These backer strips provide additional protection against water penetration. When inspecting a sidewall, you may find sections of backer strips that have slipped out of place or are hanging loose between the shingles. Since the shingles are normally installed over sheathing paper, which is waterproof, replacing the loose backer strips is usually not necessary.

### Asphalt Siding

Asphalt siding is made by impregnating an organic felt material or glass fiber mat with asphalt. The siding is available either as shingles or as roll products. The exterior surface of the roll material is coated and embossed so that, from a distance, it looks like bricks. As the siding ages, it becomes dry and brittle and cracks easily. For the most part, asphalt materials are no longer used for siding or re-siding residential structures. However, they can be found on existing buildings. When inspecting asphalt siding look for cracked, chipped, and eroded sections. Also check for open and lifting joints and loose, torn, and missing sections. If you find any areas that are in need of repair or replacement, record them on your worksheet.

### Stucco

A stucco finish on an exterior wall is basically a concrete sheet that has been built up in layers. It is usually made from a mixture of cement, lime, sand, and water. Stucco is weather-resistant, immune to termite and fungus attack, rigid, and durable, qualities that are very desirable for an exterior wall finish. In addition, it can be applied to curved or irregularly shaped surfaces and also to wood-frame walls that have been prepared with backing (sheathing) paper and metal lath. The backing paper is needed to resist water penetration through open joints or

FIGURE 5-3 Cracked stucco wall. If wall was covered with vines, these cracks would be concealed.

through cracks that may develop in the stucco. The metal lath provides the means for bonding and reinforcement for the stucco mix.

Stucco is generally applied in two coats on a masonry wall and three coats on a wood-frame wall. The minimum thickness for a three-coat wall is $\frac{7}{8}$ of an inch and for a two-coat wall, $\frac{5}{8}$ of an inch. The top layer of stucco is the finish coat and can be relatively smooth or can have a rough texture. In addition, it can be prepared in a wide range of colors or it can be painted.

Because stucco is a rigid material, cracks can develop as a result of a slight movement of the house. (See Figure 5-3.) Movement will occur from foundation settlement and also from wind forces. You will generally find more cracks in stucco on a wood-frame house than in stucco on a solid masonry house. Shrinkage of the wood-framing members creates stresses in the stucco that often results in cracks. Once a crack develops, water can penetrate into the wall (during a driving rain) and can cause problems. Over a period of time, the portion of the metal lath around the crack will rust and deteriorate and, depending on the condition of the backing paper, the wood framing and sheathing may rot. In addition, in cold climates, accumulated water behind the stucco can freeze, causing further deterioration as a result of frost action.

All cracks should be sealed. Hairline cracks and cracks up to $\frac{1}{16}$ of an inch can generally be sealed by coating them with a cement-based paint. The only difficulty is in matching the color of the wall. Larger cracks can be sealed by filling them with a mortar mix. Broken and loose sections of stucco must be rehabilitated—by a skilled craftsman. When inspecting a stucco wall, look for chipped, cracked, loose, and broken sections. If you find areas that are in need of repair, record their location on your work-

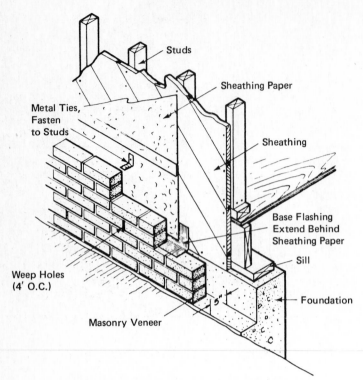

FIGURE 5-4  Components of a brick-veneered exterior wall.

sheet. Stucco does not require painting. But if it has been painted, check the condition of the paint. Once a stucco wall has been painted, periodic repainting will be required for cosmetic purposes, although at less frequent intervals than wood.

### Veneer Wall

A veneer wall is a wood-frame wall with an attached masonry facing. Unlike exterior siding, which is held in position by being fastened to the sheathing or studs, the masonry rests on top of the foundation wall and supports its own weight. It is attached to the wood backing by means of corrosion-resistant metal ties. The ties are considered the weakest point in this type of construction. If the ties have deteriorated or are not properly attached, the masonry facing can pull away from the wood frame.

The masonry, which is usually clay brick, concrete brick, or split stone, is normally positioned so that there is a 1-inch air space between the veneer wall and the wood backing. (See Figure 5-4.) Small holes, called "weep holes," are usually installed at the base of a veneer wall. These holes are needed to allow water that might accumulate in the air space to drain. When the masonry facing is brick constructed, the weep holes are generally formed by eliminating the mortar in a vertical joint.

Depending on the manufacturing process, some bricks will absorb more water than others. Bricks with high absorption should not be used for the exterior facing of walls, especially in colder climates. Unfortunately, however, occasionally they are used. Alternate freezing and thawing of bricks that have absorbed water will cause them to deteriorate. Depending on how much water has been absorbed, it is possible for the interior walls to become damp—a condition that can usually be detected during the interior inspection. If this condition exists, it can often be controlled by coating the bricks with a silicone sealant.

When inspecting a veneer wall, look for chipped, cracked, loose, deteriorating, and missing bricks and/or stones. In addition, check for cracked, chipped, and deteriorating mortar joints. Pay particular attention to the mortar joints. Occasionally, because of excessive shrinkage of the wood framing or slight foundation settlement, you may find large, open cracks—especially around window and door frames. Also look for loose and bulging sections of the veneer wall. If you find any of the above items, record their location on your worksheet for later correction.

### Masonry Wall

Unlike a wood-frame wall, where the structural support and the weather barrier are provided by two separate components, studs and siding, the masonry units in a masonry wall (clay tile, brick, stone, or concrete block) provide both the support and the weather protection. Because of the low thermal resistance of masonry, there will normally be a greater heat loss through a masonry wall than through a wood-frame wall.

In order to reduce the heat loss through the masonry wall, insulation can be added by applying a rigid foam insulation board to the interior side. In addition to providing insulation, the board can also be used as a base for plastering. Another approach is to apply furring strips to the inside wall. The furring strips create an air space into which insulation can be placed prior to installing the 'finishing wall panel.' In some cases, however, the interior side of the masonry wall is left completely exposed and serves as a decorative element or as a base for direct plastering. This is quite wasteful from an energy conservation point of view.

Because of the rigidity of masonry walls, differential movement within the wall may cause serious cracking. Wall movement may be the result of unequal foundation settlement or expansion and contraction as a result of temperature and humidity changes. Many cracks that develop are not of a structural concern, although they should be sealed to eliminate the possibility of water penetration. If there is any doubt in your mind about the severity of a crack, have the condition checked by a professional.

A common problem with masonry walls is efflorescence on the exterior surface. Efflorescence is a deposit of soluble salts that were originally within the masonry and is usually brought to the surface by water in the wall. When the water evaporates, the salts are deposited. Efflorescence can generally be removed by scrubbing with a stiff brush or washing with a dilute solution of muriatic acid. However, if the condition is a recurring problem, it is an indication that water is penetrating the wall either through cracks or through faulty joints or flashing.

When inspecting a masonry wall, pay particular attention to the joints around window and door frames. All joints should be weathertight. Are there any cracks around the corners of window or door openings? These are areas of high stress concentration and are vulnerable to cracking. Cracked and chipped mortar joints and deteriorated masonry should be indicated on your worksheet for later repair. If you notice bulging sections in the exterior walls or large, cracked sections, have the condition checked professionally, as it may indicate structural problems.

FIGURE 5-5   Exterior trim on a house: A. gable louvers, B. fascia, C. soffit, D. shutters, E. widow's walk balustrade, F. decorative columns.

## TRIM

All portions of the exterior finish, other than the wall covering, are generally classified as exterior trim. This includes the moldings and sills around windows and doors, fascia boards, soffits, louvers, shutters, and decorative columns. (See Figure 5-5.) Trim does not serve a structural function. It is used as finishing around openings and also as a means to protect joints, edges, and ends. Most exterior trim is made of wood or wood products, although aluminum and vinyl trim are becoming quite popular. Many older, traditionally designed homes have decorative sheetmetal cornices, which are considered part of the trim. The problem with sheetmetal trim is that if it is not maintained and kept adequately painted, it will rust and deteriorate.

Wood trim that is exposed to the weather should be decay-resistant so that it will not rot as a result of periodic wetting. (See section on rot in Chapter 8.) Some types of preformed trim are factory-treated with a water-repellent preservative to make them water- and decay-resistant. When the trim is cut to size during construction, the ends or miter joints must be treated to make them water-resistant. All too often, they are not treated, and the joints, which readily absorb water, begin to rot. When inspecting wood trim, pay particular attention to the joints that are vulnerable to decay. A house with a wide roof overhang at the eaves and gables will provide greater weather protection of the sidewalls and trim than one on which there is no roof projection beyond the walls. All nontreated wood that is continually exposed to moisture is prone to decay. The trim around the edge of the roof is particularly vulnerable. Although the Asphalt Roofing Manufacturers Association recommends the installation of a metal drip edge along the eaves of a roof deck, in practice, it is often omitted. The drip edge is designed to allow water runoff to drip free of the underlying trim. Without it, water tends to curl back under the shingles, wetting the edge of the roof sheathing and trim.

Wood trim should be inspected for cracked, loose, missing, and rotting sections. If the trim is painted, are there sections with peeling and flaking paint? Does the trim need repainting for weather protection? In older Tudor-style houses with timbers imbedded in the stucco siding, inspect the timbers at the stucco joints for decay, especially if the joint is horizontal. Over the years, the joints tend to open slightly, allowing water to penetrate. With nonwood trim, check for loose, missing, and deteriorated sections.

## WINDOWS

The windows should be checked during both the exterior and interior inspection. The overall condition of the windows should be checked during the exterior inspection, while the operation of the windows should be checked during the interior inspection. (See section on windows in Chapter 10.)

There are many types of windows used in residential structures. The most common types, as shown in Figure 5-6 are double-hung, horizontal

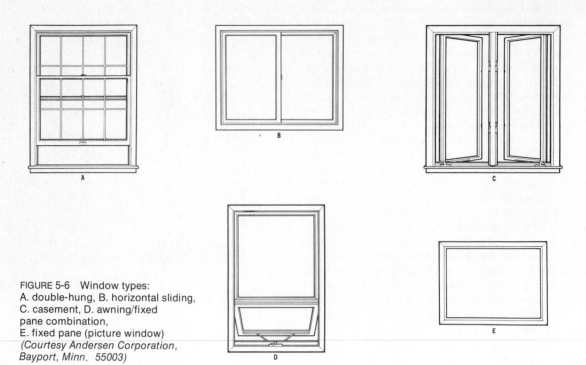

FIGURE 5-6   Window types:
A. double-hung, B. horizontal sliding,
C. casement, D. awning/fixed
pane combination,
E. fixed pane (picture window)
*(Courtesy Andersen Corporation,
Bayport, Minn. 55003)*

sliding, casement, awning, jalousie, and fixed-pane.

The *double-hung window* is the most commonly found window unit in older and newer homes. It consists of upper and lower sashes that slide vertically past one another. The sashes are held in a fixed position within the window frame by a friction fit, counterweights, or spring balances. In some windows, the sashes are removable for ease of maintenance, such as for cleaning or painting. One variation of the double-hung window is the single-hung window. In this case, the upper sash is fixed and the lower sash is movable.

The sashes in a *horizontal sliding window* slide horizontally on separate tracks. The most common design consists of two sashes, both of which are movable. However, sometimes one sash is fixed. In most of these windows, the sash can be removed for cleaning.

*Casement windows* consist of two or more sashes that are hinged at the side and, generally, are mounted so that they will swing outward. The sashes are opened and closed either by a cranking mechanism, a push bar mounted on the frame, or a handle fastened to the sash. Because the sash opens outward, a storm sash or screen must be attached to the inside of the window.

*Awning windows* have one or more sashes that are hinged at the top and mounted so that they swing out at the bottom. They are opened by push

bars or cranking mechanisms similar to those on casement windows. As with casement windows, screens and storm sashes are mounted on the inside.

*Jalousie windows* are basically adjustable louvers. The louvers are glass slats (several inches wide) that are held by an aluminum frame at each end. The frames are interconnected by levers so that the slats open and close in unison, similar to venetian blinds. Jalousie windows are crank-operated and provide good ventilation. However, because of the many glass slats, they are troublesome to wash and are not weathertight. Even with a storm sash, there often is cold air leakage around the windows. In northern climates, jalousies are usually limited to use on porches and breezeways.

Unlike the preceding windows, which are movable and provide ventilation, *fixed-pane windows* are stationary and are only used to provide daylight and viewing of the outdoors. They can be used alone or in combination with sliding, double-hung, or swinging windows to achieve a custom design.

With the exception of the jalousie windows, which are only available in aluminum, all of the windows are available in wood, metal (steel or aluminum), and vinyl-clad frames. If you are not sure whether the metal window frames in the house that you are inspecting are steel or aluminum, you can always tell the difference by using a magnet. The magnet will stick to a steel frame but not to an aluminum one.

Metal frames get quite cold during the winter months. Consequently, some of the water vapor in the air inside of the house will tend to condense on the frames. In order to reduce this condensation, several manufacturers are producing metal-framed windows with a thermal barrier that prevents the outside frame from touching the inside frame. This substantially reduces the condensation but does not eliminate it. Since wood has a greater thermal resistance than metal, wood window frames normally do not get cold enough for condensation to form on their inside surface.

Although wood windows provide a better insulation value than metal windows, they do have a tendency to swell or shrink with changes in moisture content. A wood sash that absorbs moisture will expand and bind in the frame so that it does not operate freely. Wood windows should be treated (by the manufacturer) with a water-repellent preservative to resist decay and moisture absorption. In the past, not all windows were so treated; thus rotting sections and binding sashes are occasionally found during an inspection.

The sheet glass used in windows must be of sufficiently high quality to minimize distortion. Years ago, because of the difficulty of manufacturing large distortion-free panes, window glass was only available in small sheets. Consequently, in order to fill a large opening such as a window sash, small panes of glass were used and held in position by framing strips called "muntins." Today, even though large windowpanes are available, muntins are still used to create a special architectural effect. Some window manufacturers provide preassembled wood or plastic dividers that simulate muntins. The dividers merely overlay the large windowpane and snap in and out of the sash.

Windowpanes are also available with single and double glazing. A double-glazed window is a thermal (or insulated) pane. It will reduce the heat loss or gain through an equivalently sized single-pane window by about 50 percent. It will also reduce condensation on the inside surface. With some windows, triple glazing is also available.

### Inspection

When inspecting the windows, look for cracked, broken, and missing panes. Check the joints between the sash and the window frames to see whether they are filled with paint. If they are, the windows may not open and minor maintenance will be needed. The condition of the joints between the glass pane and the sash should be inspected. Are there any loose panes? Most windowpanes are

secured to the sash by bedding and sealing with a glazing compound such as putty. If putty is used, are there any cracked, loose, chipped, and missing sections? Some panes are secured to the sash by wood strips (trim). The strips should be checked for cracked, loose, and missing sections. If any of the above items are found, they should be noted on your worksheet for later correction.

Look at the overall condition of the window frames and sash. Windows that are exposed to the elements are vulnerable to weathering deterioration. Are any wood sections cracked and rotted? Steel windows, if not maintained, will rust. Depending on the extent of the deterioration, some windows will require simple repair, while others may require replacement. All of the windows will generally not be visible and/or accessible during your exterior inspection, especially the windows on upper levels. The exterior portion of those windows, along with their operation, should be checked during your interior inspection.

### EXTERIOR DOORS

There are two basic types of exterior wood doors: flush doors and stile-and-rail doors. Flush doors are made by bonding face panels to solid or hollow cores. Stile-and-rail doors, also referred to as panel doors, are solid doors that consist of vertical and horizontal members (called "stiles" and "rails," respectively) that enclose wood or glass inserts. (See Figure 5-7.)

Most *flush doors* have hardwood veneer face panels, although hardboard and softwood panels are also available. Some doors are made with cutouts for windows or louvers. Flush doors are used as both interior and exterior doors. When used as exterior doors, they should be made with waterproof adhesives rather than water-resistant adhesives. You can often tell whether the proper adhesive was used in constructing the door by looking at the top edge. In many quality doors, you will find a small red plastic plug in the edge. This indicates that the door was bonded with a waterproof adhesive that is suitable for exterior use. When an improper adhesive is used, the exterior face panel will eventually begin to delaminate and peel.

A solid-core flush door provides greater heat and sound insulation, fire resistance, and dimensional stability than does a hollow-core door. The solid core of a flush door may be made of wood blocks or a composition material that has been formed into a rigid slab; a hollow core is generally made of wood or wood derivatives (cardboard) that have been formed into a honeycomb or parallel strips. When resistance to heat, sound, and fire are not critical factors, the hollow-core flush door is sometimes used as an exterior door. This, however, is not considered quality construction. When used on the exterior, the door should be treated with a water-repellent preservative and should also be bonded with a waterproof adhesive. Unfortunately, this is not always the case.

One variation of the flush door is the metal-clad insulated entrance door. This door is available in a selection of surface styles and is becoming more popular. Basically the door consists of metal face panels with an insulating core. Some doors are provided with a thermal-break to separate the interior parts of the frame and door panel from the exterior parts, thereby minimizing condensation during the winter months. Because of the insulating characteristics of this type of door, the need for a storm door is essentially eliminated.

Although *stile-and-rail doors* are not as commonly used as are flush doors, they are available in a greater variety of designs. Because of the number of panels and joints, the stile-and-rail door is not as effective an insulator as is a flush door. Also, depending on the quality of the door, one or more panels may crack as a result of shrinkage. If you stand inside of the house looking at the door, cracked sections will become very noticeable. Daylight will be visible through the cracks.

Some exterior doors are not considered secure because of the location of the glass panes (relative to the door lock). If the door lock can be reached by breaking a glass pane either in the door or in side panels, then an auxiliary lock is recommended. This lock should be positioned where it is not accessible from the outside. Since you will normally not know whether you were given all of the keys to the exterior door locks, it is recommended that, after you take possession of the house, you replace all of the door locks or, at least have the locks rekeyed.

The condition of the exterior doors should be checked during your exterior inspection, and the operation of the doors should be checked during your interior inspection. On the exterior, inspect for cracked, chipped, broken, delaminating, and rotting sections. When inside the house, check the doors for cracks (visible daylight) and ease of operation. Does the door open and close easily or does it bind? Also check for weatherstripping around the exterior joints. Weatherstripping is desirable, as it will minimize air infiltration. If you find any problems with the doors, record them on your worksheet.

## STORM WINDOWS, SCREENS, AND STORM DOORS

### Storm Windows

Windows are a major source of heat loss in a house. On a per-square-foot basis, more heat is lost through windows than through any other area. In fact, the amount of heat lost through a single-pane window is approximately fourteen times greater than that lost through a well-insulated wall of com-

FIGURE 5-7  Exterior doors: flush (*top*); stile-and-rail (*bottom*).

parable size. However, through the use of storm windows, the heat loss can be reduced by about 50 percent.

There are three basic types of storm windows: storm sashes, storm panels, and combination units. A *storm sash* is a removable sash, usually made of wood and containing a fixed-pane window. The storm sash fits over the operating window either on the outside or inside, depending on how the window opens. Storm sashes are most commonly found on the outside of older double-hung windows. They are not desirable for year-round use because they cannot be opened to admit breezes during the warmer months. Consequently, the storm windows are generally taken off in early spring, and reinstalled in late fall—a task that can be somewhat awkward and time-consuming.

A *storm panel* looks like a storm sash except that it is usually mounted in a narrow metal frame and is attached to the movable window sash rather than being fitted over the entire window opening. Since storm panels are attached directly to the movable sash, they do not interfere with the operation of the window and need not be removed during the warmer months.

*Combination units* refer to storm and screen sashes combined in a single frame. The unit is mounted over the outside of the window and, as such, is effective in reducing air infiltration around the window joints in addition to reducing heat loss. Combination storm and screen windows are available in two- and three-track units. With two-track units, the outside track contains the storm sash in the upper half and a screen sash in the lower half. With the screen in position, the upper storm sash cannot move. The inside track contains the lower storm sash, which can slide up and down. In a triple-track unit, there is a separate track for each of the two storm panes and for the screen. Combination storm and screen units are generally found on double-hung and horizontal sliding windows. Since these units do not interfere with the operation of the movable sash and can also be opened to provide ventilation, they are not normally removed once installed.

Combination units are available in aluminum, steel, or solid vinyl. The aluminum frame with a baked enamel finish looks like a vinyl frame. You can tell the difference by looking at an edge or joint. The aluminum edge will have a silvery color, whereas the vinyl edge will be the same color as the frame. Over the years, many aluminum frames with a mill finish (plain aluminum) show the effects of weathering such as pitting, corrosion, and a degraded appearance. An anodized or baked enamel finish will offer greater protection against weathering. Combination storm and screen windows

made of steel have a tendency to rust and require periodic painting.

### Screens

Most window screens for residential structures are either mounted on a wood sash or are rimmed with a metal or plastic frame. The wood-framed screen is usually used in conjunction with a storm sash, and the metal- or plastic-framed screen is used in the combination storm and screen unit. Metal- or plastic-framed screens are also used for casement and awning-type windows. However, for these windows, the screen must be equipped with panels that provide access to the cranks or push bars.

Another type of screen that is available (although not very common) is the roll-up screen. This screen is mounted on the inside of the window and is similar in operation to a roll-up shade. When the screen is not being used, it can be rolled up and hidden from view. The sides of the screen move in metal tracks to prevent insects from flying in around the edges. As the screen ages, the joint between the screen and the track tends to open and become less effective.

### Storm Doors

In colder climates, unless the exterior doors are the insulated type, they are often used with storm doors in order to reduce heat loss and cold air infiltration around the joints. Storm doors are generally lightly constructed wood or metal stile-and-rail-type doors with a glass panel insert. On many of these doors, the glass insert is interchangeable with a screen panel so that they can function as both storm and screen doors. Because of the nature of storm doors (constantly being opened), they are not as effective as storm windows in reducing heat loss. Nevertheless, they are effective from an overall energy conservation point of view.

### Inspection

When inspecting the house, look for storm windows. If you do not see any, or if the inspection is being performed during warmer weather when storm sashes are normally not installed, ask the owner whether or not there are storm sashes for all of the fixed and movable windows. If there are no storm windows or only a few, record the fact on your worksheet. Installing a complete set of storm windows can be quite costly.

Storm windows should be inspected for cracked, broken, and missing panes. When the storm sash is wood, check for cracked, broken, and rotting sections. On combination units, look specifically at the corner joints. These joints should be tight so that there will be no cold air leakage into the unit. Check the overall condition of the frames. Are there loose, broken, rusted, or corroded sections? Are any of the panes loose in the sash? When inspecting the screens, look for torn sections and holes. In metal- and plastic-rimmed screens, the screening is normally held in position by a spline that has been forced into a groove around the frame. Periodically, I find splines hanging loose within the frame of the combination unit. If you find loose splines, it is an indication that the joints in the associated screens must be resecured.

Storm doors should be checked for ease of operation and overall condition. Are there cracked, broken, loose, rotted, or corroded sections? Is the glass panel loose, cracked, broken, or missing? If you find any problems with the storm windows, screens, or storm doors, record them on your worksheet as a reminder for later correction.

## CAULKING

As you walk around the house inspecting the walls, windows, trim, and doors, look for cracked and open joints. All exterior joints should be caulked (sealed) so that they are watertight and airtight. If they are not adequately caulked, wind-driven rain can enter and cause wood members to rot, metal ties to rust, and masonry sections to crack and chip. In addition, cold air can infiltrate into the house, resulting in higher heating costs. A vulnerable joint for cracking is one that joins two dissimilar materials, for example, the joint between a brickfront facing and a nonmasonry sidewall. Dissimilar materials usually have different expansion and contraction characteristics that often cause the joints between them to crack and open. These joints should be sealed with a nonshrinking, flexible caulking compound.

There are several types of caulking compounds. The four most popular types are oil base, acrylic latex base, butyl-rubber base, and silicone base. *Oil base* caulking compounds are the cheapest and will readily bond to most surfaces—wood, masonry, and metal. However, they are not very durable, as they tend to dry and crack after a short period of time. Joints sealed with this type of caulk require periodic inspection and maintenance. *Acrylic latex* caulking compounds are medium priced, durable, flexible, and should last for many years. *Butyl-rubber* caulks are medium priced, durable, and paintable. However, they exhibit a high shrinkage—a characteristic that is acceptable when caulking narrow cracks and inside corners. *Silicone base* caulks are the most expensive. They are very pliable and, as such, are good for sealing joints that are subject to movement. No one caulking compound is ideally suited for every application. However, based on cost, durability, and ease of application, acrylic latex caulks are considered by many to be the best overall choice.

When inspecting the exterior joints. check the condition of the caulking. Look for cracked, chipped, crumbly, and missing caulking compound. The location of joints that need recaulking should be recorded on your worksheet. Recaulking is a relatively simple task and can be done after you move into the house.

## CHECKPOINT SUMMARY

### GENERAL CONSIDERATIONS

- Inspect exterior walls for sagging and bulging sections, and for corners that are not vertical.
- Check for window and door frames that are not square.
- Structural problems for which the cause cannot be determined should be evaluated by a professional.
- Note wall locations that have pipe or hood projections.
- Determine their usage (i.e., sump pump discharge, condensate line, dryer vent, etc.).
- Check for vines that are growing up the exterior walls.

### EXTERIOR WALLS

**Wood Siding (Shingles/shakes, boards, plywood panels, hardboard)**
- Check bottom course of siding for sections in contact with, or close proximity to, the ground (less than 8 inches).
- Check wood shingles/shakes for open joints, cracked, chipped, loose, or missing sections.
- Note areas of rot or discolorations.
- Check for peeling and flaking paint and warped shingles, particularly on sidewalls with a southerly or southwesterly exposure.
- Inspect for poor-quality shingles and for shingles that have been improperly nailed.
- Check wood boards for open joints, cracked and rotting sections, loose or missing knots, peeling paint, and blistered sections.
- Inspect plywood panels for open joints, loose, warped, cracked, delaminated, or rotting sections.
- Check hardboard siding for cracked, deteriorated, or loose sections.

**Aluminum/Vinyl Siding**
- Check aluminum siding for loose, missing, torn, or dented sections.

- Check joints for open sections and weathertightness.
- Does siding contain insulation backer boards?
- Check siding for an electrical ground connection. (This requirement can be verified with the local Building Department.)
- Check vinyl siding for open joints, loose, cracked, or sagging sections.

### Asbestos-Cement Shingles/Asphalt Siding

- Check asbestos-cement shingles for loose or missing sections, cracked, chipped, and broken areas.
- Inspect asphalt siding for open/lifting joints, missing, loose, torn, cracked, chipped, or eroding sections.

### Stucco-Cement Finished Walls

- Check for bulging, missing, loose, cracked, or chipped sections. Note areas in need of rehabilitation.
- If stucco is painted, check condition.

### Veneer and Masonry Walls

- Inspect for loose or bulging sections and large, open cracks, particularly around door and window frames.
- Check for cracked, chipped, or missing sections of brick or stone.
- Inspect mortar joints for deterioration, cracked or loose sections.
- Check exterior surfaces on masonry walls for signs of water seepage (efflorescence).

## TRIM

- Check trim for cracked, loose, missing, or rotting sections.
- Inspect for areas of bare wood, blistered and peeling paint.

- Check nonwood trim for cracked, torn, missing, or loose sections.

## WINDOWS

- Check for cracked, broken, or missing panes.
- Are any of the windows painted shut?
- Are the panes properly secured to the sashes?
- Check the condition of the window frames and sashes.

## EXTERIOR DOORS

- Check for cracked, chipped, broken, or delaminating sections.
- Check for weatherstripping around exterior joints.

## STORM WINDOWS, SCREENS, AND STORM DOORS

- Check for missing units and/or partial installations.
- Inspect storm windows for loose, cracked, broken, or missing panes.
- Inspect wood units for cracked, broken, or rotting sections.
- Inspect combination units for loose, broken, rusting, or corroded sections.
- Inspect screens for torn sections and holes.
- Inspect/check doors for ease of operation; missing glass; cracked, broken, rotting, or corroded sections.

## CAULKING

- Check joints for cracked, chipped, crumbly, missing, or loose areas of caulking compound.

# 6. LOT AND LANDSCAPING

In addition to all of the items mentioned in the previous chapters, you should also inspect the drainage around the house and the landscaping. If there are retaining walls, decks, or fences, they too should be inspected.

## DRAINAGE

As housing developments and shopping centers sprout up in the countryside, they affect the drainage characteristics of the surrounding area. Normally, in undeveloped areas, a large portion of the water falling to the earth soaks into the ground. The remaining portion flows over the surface into lakes, rivers, and streams or accumulates in low-level areas forming ponds. In built-up areas, thousands of acres that had been soaking up rain have been rendered impervious to water because of the buildings and paved areas. The surface water runoff in these areas may be two to ten times more than it was when the same land was undeveloped.

In built-up areas, surface water usually flows into storm drains (catch basins) that, in turn, discharge into rivers and streams. There have been cases where established housing developments have been inundated with surface water after a heavy rain because their storm drainage facilities were not adequate for the increased water flow resulting from new, adjacent housing developments. In most cases, the increased runoff results in the rivers and streams swelling, although they are usually contained within their banks. The possibility does exist, however, that after heavy prolonged rain, a river or stream can overflow its banks and flood the surrounding area. Many people do not realize that even a small creek, which may be a trickle when they see it, can become a raging, destructive torrent following an excessively heavy rain.

The area normally flooded when a river or stream overflows its banks is called a "flood plain." Between 5 and 10 percent of the land in the United States is on a flood plain. Much of this land is level and, from all other outward appearances, seems to be desirable. As land in urban and suburban areas became more and more scarce, builders constructed homes directly on the flood plains of streams and other waterways. These homes are all vulnerable to flooding. (See Figure 6-1.) In many parts of the country, there are owners who do not realize that their homes were built in a flood-prone area, and they probably will not realize it—until it is too late.

If you have any doubts about whether or not the house that you are inspecting is located on a flood plain, you should check with the local town or county engineer. If the engineer is not available, very often the local Highway Superintendent can tell you whether or not the area periodically floods. In many communities, Federal flood insurance is available for those homes located on a flood plain. If you are considering such a home, you should also consider purchasing flood insurance.

Surface runoff is of concern to the homeowner because it can also result in soil erosion, ponded water, and water penetration into the basement or crawl space. Soil erosion occurs whenever water flows over bare earth. Soil particles are loosened and are carried away by the flow. Water seeks its own level and will, therefore, flow from a point of higher elevation to one of lower elevation. The paths that the water takes when flowing to a lower level are called the "natural drainageways." Areas that are particularly vulnerable to erosion are steep banks and drainageways. (See Figure 6-2.)

The basic principle for preventing or minimizing erosion is to have the grounds covered, as much as possible, with growing vegetation such as grass, trees, bushes, shrubs, and even weeds. If the vegetation does not root and keeps washing out, a substitute cover such as gravel, stones, or mulch can be used. This cover is not as effective, but it does reduce the erosion. In some cases, the banks are too steep for a ground cover of any kind; in this case, they must be stabilized by terracing and/or by using retaining walls.

In addition to a ground cover, erosion can be reduced by slowing down the water flow. As an example, if there is a concentrated surface runoff along a natural drainageway, the water can be diverted to a man-made channel or ridge that follows a level contour. This spreads out the water and slows down the flow so that the water does not scour and erode the soil.

The effects of surface runoff can be minimized, if needed, by reshaping the ground surface. This can be done by terracing and/or regrading the lot into gentle slopes with diversionary ridges and swales. A swale is a depression in the ground that, like a ridge, will intercept surface runoff and redirect it to an area where the water will not cause any damage. When a house is located on a sloping lot, there should be a swale or ridge in the portion of the lot that slopes toward the house. This type of a diversion will prevent surface water from accumulating around the house. Otherwise, the possibility does exist that the surface runoff will seep into the basement or crawl space. (See Chapter 11.)

Many building lots have low, level areas that will tend to accumulate water after a rain or as a result of surface runoff. When the soil is slow draining, as in the case of clay and silt, the water will pond rather than soak into the ground. The ponded areas retain the water until it evaporates or eventually seeps into the ground. Depending on the location of the pond, the accumulated water may or may not be a problem. If the pond is over the leaching field of a septic system or is located in an area that normally has a lot of foot traffic or is used for play by children, then corrective action is necessary. The problem can often be corrected by bringing in fill and regrading the area. However, when regrading is not practical, the area can be drained by laying a line of perforated drain pipe through the affected area and directing one end of the pipe to another low spot. The pipe is generally encased in a bed of gravel or broken stones. If the conditions warrant it, a concrete block catch basin with radial spokes of perforated pipe can be installed at the low point. (See Figure 6-3.) Water collected in the pipes and catch basin can then be directed away to another area. If there are no other low areas to which the ponded water can be redirected using a pipe with gravity flow, then the water can be directed to a sump pit and pumped to the desired location.

## Groundwater/Water Table

That water that soaks into the ground eventually percolates downward, under the influence of gravity, until it reaches an impervious layer through which it cannot penetrate. After the water reaches the impervious layer, it begins to move in a lateral direction. This underground flow is known as "groundwater," the top surface of which is commonly called the "water table." The level of the water table will vary with the amount of rainfall. Consequently, the water table may be several feet higher after a prolonged rainy period than during a prolonged spell of dry weather.

FIGURE 6-1   Backyard flooding of a house located in a flood plain. *(Courtesy USDA-Soil Conservation Service)*

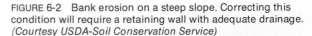

FIGURE 6-2   Bank erosion on a steep slope. Correcting this condition will require a retaining wall with adequate drainage. *(Courtesy USDA-Soil Conservation Service)*

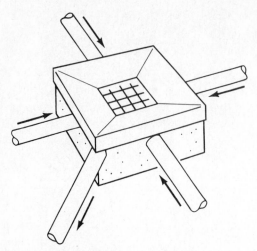

FIGURE 6-3   Concrete block catch basin with several perforated inlet pipes and a solid outlet pipe that drains to a suitable location. Used for draining low level lawns that are collection ponds for rain water.

The level of the water table is of concern to the homeowner in that a high water table can result in a flooded basement or failure of the septic system's leaching field. In many parts of the United States, the seasonal high water table is only 2 to 5 feet below the ground surface. In those areas, houses should be built on a slab or over a crawl space rather than over a full basement. Unfortunately, however, houses with full basements have been built in areas where the water table (during the wet season) is above the level of the basement floor. This invariably results in water penetration into the basement. In fact, depending on the soil, even when the water table is several feet below the basement floor, there may be some water seepage into the area as a result of the capillary rise of groundwater. (See Chapter 11.)

Homes located in areas where the seasonal high water table is only a few feet below the ground surface should not have septic systems for waste disposal. Ideally, they should be connected to a sewer system. For proper operation of a septic system, the water table during the wet season should be at least 4 feet below the bottom of the leaching field or seepage pit. The operation of a septic system is explained in Chapter 13.

Basically, the top surface of flowing streams, rivers, lakes, and also the ocean is the water table. Consequently, the terrain that gradually slopes into the waterway will have a high water table. Homes built in these areas are not only vulnerable to problems associated with a high water table, but they are also vulnerable to flooding. The water table tends to follow the general contour of the land and, in some areas, may intersect the ground surface,

thus forming marshy, wet lands. To a homeowner, these wet lands are quite undesirable, for not only are they costly to drain, but they are also a breeding place for insects.

Excessive grading or reshaping of the ground surface (such as cutting out the side of a hill to locate a house, Figure 6-4) can change the natural drainage patterns and cause groundwater to seep to the surface. I have inspected many such houses and have found (in the early spring or after an excessively heavy rain) water oozing out of the cut side of the hill. This water, if not redirected away from the house, can work its way into the basement or crawl space.

In areas where there is a seasonal high water table, if the topography is such that the land slopes toward one side of the house, then in addition to surface water runoff, there will also be subsurface water flowing toward the house. This water, if allowed to accumulate around the foundation, can seep into the basement or crawl space. This condition can usually be controlled by installing a "curtain drain" in the hillside parallel to the house in order to divert the water away from the house.

A curtain drain consists of a perforated drain pipe installed in a trench that is filled with gravel and covered with soil. The trench normally extends several feet beyond the house, with one end leading to a suitable disposal area. Incidentally, the perforations in the pipe should be facing downward and not upward, as is popularly believed. As the subsurface water level rises, it enters the holes along the length of the pipe. Since water always takes the path of least resistance, once inside the pipe, it flows to the outlet, which must be located away from the

FIGURE 6-4   House located on the cutout side of a hill. Building site requires special provisions to minimize erosion and drainage problems. *(Courtesy USDA-Soil Conservation Service)*

house and which must also be unobstructed. The outlet, however, should have an animal screen to prevent a small animal (such as a rabbit) from entering, becoming lodged, and blocking the flow.

In areas where there is a seasonal high water table or where there is a potential for surface water to accumulate around the foundation, it is advisable to have foundation footing drains. These are perforated drain pipes that are installed parallel and adjacent to the foundation footing. (See Figure 6-5.) As with curtain drains, the footing drains are installed with the holes facing downward. The purpose of the footing drain is to channel the water that accumulates around the foundation away to another location. Footing and curtain drains either must have a free-flowing outlet or must discharge into a sump pit where the accumulated water can be pumped to the desired location.

## Inspection

The drainage inspection should begin as you are driving up to the house. When you are approaching the house, take notice of the overall topography. Is it level or inclined? If it is inclined, is it a gentle slope or a steep slope? With inclined topography, there is some concern about the possibility of surface and subsurface water movement toward the house. If the house is located near the bottom of an inclined street, is there a storm drain (catch basin) in the street at the low point? There should be, especially if the street is paved. Otherwise, after a rain or snow melt, water will accumulate at the low area and, depending on the amount, will flood the adjacent yards and driveways. Did you notice a waterway (stream, brook, etc.) on the street as you approached the house? If you did, the house may be located on a flood plain.

When you arrive at the house, notice whether the land between the house and the street is above or below the street level. If the land slopes downward from the street to the house, the house will be vulnerable to drainage problems. In this case, the surface water, if not properly controlled, can accumulate around the foundation or can pond on the lawn or over the entry path. If the house is inspected when it is not raining, you may not actually see any problems. However, based on the slope and overall grading of the land around the house, you can at least determine any potential for a problem.

As you walk around the house, notice whether or not the ground immediately adjacent is graded so that it slopes away from the house on all sides. It should be. Otherwise, surface water can run directly up to the foundation (see Figure 6-6), seep down along the foundation walls, and accumulate at

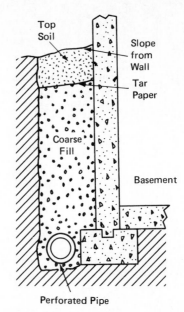

FIGURE 6-5 Foundation footing drain, used for channeling water that accumulates around the foundation to another location.

the lower section. When this happens, it usually results in water seepage into the basement or crawl space. A rule of thumb for grading this area is a drop of about 1 inch per foot. The lawn should slope away from the house for at least 10 feet and should be pitched so that there is approximately a 10-inch drop over that distance. (See Figure 6-7.) Because of normal soil settlement and compaction, an occa-

FIGURE 6-6 Improper grading of the land adjacent to the house. The lawn pitches toward the door, resulting in surface water ponding in front of the entry area.

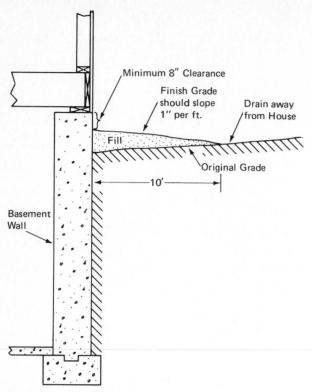

FIGURE 6-7  Finish grade of the ground adjacent to the foundation, sloped for proper drainage.

sional clogged gutter or faulty downspout, and foot traffic (especially when the ground is wet), the slope of the ground adjacent to the house usually changes with time. Consequently, the area around the foundation should be periodically checked for proper grading.

When checking the grading around the founda-

tion, you may occasionally see a pipe protruding through the foundation wall or, possibly, out of a basement window. If you do, record the fact on your worksheet for further investigation when you inspect the basement. Usually, this pipe is connected to a sump pump and is used for discharging the water that accumulates in the sump pit. The end of the pipe should be extended away from the house so that the water will not accumulate around the foundation. Sometimes, however, the pipe terminates just beyond the foundation wall. This termination basically negates the advantage of a sump pump. The discharging water accumulates around and under the foundation and reenters the sump pit, only to be pumped out again. (See Figure 6-8.)

If you find a stream on the property, you should realize that there is a potential for flooding. As discussed previously, flooding can occur because of the increased surface runoff resulting from a prolonged, heavy rain. In addition, if there is a blockage in the stream channel because of fallen trees, tree limbs, sediment, or trash that restricts the water flow, flooding can result. Depending on the location of the stream relative to the house, occasional overflowing of the stream banks may or may not be a problem.

As you walk around, look at the overall landscape. If there is sloping topography, is there a natural drainageway to direct surface runoff away from the house, or is there a need for a swale or ridge? If there is an abrupt change in the grading, is there a need for a retaining wall? Are any areas eroding to the extent that corrective action is necessary? Are there low or level areas that are vulnerable to water ponding? Ponded water on the lawn does not necessarily indicate a drainage problem. It

FIGURE 6-8  Sump pump discharge pipe. *Left:* Pipe terminates just beyond the foundation wall. *Right:* Discharge pipe has been extended so that effluent will discharge away from the foundation.

may be caused by a malfunctioning septic system, a faulty sewer hookup, or, possibly, a break in the main water supply pipe. If you find ponded water during your inspection, you should try to determine the cause.

If there are footing drains around the house foundation and/or curtain drains in a hillside, they would not be visible during your inspection. In order for these drains to function properly, they must have a free-flowing outlet. (See Figure 6-9.) Ask the seller if there are drains and, if so, ask for the location of the outlets. Unfortunately, most homeowners do not know whether or not there are footing and/or curtain drains. When a house is sold, this type of information is usually not discussed, although it should be. Consequently, the location of the drain outlet is lost for the new and all future owners of the house. If you are lucky enough to have a seller who knows the location of the drain outlet, you should inspect the opening to make sure that there is no obstruction. On occasion, in new homes, the drain outlet is inadvertently blocked when the lawn is landscaped. If you are buying a new house, ask the builder to show you the location of the drain outlet.

## RETAINING WALLS

Retaining walls are mostly used for stabilizing and controlling erosion on steep banks. In some cases, however, they are used in conjunction with terracing of rear or side yards to provide a level area for recreation. In either case, they must be designed to withstand the lateral pressures being exerted on them by the soil.

Retaining walls are normally built with construction timbers, railroad ties, stone, concrete, or concrete blocks. Some concrete and concrete block walls have stone or brick veneer facing. On occasion, you may find a "gabion" retaining wall. Gabions are steel baskets filled with stones. (See Figure 6-10.) As gabions age, the steel baskets tend to corrode and deteriorate—especially on the side facing the embankment. Over the years, however, soil sediment usually fills the voids between the stones and tends to hold the wall in place.

Stone retaining walls are often referred to as dry or wet, according to whether or not mortar was used between the stones. A dry retaining wall is one that has been constructed without mortar. It depends on the weight and friction of one stone upon another for stability. Frost heaving is not a problem with this type of wall. The stones are not bonded together and will, therefore, be raised and lowered with the frost. Consequently, the bottom course of the wall is usually only about 6 inches below grade rather than below the frost line.

FIGURE 6-9 Free-flowing outlet of curtain drain. Note water discharging from pipe.

A wet wall is one with mortar between the stones. The mortar secures one stone to another and, thereby, achieves a monolithic wall with greater stability. Because this is an integral wall, frost heaving will cause cracking. To prevent frost heaving, the bottom of the wall must be below the frost line. A wet wall offers greater solidity and, as such, there will not be any loose soil washing out or running through the voids. Also, a wet wall is less

FIGURE 6-10 Gabion retaining wall.

of a hazard because no loose stones can be kicked out of place or fall off the top.

When constructing a retaining wall, provisions must be made for draining the water that normally accumulates behind the wall. Otherwise, there may be a hydrostatic pressure buildup that, if great enough, can cause a structural failure of the wall. Drainage should be provided by installing a continuous perforated drain pipe at the lower portion of the wall and backfilling the area with broken stones or gravel. The pipe should be directed so that the effluent flows to a suitable location away from the wall. In many monolithic retaining walls, the perforated pipe is replaced by "weep holes." These are holes in the wall that run from the front through to the gravel backfill. The weep holes allow the water that accumulates in the gravel to drain out through the wall. Weep holes should be placed at a 5- to 10-foot spacing and should be 4 inches in diameter (the same diameter as the drain pipes).

Unfortunately, retaining walls are often built without adequate drainage provisions. The gravel backfill and/or drain pipe may be omitted, or the weep holes may be too few in number or too small in diameter to be effective. The weep holes must be kept clear so that the water behind the wall can be adequately drained.

A retaining wall built with construction timbers or railroad ties should be anchored into the hillside in order to provide the resistance needed to overcome the lateral forces that are exerted on it. Depending on the forces, if the wall is not tied back into the earth, it can bow, buckle, or heave and eventually collapse. Anchoring of the wall is achieved by using "tie backs" and "dead men." A tie back is a construction timber that has been placed perpendicular to the wall. The front end is flush

with the wall and is fastened to it with large spikes. The rear end is fastened to a dead man, which is a small section of timber that is perpendicular to the tie back (and parallel to the wall). When the area around the wall anchor is backfilled with soil, a force is developed on the anchor that resists the lateral force on the wall. Because of the open joints between the railroad ties, weep holes are not needed for drainage.

Many railroad tie or timber retaining walls are not constructed with anchors. You can tell whether or not there are anchors by looking at the wall. If there are tie backs, then there will be end sections visible in the face of the wall. (See Figure 6-11.) However, from a visual inspection, you cannot tell the length of the tie backs or whether dead men have been installed. Your inspection, therefore, should concern itself with the condition of the wall rather than its construction, unless it is a new wall. If it is newly constructed, you should inquire about a guarantee.

### Inspection

When inspecting a retaining wall, look at its overall condition. With a dry stone wall, look for missing and loose stones and crumbled sections. This type of wall is relatively easy to repair and generally does require periodic maintenance. With a wet stone wall, check the mortar joints for cracked, loose, and deteriorated sections. Are there weep holes in the wall? If so, are they adequately sized and unobstructed? Concrete and concrete block walls should also have weep holes. Are there any cracked and heaved sections? Wood-constructed retaining walls should be checked for cracked, rotting, loose, and heaved sections. Some retaining walls are completely covered with vines. If you do see a vine-covered wall, try to push the vines aside so that you can inspect the wall. Quite often, I have found cracked sections in the wall through which the vines were growing. While inspecting the wall, look for loose, heaved, and deteriorated sections.

All retaining walls should either be vertical or inclined slightly toward the embankment. They should not be leaning forward. When they are leaning, it is an indication that they could not withstand the lateral forces being exerted on them by the terraced or sloped earth behind. Once a wall cracks and heaves, the pressure that caused the condition is relieved, and it may then be possible for the wall to stay in the leaning position for many years. (See Figure 6-12.) However, additional forces may cause the wall to continue to heave and eventually to collapse. If you see a retaining wall that is leaning slightly, do not be alarmed. It does not mean that immediate corrective action is necessary. Usually, a

FIGURE 6-11 Timber (railroad tie) retaining wall. Note end sections, indicating tie backs used for anchoring the wall.

wait-and-see attitude is best since the heaving may be dormant. If the heaving is excessive and/or if, by the wall collapsing, someone can get hurt, then the wall must be rehabilitated or braced. If there are any questions in your mind about what is excessive heaving, have the wall inspected by a professional.

## LANDSCAPING

As you walk around the house, inspect the landscaping in the front, rear, and side yards. Specifically, look at the lawn, shrubs, and trees. A nicely landscaped area will greatly enhance the beauty and value of the house. However, do not jump to a hasty conclusion about the house based on the landscaping. I have seen many neglected houses with beautiful landscaping and many well-maintained houses with poor landscaping.

### Lawn

A lawn serves two purposes. It adds to the aesthetic beauty of the property, and, more important, it prevents erosion and washout of the topsoil. If you find that a large portion of the lawn consists of crab grass and other weeds, do not be distressed. With a planned program of weed control, seeding, and fertilizing, you can upgrade the lawn so that it can be the "showcase of the neighborhood" within a few years and at not too great an expense.

If you find any holes or sunken sections in the lawn, they should be filled in, as they represent a potential tripping hazard. Occasionally, sunken sections are caused by the collapse of rotted, decayed, or deteriorated construction debris that was buried on the site years before. In new homes, all construction debris should be removed from the site rather than buried there.

In some parts of the country, moles are a problem in lawn maintenance. They burrow in the ground near the surface in search of food (grubs, caterpillars, and insects) and, in the process, create soft ridges (mole hills) that spoil the lawn's appearance. If you see ridges over portions of the lawn and they feel soft when you walk over them, suspect moles. This condition can generally be controlled through soil treatment and should be discussed with the proprietor of a local nursery.

Some lawns have steep sloping areas that, from a maintenance point of view, are quite difficult to mow, even when mowing across the slope. Because of the danger involved, sit-down riding power mowers should not be used when cutting the grass on a steep slope. These mowers have been known to topple over and severely or fatally injure the driver. In some homes, the steep, sloping sections of the lawn have been replaced by terraced areas with steps

FIGURE 6-12 Cracked and heaved retaining wall.

that lead from one level to another. If there are terrace steps on the lawn of the house that you are inspecting, you should inspect them for cracked, loose, missing, and deteriorated sections. Also, check for uneven treads and dimensional variations in the risers (a tripping hazard). In addition, if there are more than two steps, a handrail is recommended.

If you are planning to buy a newly constructed house, find out whether it will be your responsibility or the builder's to establish a new lawn. If it is your responsibility, it can be quite expensive, depending on the size of the lawn and whether or not topsoil will have to be added. Over 100 tons of topsoil is needed to cover an area one third of an acre to a depth of 2 inches.

### Shrubs

Quite often, when new homes are landscaped, the shrubs are intentionally planted very close to one another in order to produce an overall immediately pleasing effect. Many homeowners do not plant shrubs with the future overall appearance in mind. Consequently, in those homes, as the shrubs grow and fill out, they tend to crowd one another, losing their individuality. Eventually, they become unsightly, with portions dying off for lack of sunlight. In addition, the growing shrubs often block walkways and produce so much shade that the area around the house is always damp—a condition conducive to the growth of decay fungi and mildew. By extensive pruning of some of the shrubs and transplanting of others (if you want to save them), the area can often be completely rejuvenated and restored to its original beauty. For some people, their dream house is one that is covered with ivy. Actually, vines of any type growing up along the outside walls of a house are quite undesirable. If you see vines on the house that you are inspecting, you should consider their removal.

### Trees

If there are trees on the property that you are inspecting, they should be checked to see if any are dead or if there are any large, dead branches. All dead trees should be taken down. Because they are vulnerable to insect damage and decay, they are a potential hazard, especially if they are located near the house. Large, dead branches are also a potential hazard. On a windy day, they can break off the trees and fall to the ground or, worse, onto the house.

After a deciduous tree has lost its leaves, it may be somewhat difficult to determine whether it is dead or has any dead branches. However, if you see any limbs with the bark peeled off, you can assume that those branches are dead. If there is any doubt in your mind, after you move into the house, you should have the tree(s) checked by a professional or wait until spring and summer when all the trees are in full bloom.

If you find any dead trees or dead branches, record their location on your worksheet for later removal. Depending on the size and location of the dead tree, its removal can be somewhat costly. This type of work should only be performed by a professional who carries insurance, in the event that the tree causes damage when falling to the ground. In addition to dead branches, all limbs that are overhanging or resting on the roof should also be pruned back. Otherwise, they may eventually damage the roof.

If you are buying a newly constructed house with trees on the property, you should be aware that the roots of some of the trees may have been damaged during construction. This could occur as a result of heavy equipment (such as tractors or trucks) being driven too close to the tree. Trees that have had root damage during construction will not necessarily show any immediate effects. However, within a year or two and depending on the amount of damage, the trees may die. If care is taken during construction, this problem can be avoided. Your best bet is to buy a house from a quality builder.

## DECKS

There are many types and styles of decks. However, from an inspection point of view, your main concern should be safety rather than appearance. When inspecting a deck, unless it is a rooftop or cantilever type, you should begin with the supports on the underside. If the deck is more than a few feet above the ground, it will generally be supported by wood or metal columns (posts). Unless wood posts have been pressure-treated, they should not be in direct contact with the soil. Untreated wood in contact with the ground is vulnerable to rot and termite activity. Also, the dampness normally associated with the soil can promote rust deterioration of a metal column.

Each column should be resting on a concrete pad that has a footing below the frost line. Otherwise, the footing is subject to frost heave. Probe the base sections of the columns with a screwdriver to determine whether or not there is deterioration. If the screwdriver can penetrate the column beyond the surface, a problem condition exists that should be corrected. In some cases, the column may require replacement. Push the column to see if there is any movement. There should not be. Occasionally, I find columns that are loose and are not adequately supporting the deck. (See Figure 6-13.) These columns should be shimmed and fastened securely to the

FIGURE 6-13 Inadequately supported deck. Column is loose and can easily be knocked over.

deck. The condition usually results from uneven settlement of the support footings and inadequate fastening at the top or bottom of the column.

When the deck is less than a few feet above the ground, it is usually supported by masonry piers. Inspect the piers for cracked, broken, loose, and/or deteriorated sections. If you find any, they must be repaired. With some "ground-hugging" decks, usually less than a foot above the ground, this inspection may not be possible. Most of the support piers are not visible.

When one side of the deck is attached to the house, there are usually no support posts below that section. Consequently, if the joint between the house and the deck should weaken, there is a potential for that portion of the deck to collapse. Check the joint between the deck and the house to see if it is securely fastened. Is it pulling away from the house? It should not be. In some cases, the deck is fastened to the house with undersized or an inadequate number of nails. I know of one community where this type of installation resulted in two decks collapsing. Because of these failures, that town passed an ordinance that requires using lag bolts rather than nails to secure the deck to the house. (See Figure 6-14.)

Next, check the joist supports at the portion of the deck that is attached to the house. Since there are no posts, there will not be a girder to support the joists. In this case, the joists should be supported either by metal brackets fastened to the header or by being toe-nailed into the header with a ledger below them. The former method is preferred because the ledger used is often skimpy. I have seen many decks where the joists were toe-nailed into the header, but the ledger was never installed. If you find this type of installation, you should install angle brackets to support the joists, or, at the very least, install a ledger as a precautionary measure.

In addition, depending on the size of the deck, there may be a need for diagonal bracing. This provides additional rigidity to the deck and can be achieved by placing a board (2 × 6) between two diagonal corners and nailing it to the underside of each joist.

When deck planks are installed, there should be a space of about ¼ of an inch between them. This space allows rainwater and melting snow to drain. In some cases, the planks are butted up against one another so that there is virtually no space between them other than the crack of the joint. Water entering this crack does not readily drain and, instead, promotes decay. If you can reach the underside of the deck planks and the top portion of the joists, probe them for rot. If there are rotting sections and the decay is in an advanced stage, you may see the fruiting bodies of the decay fungi. (This is discussed

FIGURE 6-14 Lag bolts *(arrow)* are used to secure the deck to the house. Note that joist is resting on a ledger board for support.

in detail in the section on rot in Chapter 8.) If there are steps leading to the deck, the treads, stringers, and handrails should also be inspected for decay. As with the deck support posts, the stringers should be resting on a concrete pad rather than being in contact with the soil.

After inspecting the underside of the deck and the steps, you should inspect the top portion. When the deck is more than 4 feet above the ground, there should be a guard rail around the perimeter as a safety precaution. Naturally, the higher the deck, the greater the need for a railing. If the deck is to be used by small children, then additional protection is needed to block the open area between the railing, railing posts, and the deck planks. The guard rails and deck planks should be inspected for cracked, rotting, and loose sections. (See Figure 6-15.) Depending on the quality of the wood and the upkeep, a deck need not deteriorate to a point where

FIGURE 6-15 Cracked and rotting deck planks. Planks should be replaced on an as-needed basis.

it requires complete rehabilitation. Repairs and/or replacement of deteriorated sections should be performed on an as-needed basis. If you find sections of the deck that are in need of repair, you should indicate those areas on your worksheet.

## FENCES

If there is a fence on the property that you are inspecting, you should check its overall condition. The problems encountered with fences are normally not major ones and are usually not costly to correct. However, you may find a fence that has deteriorated to a point where it is in need of complete rehabilitation or replacement.

Wood fences should be inspected for cracked, broken, loose, and missing sections. In addition, they should be checked for deterioration as a result of rot and termite infestation. (Termites and rot are discussed in Chapter 8.) The gate(s) for the fence should also be checked for cracked, loose, or broken sections and for ease of operation. Wooden gates often sag as they age and require periodic maintenance.

Metal fences should be inspected for rusting, loose, and deteriorated sections. Rusting sections should be scraped, primed, and painted. Chain-link fences are generally constructed of galvanized steel. Galvanizing (zinc coating) protects the steel against rusting and is usually applied by hot dipping or electroplating. The hot-dipped process produces a heavy zinc coating, which is very effective, in contrast to the thin coating produced by electroplating. Chain-link fences that have been galvanized by electroplating have a tendency to rust and will require periodic maintenance. Some chain-link fences have a vinyl coating that protects against rust. The vinyl coating is quite effective and lasts for many years.

If there is an "in-the-ground" swimming pool on the property, there should be a fence around the pool area. Most communities have an ordinance requiring a fence of a specific height as a protective barrier. If you do not see a fence around a pool area, you should check the requirements with the municipal Building Department. Otherwise, you may find out, after buying the house, that you are legally obliged to install one.

## CHECKPOINT SUMMARY

### DRAINAGE

- When approaching the house, take note of the overall topography.
- Is it level or inclined?
- Are there gently or steeply sloped areas?

- Is the house located near or at the bottom of an inclined street?
- Note if there is a storm drain (catch basin) nearby.
- Are there nearby streams or brooks?
- Are you able to determine if the house is located in a flood plain or flood-prone area?
- Is the ground immediately adjacent to the house graded so that it slopes away on all sides of the structure?
- Are there natural drainageways to direct surface water away from the house?
- Are there low or level areas that are vulnerable to water ponding?
- Are there areas of ponded water on the lot?
- Are you able to determine if the house has footing drains?
- Can you locate the outlet for these and any other drainage pipes?

### RETAINING WALLS

**Timber, Railroad Tie, Dry Stone Wall, Gabion**
- Inspect for missing, loose, and crumbling sections of stone.
- Check timber and railroad tie walls for cracked, loose, rotting, and heaved sections.
- Are the wood-constructed walls properly anchored (tie backs)?

**Concrete, Concrete Block, Wet Stone Wall**
- Inspect for cracked and heaved sections.
- Check for loose, deteriorated, and missing mortar joints.
- Is the wall vertical or does it lean?
- Are portions of the wall heavily covered with vines?
- Did you inspect these areas for cracked and heaved sections?
- If possible, try to determine whether the area behind the retaining wall is adequately drained.
- Are there weep holes at the base of the wall? Are they blocked?
- Are the weep holes adequately sized and spaced?

### LANDSCAPING

**Lawn**
- Inspect for holes, sunken sections, bald spots, and eroding areas.
- Estimate areas that will require recultivation.
- Note soft sections or ridges (possibly due to moles).
- Inspect terrace steps for cracked, loose, rotting, or missing sections. Check steps for handrails, uneven treads, and variations in riser heights.

**Shrubs**

- Inspect shrubbery for overcrowding, dying sections, blocked walkways/steps.
- Note areas in need of pruning, transplanting, and/or removal.
- Note areas of the house that are covered with vines.

**Trees**

- Check for dead trees and limbs, especially those that are close to the house.
- Note tree limbs that are overhanging or resting on the roof.
- Note, for future professional evaluation, any trees that show evidence of rot, split sections, or insect infestation.

## DECKS

- Check and inspect the various deck components for safety rather than appearance.
- Check concrete/brick piers for cracked, loose, and deteriorated sections.
- Inspect/probe wood columns for rot and/or termite activity.
- Inspect metal columns for rust deterioration.
- Are columns supported on concrete pads or are they in contact with the ground?
- Note any loose columns.
- Check for open and weakened joints between the deck and the house.
- Is the deck attached to the house with nails or lag bolts? (Lag bolts are preferred.)
- Inspect deck joist supports at the portion of the deck that is attached to the house.
- Are deck joists supported by metal brackets (preferred) or are they toe-nailed into a header beam with a ledger board below the joist?
- Where the joists have been toe-nailed, check for missing ledger boards.
- Does deck contain diagonal bracings?
- Inspect/probe the underside of deck (girders, joists, floor planks) for missing, cracked, and rotting members.
- Inspect/probe wood step treads, stringers, and handrails for cracked, loose, missing, and rotting sections.
- Are the stringers supported on a concrete pad or are they in contact with the ground?
- Check top portion of deck for cracked, loose, missing, and rotting sections of deck planks, railings, and railing posts.

## FENCES

- Inspect wood fences for cracked, broken, loose, and missing sections.
- Check/probe for areas of rot and insect damage.
- Inspect metal fencing for loose, missing, and rusting sections.
- Check gates (metal and wood) for sag, missing hardware, and for cracked, loose, broken, and missing sections.
- If property contains an in-the-ground pool, is the area around the pool adequately fenced off? (It may be a legal requirement.)

# 7. GARAGE

The garage should be inspected after the exterior inspection has been completed. There are two basic types of garages, namely, attached and detached. An attached garage is a physical part of the main building. It may be located so that it is below a habitable portion of the structure or connected to the side of the building. A detached garage, on the other hand, is a separate physical structure and is not part of the main building. Occasionally, there may be a connecting breezeway or porch between the two structures.

## ATTACHED GARAGE

Since the principle use of the garage is for car storage, the possibility of dripping oil and/or gasoline presents a potential fire hazard. Because the attached garage is physically connected to the main structure, certain precautionary measures should be taken during construction to minimize the haz-

FIGURE 7-1 Steps connecting the garage floor slab to the adjacent living area, which is at a higher level.

ards. Look around the garage to see if there are any potential problems.

### Fire and Health Hazards

Is there an interior door between the garage and the house? If there is, is there at least one step leading up to the door? There should be. (See Figure 7-1.) It is surprising how many times I find that the garage floor slab is either at the same or at a higher level than the adjacent living area. (See Figure 7-2.) The living area should be above the level of the garage floor in order to prevent toxic exhaust gases and gasoline vapors, which are heavier than air, from entering the house whenever the interior door is opened. As a precautionary measure, the interior door should have a tight seal around the joints in order to prevent seepage. This door should be a fire-resistant type such as metal clad, solid wood, or hollow core, with a sheetmetal covering on the *garage side*. As a safety feature, the interior door should also be self-closing. In most homes, however, it is not. It seems that homeowners have found self-closing doors inconvenient, especially when carrying in packages from the local supermarket. Nevertheless, safety should not be sacrificed for convenience.

Next, look at the walls that separate the garage from the living area. Are there any exposed wood-frame members? There should not be any. Exposed wood framing in this area is considered a fire hazard and should be covered with a fire-resistant material such as plaster/stucco on lath or ⅝-inch gypsum wallboard. This wall should also be insulated to reduce heat loss. If there is a living area above the garage, the ceiling should also be insulated and have a fire-retardant covering.

In some garages, an access hatch to the attic is located in the ceiling. During inspections, it is occasionally noted that the hatch cover for this opening is missing or open. (See Figure 7-3.) This is a fire hazard. If a fire should start in the garage, the open area in the ceiling could act as a flue and draw the flames up into the attic where they would quickly engulf the house. The attic hatch cover *must* be in place at all times.

Some homes have a garage literally in the basement. The garage is at the basement level with no partition walls separating the garage area from the basement area. This is a fire and health hazard, in addition to being inefficient in design from an energy conservation point of view. When the garage doors are opened, there will be a loss (from the basement) of warm air in the winter and cool air in the summer.

Occasionally, the heating plant (furnace or

FIGURE 7-2 Garage floor slab at a higher level than the adjacent living area—a potential hazard.

might not see them. Ceiling stains are often caused by leakage from a bathroom above the area. When you do the interior inspection of the house, all of the plumbing fixtures (sinks, bowls, and tub/shower) should be operated. After that portion of the inspection is completed, if the garage ceiling showed signs of past problems, you should reinspect it for indications of current leakage.

In some cases, there are exposed drain pipes and/or water pipes in the garage. If your home is located in the northern part of the United States, the water pipes should be insulated as a precautionary measure against freezing during the winter months.

Depending on the location of the sewer or septic tank, there may be a pit in the garage floor that is covered with a metal plate. If there is such a pit, it may contain a cleanout and trap for the house waste line. Sometimes, the water inlet pipe is also located in this pit. (These items are discussed in detail in Chapter 13.) Lift the cover and look inside the pit. Often, the builder neglects to remove the wood framing around the sides of the pit. The wood is used as a form when constructing the open area. Because of the dampness in the pit, a wood liner will eventually rot and may be termite infested. (This is an area where termites are often found; see Chapter 8 to learn how to determine their presence.) If there is wood in the pit, it should be removed, regardless of its condition.

FIGURE 7-3 Open attic access hatch in the garage ceiling.

boiler) is located in the garage. (See Figure 7-4.) This is, perhaps, the least desirable location for a heating unit. There is always the possibility that a leak could develop in the gasoline tank or fuel line of an automobile. Should this occur and if the garage is inadequately ventilated, the resultant flammable vapors could be ignited by the flame in the heating system. Of course, this risk can be minimized by locating the heating unit on a platform (since gasoline vapors are heavier than air and will accumulate at the ground level) or by enclosing the heating unit in a room with a tight seal on the door. If the heating unit is enclosed, the area must be vented to provide outside air for combustion. Another problem with a hot-water heating system located in the garage is that the pipes are more vulnerable to freezing there should the system malfunction or run out of fuel oil.

### Plumbing Check

While looking at the walls and ceiling of the garage, look for signs of plumbing leaks. Check the ceiling for water leakage stains. If the garage has an overhead-type door, be sure to close the door and then look at the ceiling. In the open position, the overhead door will block about 25 percent of the ceiling; if there are leakage stains in that section, you

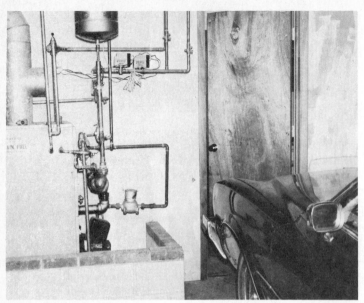

FIGURE 7-4 Heating system (oil-fired, forced hot water) boiler located in the garage.

## Flood Potential

The bottom of the pit should be relatively dry in all but very wet weather. If the bottom contains water, it is an indication that the level of the subsurface water (water table) in the overall area of the home is high. When this condition exists, there is a possibility that, during rainy periods, the water level can rise and seep into the garage through the pit or through cracks in the floor slab. (Water seepage into this area is discussed in detail in Chapter 11.)

Cracks in the floor slab may be caused by shrinkage or differential settlement and are usually not a concerning factor. They should, however, be sealed because they can allow water to seep into the garage. An extensively cracked or heaved floor slab is of concern because it may indicate a water problem. Heaving and extensive cracking are very often caused by water pressure being exerted on the underside of the floor slab. If this condition exists, it should be evaluated by a professional.

Note whether or not there is a drain in the floor slab. If there is, the floor should be pitched toward that drain. If there is no drain, then the floor should have a slight pitch toward the automobile entry door. This will allow water from melting snow to drain to the exterior rather than puddle on the floor. Also, the floor slab should be slightly above the level of the driveway to reduce the possibility of water entry. It should be noted that a garage at the base of an inclined driveway is *always* vulnerable to water penetration. (This condition is discussed in the driveway section of Chapter 4.)

## Doors

When you inspect the garage, you should always check the operation of the exterior door or doors. Open and close each door and note whether it operates relatively easily. The most common type of door for an attached garage is the overhead type. This door has the advantage of not taking up usable space when open. Look for obvious deficiencies such as broken or missing springs or guide wheels, loose and misaligned tracks, and so on. Check the door's operation. If it is difficult to lift, stuck in a fixed position, out of plumb, or will not stay in the up position, some minor maintenance is needed. When closing the door, give it a start and let it come down by itself. If the door closes rapidly and heavily, it is a hazard, especially for small children. Adjustment is needed to the spring tension. When the door is closed, use the lock mechanism. You may find that the lock bars are in need of resetting.

Some overhead doors are the one-piece, swing-up type rather than the sectional, roll-up type. These doors often require additional efforts to open, particularly during periods of snow and wind. Many overhead doors are opened by an automatic control. Operate the control. The doors should open and close smoothly without binding in the tracks. Make certain that the radio controller(s) work. Ask the owner to demonstrate that they exist and work.

Other doors found on a garage are the sliding and folding types. Sliding doors usually hang from overhead tracks. One disadvantage of such doors is that they take up valuable wall space when open. Also, small pieces of debris on the ground can interfere with their operation. Fold-out doors often sag, have loose hinges, and drag on the ground, making opening and closing quite difficult. In general, they require more frequent maintenance. If these conditions exist, they can and should be corrected.

## General Considerations

Look around the garage for an electrical outlet. There should be at least one three-prong convenience outlet. Also, there should be overhead light(s) controlled by a switch near both the interior door and the exterior door. Two desirable features, although not necessary, are windows that provide daylight and ventilation and a service door that can be used as access to the garage without opening the automobile entry door(s).

Depending on the location of the house, the garage may be heated. Heat is usually provided by extending the central heating system (hot water, steam, or warm air) into the garage area. The radiators or heat registers providing the heat should be checked as part of the overall heating system inspection. If there are warm air ducts in the garage, look for return grilles. There shouldn't be any because through them, poisonous exhaust fumes could be brought back into the system and circulated throughout the house. When a garage is used solely for storage of automobiles, it is only necessary (and not even always) to bring the temperature above freezing. Heating the garage above that temperature is considered wasteful of energy.

Last, when inspecting an attached garage, look for termites in any exposed wood-frame members. The area most vulnerable to termite infestation (aside from wood found in a sewer cleanout pit) is the wood framing around the base of the exterior door.

## DETACHED GARAGE

If your house has a detached garage, you need not be as concerned with the fire and health hazards mentioned with the attached garage. True, the area is still considered a potential fire hazard. However, since the structure is physically apart from the main building, a fire, although unfortunate, would not usually result in the loss of a life. The main concern with this type of garage is its structural integrity.

### Exterior

The exterior of the detached garage is checked the same way that you inspect the main house. Walk around the outside of the building twice. The first time, look at the roof and gutters. Do any of the roof beams appear to be sagging? If so, additional bracing may be needed. Have a professional make this determination. Do not assume that the roof over the garage and the roof over the house are in the same condition. Although the roof covering on the main house may be in good condition, the covering of the garage roof may be badly worn and may require replacement. (The garage roof is inspected as discussed in Chapter 2.) Are there gutters all around the base of the roof? If not, make sure you check all wood siding and trim for rot. The rain run-off from the roof can promote rot. A wood-frame garage with a pitched roof should have gutters. If there are long, overhanging eaves or if the garage is masonry constructed, gutters are not a necessary feature, although they are often desirable. If there are gutters and downspouts, see if they are in need of repair. (These items are inspected as discussed in Chapter 3.)

After looking at the roof and gutters, walk around the building once more. This time, look at the walls, windows, and doors. If the exterior walls are covered with a wood siding, does the base of the

siding extend to the ground? It should end about 8 inches above the ground. If the siding is in contact with the ground, it should be checked for termites and rot. Pay particular attention to the rear wall. On some occasions, you may see a wall that is bowed. This is usually caused by a car that did not stop in time. The wall stopped the car and, in the process, the supporting studs were broken. If such is the case, the wall is in need of rehabilitation. Also, you might sometimes see a wall that is offset. The bottom section of the wall extends about 3 feet beyond the upper section. This is done to accommodate longer cars than those for which the garage was constructed.

Finally, check the base of the wood framing and trim around the garage door(s). This area is *particularly* vulnerable to rot and termite activity. (See Figure 7-5.)

### Interior

When entering the garage, check the doors first. Look for broken and cracked sections of wood framing and glass panes. Open and close the doors; they should operate smoothly and have all necessary hardware (see page 50).

Depending on the location of the garage, there are times when the entire roof is not visible from the outside. After you enter the garage, look up at the underside of the roof. If you can see daylight through a hole or crack, there is a problem with the roof. Look for signs of past water leakage stains on the wood framing. These stains appear as dark streak discolorations on the wood. Leakage stains do not necessarily indicate a current leak—the problem may have been corrected. If you see stains on the wood framing, ask the homeowner whether

FIGURE 7-5 Termite infestation and rot at base of garage door frame.

FIGURE 7-6   Heaving garage wall. Section of wall was located below grade level.

repairs to the garage roof have been performed. Next, look at the walls. If the garage is located on an incline, look at those sections of walls that are below grade. These walls are usually constructed of brick, concrete, or rubble and also function as retaining walls. If proper drainage provisions have not been made, the walls will tend to crack and heave. (See Figure 7-6.) If you see cracked and heaved walls, you should have a professional make a determination of whether or not rehabilitation is required. Often, the walls are covered with a stucco or plaster finish and the wood-framing members that form the walls are not visible. However, any exposed studs and bottom plates should be checked for cracked and broken sections, rot, and termite activity.

To reduce the vulnerability of the bottom plate of a wood-frame wall to rot and termite infestation, the plate should be resting on a foundation wall that is at least 4 inches above the garage floor. In many older, detached garages, this plate is found *directly* on the floor or in contact with the ground. If this is the case, look carefully at the plate and probe it with a screwdriver or ice pick. If it can be penetrated, there is probably rot, termite, or carpenter ant activity.

Look at the condition of the floor. If there are cracked, broken, and settled sections, as are often found in older, detached garages, then rehabilitation is in order. This condition will usually not indicate an undermining of the structural integrity of the garage but rather a poor-quality installation of the floor slab. In some garages, you will find a dirt floor rather than one of concrete or asphalt. This is not desirable because the dampness associated with this type of floor will promote rot in the wood-framing members, as well as premature rusting of any items stored in the garage.

## Heat/Electricity

Most detached garages are not heated. However, when they are, heat is usually provided by a space heater rather than by extending the central heating system. The heater should be checked to see if it is operational. This can be done by turning up the thermostat. The thermostat will be either wall-mounted or mounted directly on the unit. Most non-electric heaters must be vented to the outside and should not have wood framing in contact with the exhaust stack, which would be a fire hazard. If the heater is not vented to the outside, ask the owner to show you proof that the unit has been specifically approved for installation without a flue connection.

In new detached garages, the electrical service and wiring is usually not a problem. There should be an overhead light that is controlled by a wall switch and at least one three-prong convenience outlet receptacle. If the garage is a distance from the house, a desirable feature would be to have either spotlights or row lights along the path between the two structures. The lights should be controlled by two three-way switches, one at the garage and one at the house. In many older garages, the electrical wiring and service is often makeshift and, in many cases, nonoperational. Look around. If you see loose and hanging wires, exposed junction boxes and wire splices, you are looking at electrical violations. In some cases, the service wire from the main house to the detached garage is interior-type wire and not exterior-type. This is a potential hazard and must be corrected. If electrical problems are found during the garage inspection, then you should require that the seller provide you, at contract closing, with a Certificate of Approval for the electrical system. The approval should be made by the Municipal Electrical Inspection Agency. (See Chapter 12.)

## CHECKPOINT SUMMARY

### ATTACHED GARAGE

#### Inspecting for Fire and Health Hazards
- Are the garage and basement area combined into one open area?
- Is the interior garage door located at least one step up above the garage floor?
- Does this door have a tight seal? Is it self-closing?
- Is this door fire-resistant or does it have a sheetmetal covering on the garage side?
- Is the boiler/furnace unit located in the garage?
- Has it been placed on a raised slab?

- Inspect garage ceiling and walls for exposed wood-frame members.
- Check ceiling area for open and/or missing attic access hatch.
- Check for return grilles in warm-air heating systems.

### General Considerations

- Inspect ceiling area for signs of plumbing leaks, stains, and patched sections.
- If garage is unheated, are there uninsulated water pipes that are vulnerable to freezing?
- Inspect floor for extensively cracked, settled, and heaved sections.
- Check these areas also for evidence of water seepage, and silt deposits.
- Does driveway incline make garage vulnerable to flooding?
- Is there a drain protecting the garage entry? Is it adequate?
- Does garage floor contain a drain?
- Inspect exterior doors and trim for cracked, missing, rotting, and insect-damaged sections.
- Operate door(s). Note broken and missing springs, guide wheels, locks, and misaligned tracks.
- Check overhead lights, wall switches, and convenience outlets.

### DETACHED GARAGE

#### Exterior

- Inspect walls/siding for bulging, cracked, loose, missing, and rotting sections.
- Note broken windows and patched sections.
- Check roof beams for cracked, rotting, and sagging members.
- Inspect roof shingles (as outlined in Chapter 2 Checkpoint Summary).
- Check type and condition of gutters and downspouts. Note their absence.
- Inspect/probe wood framing and trim around doors (particularly doors that are in contact with, or in close proximity to, the ground).

#### Interior

- Check garage doors for broken, cracked, and rotting sections.
- Inspect doors for operation, sagging sections, missing hardware, and broken glass panes.
- Inspect underside of roof for damaged sheathing and signs of leakage.
- Inspect foundation/retaining walls for cracked, bowed, and heaved areas.
- Is there a concrete, asphalt, or dirt floor?
- Check concrete or asphalt floor for cracked, broken, and heaved sections.
- Probe wood sills for insect infestation/damage (particularly if these members are in contact with the ground).
- Inspect for loose and hanging electrical wires, exposed junction boxes, wire splices, extension-cord-type wiring and, in general, makeshift wiring.
- Is there a space heater? Check operation.
- Is unit properly vented?
- Are there wood-frame members in contact with the exhaust stack?

# 8. WOOD-DESTROYING INSECTS AND ROT

## TERMITES

### Subterranean Termites

There are many types of wood-destroying insects. The one that causes the most damage to residential structures in the United States is the subterranean termite. Termite infestation, for reasons that are completely unjustified, is quite often an emotional issue with many people. Home buyers generally overreact after discovering a termite condition and, on occasion, lose interest in the house. Actually, the discovery of termite infestation should not be cause for alarm—concern maybe, but certainly not alarm.

Termites work very slowly. It takes many years for termites to do serious damage to a house. A mature, well-established colony of 60,000 termites will eat the equivalent of 2 to 4 feet of a 2 × 4-inch board in one year. A termite condition can be completely controlled through the application of chemical insecticides. The chemicals most often used for termite treatment—aldrin, chlordane, dieldrin, heptachlor—have an effective life that often exceeds twenty-five years. Consequently, a house, if properly treated, will be protected from further termite damage for at least twenty-five years.

A number of states have regulations requiring a termite inspection by a professional prior to, or as a condition of, the purchase agreement. The cost of this inspection is almost always paid for by the seller. If the state that you are in has such a requirement, you should ask the seller or real estate agent to have the house inspected by a professional and to have a report of the results sent to you. In many states (even in some that do not have a pre-purchase termite inspection requirement), if a termite condition is found prior to the sale, the cost for correcting the condition (chemical treatment) is borne by the seller.

When termites are discovered in a house, they should be exterminated professionally. However, because termites work slowly, termite-proofing the house need not be done immediately upon learning of an active infestation. Take your time and get two or three cost estimates from established termite exterminating firms. After treating a house, many companies will provide a five-year guarantee against reinfestation, while some firms only provide a one-year guarantee. The guarantee can often be extended annually, at a small fee, for a period of twenty years. If the house that you are inspecting had been previously treated for termites, find out if the owner has a guarantee and whether or not it can be transferred to you.

During an inspection, all exposed wood-framing members should be checked for structural deterioration as a result of termite activity. There are very few houses on record that have been damaged by termites to a point where they are considered unsafe. Quite often, the amount of damage caused by termites (by the time termite activity is discovered) is minor, and repair or replacement of the infested wood members is not necessary. Even with a heavy infestation, usually only a portion of the house is affected. And even then, only a portion of the wood framing involved may be damaged to a point where it has lost its structural value. In this case, only the affected members will require repair or replacement. If you are in doubt as to the structural integrity of any of the affected members, you should consult a professional.

Termites play an important role in the natural ecological cycle. They feed on cellulose, the principal ingredient of wood. As a result, they help to break down dead trees in forests and other wooded areas, thus enriching the soil. Termites began attacking houses when the wooded areas were cleared for building construction and there was no other available source of food near their nest. Subterranean termites are found in every state except Alaska. Their overall distribution within the United States is shown in Figure 8-1. As their name implies, subterranean termites live in a colony (nest) that is usually located in the ground below the frost line. Even when a house is infested with termites, they usually do not have a nest in the house. They are only there to gather food. The only condition under which a nest might exist in a house (a rare occurrence) is if there is a constant source of moisture such as a leaky water or drain pipe that wets the surrounding area.

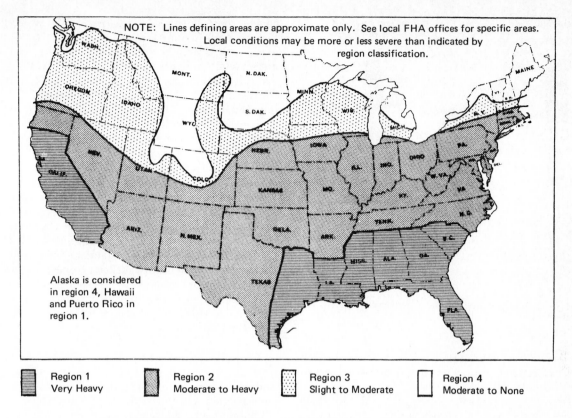

NOTE: Lines defining areas are approximate only. See local FHA offices for specific areas. Local conditions may be more or less severe than indicated by region classification.

Alaska is considered in region 4, Hawaii and Puerto Rico in region 1.

Region 1 Very Heavy    Region 2 Moderate to Heavy    Region 3 Slight to Moderate    Region 4 Moderate to None

FIGURE 8-1   Subterranean termite distribution in the United States.

Termites are social insects. Within each colony, there exists a rigid caste system consisting of a queen and king, workers, soldiers, and reproductives. Each member of the colony instinctively performs his special task. The function of the queen and king is to propagate the colony. The fertilized queen lays the eggs and may live for as long as twenty-five years. The workers care for the eggs, feed the young and the queen, and generally maintain the colony. They also forage from the nest to the wood supply and return with food. The soldiers defend the colony against attack by other insects, mostly ants. The average worker and soldier live only two or three years. The function of the reproductives is to replace the queen and king in the event of their injury or death. They also lay eggs that rapidly increase the termite population.

When a colony matures, reproductives leave the nest (swarm) to set up a new colony. Although thousands of reproductives leave the nest, only a handful survive to establish a new colony. The remainder die because of adverse conditions in the soil or because they fall prey to other insects. Reproductive termites sprout wings for the swarm. With their wings, they are only about half an inch long. They are considered poor fliers and generally flutter around before falling to the ground. Some, however, may be picked up in the wind and carried great distances. Once the reproductives land, they shed their wings, pair off in couples, and return to the soil in search of a suitable place to build their nest.

In most parts of the country, swarming generally occurs in the spring and sometimes in the fall. However, swarming termites have been found in January in some heated houses. In the warm, humid parts of the country, swarming can occur at any time. Even if there are no other outward signs of termite activity, termite swarming in a house is an indication that there is a healthy, established colony nearby from which worker termites are coming in their search for food.

Swarming termites *do not* attack wood. Their only function is to start up a new colony. Even if there is a swarm in your house, you may not see it. A swarm may last from fifteen minutes to one hour and, if you are not in the right place at the right time, it can be over by the time you enter the room. However, if there was a swarm, you can tell by the discarded wings. They are often found on windowsills, light fixtures, and beneath doors. Do not confuse swarming termites with swarming ants. To the untrained eye, they may appear to be similar, but there are distinctive differences. (See Figure 8-2.)

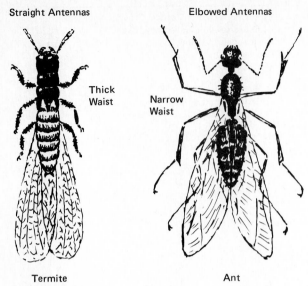

Straight Antennas          Elbowed Antennas

Thick Waist

Narrow Waist

Termite                    Ant

FIGURE 8-2    The difference between swarming ants and swarming termites. Actual size, ½ inch.

The most obvious difference is that termites have a thick waist and ants have a pinched (hourglass) waist.

Subterranean termites require a dark, damp environment. In their search for food, worker termites build shelter tubes (tunnels) that help conserve moisture and shield the termites from the light. (See Figure 8-3.) The tubes are about ¼- to ½-inch wide and provide a passageway between the ground and the food supply (wood member). They can be built at the rate of several inches per day, and are mainly composed of soil, wood particles, and excreta. Shelter tubes, which may be noted on foundation walls, on the outside of wood framing, or even free-standing between the ground and an overhead pipe or beam, are visible evidence of termite infestation. If the particular tube is active, worker termites will be busy using it to go between the nest and the house. By breaking the tube, you can see the workers who will try to repair the break. They are about ¼-inch long and have a whitish cream coloring.

Some tubes may be abandoned and no longer in use. If you find an inactive shelter tube, it does not mean that termites are no longer in the house. It may, if the house has been termite-proofed. However, if it has not, even an abandoned shelter tube, no matter how small, is sufficient evidence to consider termite treatment. Many shelter tubes emanate from a nest. There may very well be an active tube inside the voids of a concrete block wall that would not be visible during an inspection. (See Figure 8-4.)

Whether or not a new building will be attacked by termites will depend on the surrounding area and, to a large extent, the builder. There are certain construction practices that tend to increase the probability of termite attack. Some builders have been known to bury tree stumps and wood debris near the foundation or below the basement floor slab. All stumps and debris should be removed from the building site. Also, all form-boards and scrap lumber should be removed before the excavated

FIGURE 8-3    Termite shelter tubes: on foundation wall, header and subflooring (left); on house drain pipes (right). (Courtesy Velsicol Chemical Corporation)

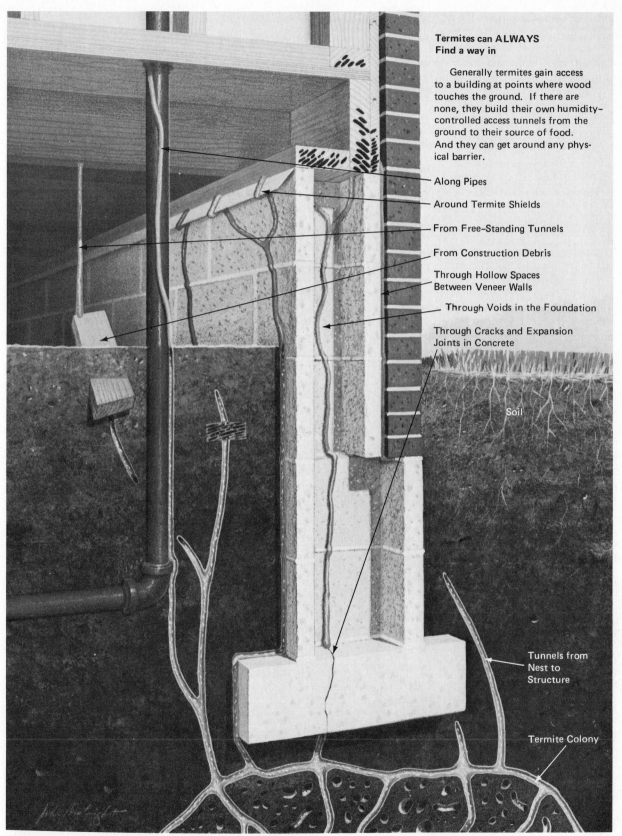

**Termites can ALWAYS Find a way in**

Generally termites gain access to a building at points where wood touches the ground. If there are none, they build their own humidity-controlled access tunnels from the ground to their source of food. And they can get around any physical barrier.

— Along Pipes

— Around Termite Shields

— From Free-Standing Tunnels

— From Construction Debris

— Through Hollow Spaces Between Veneer Walls

— Through Voids in the Foundation

— Through Cracks and Expansion Joints in Concrete

Soil

Tunnels from Nest to Structure

Termite Colony

FIGURE 8-4 Termite entry points into a house. *(Courtesy Terminex International Termite and Pest Control)*

area around the foundation walls is backfilled. There should not be any buried wood around the house. Otherwise, it will provide a source of food for a new termite colony that, when it becomes large enough, will attack the house.

Most often, termites enter a house by eating their way through untreated wood members that are in direct contact with the ground. Some of the more common points of entry are garage door frames, basement windowsills, wooden steps and supports, wood sills, and headers and studs on foundation walls that are located at or below grade. A particular area of attack is the wood framing that is adjacent to a concrete-covered, earth-filled porch, patio, or entrance slab. (See Figure 8-5.) If there is no earth/wood contact, termites can build shelter tubes to provide passageways from the nest to the wood framing in the structure.

Some homes have a strip of metal (termite shield) between the foundation wall and the sill plate, which rests on top of the foundation wall. The purpose of the termite shield is to act as a barrier between the nest and the food supply. In most cases, the termite shield gives the homeowner a false sense of security. The shield will not prevent infestation. It will only deter an attack. The problem is that the termite shield is rarely installed properly. An opening at a seam or a hole as small as 1/32 of an inch is large enough for termites to pass through. All seams should be soldered and any holes around bolts and pipes should be filled with coal tar pitch. Even if you see a termite shield on the house that you are inspecting, you should look for termite infestation.

FIGURE 8-5 Termite colonies can develop in buried wood debris and gain entrance into a building, particularly at earth-filled, concrete entrance slabs or patios.

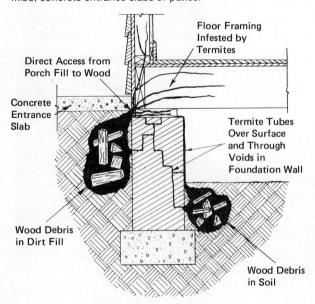

Floor Framing Infested by Termites

Direct Access from Porch Fill to Wood

Concrete Entrance Slab

Termite Tubes Over Surface and Through Voids in Foundation Wall

Wood Debris in Dirt Fill

Wood Debris in Soil

## Inspection

A complete subterranean termite inspection consists of an interior and exterior check of that portion of the house that is close to, or in contact with, the ground. The exterior termite inspection can be performed concurrently with the normal exterior inspection as described in Chapter 1. As you walk around the outside of the house, look for termite shelter tubes along the outside foundation walls. In many homes, this area is covered or partially blocked by shrubbery. Move or part the shrubbery so that you can see the wall. This is especially important for areas just below a garden hose spigot.

In some cases, the base of the exterior wood siding is in contact with the ground so that the foundation wall is not visible. This is a poor construction practice, but unfortunately is fairly common and usually occurs during final grading and landscaping. The base of the wood siding should terminate at least 6 inches above the finished grade. The exterior wood siding that is often used is redwood or cedar. Both types of siding are resistant to termite attack and to rot. However, it is important to understand that they are not immune to attack and may eventually succumb. If the base of the siding is in contact with the ground, probe it with an ice pick or a screwdriver. If the wood has not been attacked by rot, termites, or other wood-destroying insects, your probe will not penetrate much beyond the surface. If the probe penetrates the wood deeply, then the wood has been attacked. In order to determine the cause for the deterioration, it is necessary to break open a section and look at the condition of the wood. Caution: Do not proceed beyond the probing without consent of the homeowner. In fact, it would be wise to obtain the homeowner's consent for the probing.

A section of termite-damaged wood will reveal galleries (channels) that run parallel with the grain. (See Figure 8-6.) This is because termites will attack the softer portion of the wood grown during the spring and not the more dense summer wood. The channels will not look polished, as they do with carpenter ants. Portions will be lined with grayish specks that consist of excrement and earth. It is possible that deteriorated wood could be the result of a combination of causes such as rot, termites, and carpenter ants. You should become familiar with the telltale signs. If you are not certain of the cause, it is best to have the wood evaluated by a professional. The appearance of wood damaged by carpenter ants, powder post beetles, and rot will be discussed in their respective sections.

As you walk around the outside of the house, probe the attached wood trim, posts, and framing members that are on or close to the ground. Specifically probe garage door frames, basement or lower-level window frames, step stringers, deck posts, and

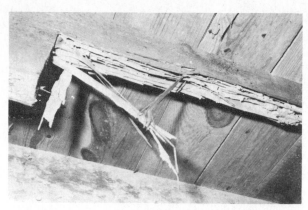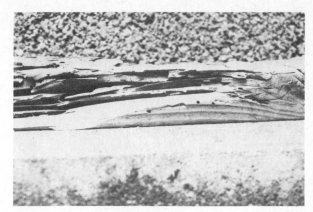

FIGURE 8-6    Termite-damaged wood. Note galleries (channels) that run parallel with the grain. *Left:* Floor joist. *Right:* 2 × 4 board that was imbedded in the ground and used for framing a concrete patio.

entry door riser. Termite activity is only of concern when it is found in the house or in an attached structure such as a garage or deck. If you find termite damage or shelter tubes on a fence post in the yard (see Figure 8-7) or in a piece of wood debris on the ground in the yard, all that means is that those pieces of wood have had termite infestation. It does not mean that the house is infested with termites and should be treated.

After checking the outside of the house for termites, the next place to look is in the crawl space beneath the house or porch. Not all houses have a crawl space, in which case this step is omitted. If the access to the crawl space is from the interior rather than the exterior, then it should be checked as part of the interior termite inspection. In the crawl space, probe the sills and headers for termite damage. Also check the first 15 inches of each joist that rests on the sill or foundation. As you move around in the crawl space, look for termite shelter tubes on the foundation walls and piers. Sometimes, the shelter tubes can be spotted between double joists. (Double joists are two joists nailed together and are used to provide additional support for a heavy load.) While in the crawl space, note any items of wood storage, remembering that they are vulnerable to infestation.

The interior inspection for subterranean termites is generally conducted in the basement and/or crawl space. If the basement is finished so that there are no exposed sections of foundation wall or wood framing, a thorough inspection cannot be performed—even by a professional. There are, however, some sections that are more vulnerable to termite attack than other areas, such as sill plates, headers, and joists that are below grade or adjacent to a dirt-filled, cement-covered patio. If the ceiling is covered with suspended tiles, the tiles can be lifted or moved to expose the wood framing. If there are no accessible areas, then termite activity will have to be determined by a swarm or exterior inspection. In areas where termite infestation is

heavy, such as the South and Southwest, a termite inspection should be performed every year. In other areas, a biannual inspection is adequate.

When the basement is unfinished, the wood framing on top of the foundation wall should be inspected by probing as described for the exterior crawl space. Also look for termite shelter tubes. You may find a tube that appears to start in the center of the foundation wall. Actually, the tube is connected to the earth through a small crack in the wall at that point. As previously mentioned, termites can work their way through cracks as small as $\frac{1}{32}$ of an inch. While in the basement, pay particular attention to the area around the furnace/boiler and pipes through the foundation or floor slab. Often activity is discovered in these areas.

Homes that are built on a slab without a basement or crawl space are also vulnerable to attack by termites. Because there are generally no areas with exposed beams or foundation, detecting termites is quite difficult, unless the infestation has advanced to the point where shelter tubes are visible within

FIGURE 8-7    Termite shelter tubes on a fence post.

the finished rooms. When inspecting a slab house, look for soft spots in the baseboard trim along the exterior wall. Also check for shelter tubes around openings in the floor slab, such as around plumbing or heating pipes.

### Drywood Termites

Homes in the South and Southwest are vulnerable to attack by drywood termites as well as by subterranean termites. Drywood termites cannot live outdoors in northern climates and have not established themselves as a pest in those areas. Isolated cases of drywood termite infestation have been found in homes located as far north as New York and Ohio, but those are rare.

Drywood termites are so called because they build their nest in perfectly good wood that is not decayed and that is not in contact with the ground. In fact, in many cases, they establish a colony in the wood-framing members of the attic. As with subterranean termites, reproductive drywood termites swarm from the nest periodically in an attempt to establish a new colony. The swarming termites often do not fly more than a few feet before settling down. However, if aided by air currents, they may fly more than a mile. Once paired, the king and queen seek cracks or checks in nearby wood, whether it is a roof or lumber pile, and set up housekeeping. In homes, drywood termites may be found in places such as rafters, studs, joists, sheathing, floorboards, window frames, door frames, and exterior trim.

Once a colony is established, it will feed on the wood around the nest. Drywood termites are general feeders and will eat spring- and summer-grown wood. As a result, the galleries thus formed will cut across the grain. The cavities will contain pellets of partially digested wood. These pellets are tiny, seedlike, and usually straw colored. On occasion, some of the pellets are pushed through openings in the wood surface. If there is not much of an accumulation, the pellets can easily be overlooked. They are, however, quite often the first sign of infestation.

The maximum population of a fully established drywood termite colony is estimated to be about 3,000. This is considerably less than the maximum number of subterranean termites in an established colony, which is estimated to be about 250,000. Consequently, it takes a longer period of time for serious damage to occur with drywood termites than with subterranean termites.

### Control

Since drywood termites do not nest in the ground, they must be chemically treated at the source of infestation. This is usually done by injecting insecticide into the galleries, a procedure that should be performed by a professional. To reach the galleries, holes are drilled in the infested wood members. The insecticide used will either be a liquid or a dust. When the wood is dry, dusting can be effective for as far as 15 feet from the point of application. However, when the wood is wet, dusting usually is not effective because the dust tends to cake in the moist galleries. If drywood termite infestation is found in a fence or pole on the property, those wood members should be treated, as the termites represent a potential source of infestation for the house.

For severe infestation, treatment is usually by fumigation. The entire house, including the roof, is wrapped with a plastic covering. After all of the openings around the house are sealed, a poisonous fumigant is introduced. The house should remain under fumigation for at least forty-eight hours. Since the insecticide used is poisonous to humans, fumigation should only be undertaken by very experienced fumigators.

### Inspection

Since drywood termites do not leave their nest in search of food, there are no telltale signs of infestation such as shelter tubes. They can be detected, however, by their pellets, which tend to accumulate in a small pile after being pushed from the wood by the termites or after falling through a crack in the infested wood. An infestation in the house can also be detected by the presence of a swarm, if you happen to be in the room during an occurrence. Since drywood termites can attack wood located anywhere in the house from the attic to the crawl space, all of the exposed wood should be checked for signs of infestation. The wood should be gently probed, so as not to break the surface. Infested wood has hollow sections and, if heavily probed, can break open, spilling the seedlike pellets. Drywood termites often consume wood up to the paint itself, forming what appears to be paint blisters. If the slightest pressure is applied to the blister, it can break. Care should be exercised to maintain the integrity of the wood surface, as a broken gallery is difficult to treat with insecticide.

## OTHER WOOD-DESTROYING INSECTS

### Carpenter Ants

As with termites, carpenter ants are social insects. They live in colonies with a rigid caste system consisting of a queen, workers, and reproductives (sexually mature males and females that periodically swarm and set up new colonies). Although worker ants may live four to seven years and the queen for as long as fifteen years, colonies have been known to last for thirty to forty years. When the queen dies or is accidentally killed, specially fed workers take over the egg-laying function.

Carpenter ants differ from termites in that they do not eat wood. They merely excavate it to build a nest. The nest consists of irregularly shaped galleries that generally follow the grain. The small fragments of shredded wood that are generated during the excavation are removed from the galleries by the ants and deposited on the outside. Consequently, the galleries do not have the earthy appearance of the termite galleries. Rather, they have a polished or sandpapered appearance.

A carpenter ant colony can be located on the ground in a decaying log or tree trunk or in the roof framing of a house. The ants also nest high in trees and will fly from there to set up new colonies in a house. They build their nests in a variety of locations, preferring wood that is moist or softened by decay. However, they will also build their nests in wood that is perfectly dry and sound.

When inspecting for carpenter ants, look specifically at sections of wood that have begun to decay as a result of a past or current moisture condition. Even though the source of the moisture may have been eliminated (such as correcting a leak), an ant colony may have already been established. Typical locations to inspect are portions of the wood framing, siding, or trim that are in contact with the ground, wood that has been dampened by the overflow from defective roof gutters, the area around a damaged section of siding or flashing, the base of hollow porch posts and columns, and areas with large, open joints such as may occasionally be found around exterior windows and doors. When these areas are inspected, they should be probed with a screwdriver or an ice pick. If the wood yields, breaks, or cracks and ants come crawling out, there is a good chance that you have located a nest.

Consider yourself lucky if you do because a carpenter ant nest is usually quite difficult to locate, as it often exists in an inaccesible location in the wall or roof assembly. One indication of the existence of a colony is unexplained piles of sawdust. Some people, however, think that piles of sawdust are an indication of termites. They are not. Subterranean termites completely devour the portion of wood that they are attacking and leave absolutely no trace of wood particles. Drywood termites also eat the wood completely. However, they do drop tiny, well-formed, seedlike pellets. If the pellets are observed closely, they can be easily differentiated from the irregularly shaped particles of sawdust.

When a house is infested with carpenter ants, there is little likelihood that the people living there are unaware of the condition. Numerous worker ants will be seen walking around the rooms as if they live there—which indeed they do, with free room and board. These ants feed on sweets, crumbs, and other foodstuffs normally found or spilled on a kitchen counter or floor. Carpenter ants are easy to recognize. They are among the largest ants in the United States, with worker ants varying in size between ¼- to ½-inch long. They are black or black with a reddish-brown midsection.

While the first sign of infestation is usually the presence of carpenter ants in the house, the fact that they are there does not mean that the nest is inside the house. It may be outdoors, and the ants may have entered the house foraging for food. A carpenter ant infestation can only be controlled by destroying the nest—either directly or indirectly. Nests can sometimes be located by watching the ant traffic. Ants continually entering and leaving a specific area are generally an indication of the nest location. If the nest is found, it can be treated directly with insecticide. If not, dusts or sprays can be used where the ants are commonly seen. The latter may not eliminate the infestation, but it should reduce it.

## Powder Post Beetles

There are many types of wood-boring beetles. The ones whose larvae or grubs feed on seasoned wood and break it down to a powdery residue are commonly called "powder post beetles." These beetles exist all over the United States, although the greatest concentration will be found in those states with a warm, humid climate. The two principal varieties of powder post beetles are the Lyctid and the Anobiid beetles. The Lyctid beetle will attack only hardwoods; the Anobiid beetle will attack both soft and hardwood timbers.

For the most part, powder post beetles are usually brought into the house via the wood that had been used in its construction. Building materials may become infested while being stockpiled in the lumber yard. The insects may also be brought into the house in finished wood products such as oak flooring, paneling, and/or furniture.

The beetles lay their eggs in the open pores, cracks, and crevices in the surface of unfinished wood. After the eggs hatch, the larvae feed and tunnel their way through the wood, reducing it to a powder. Depending on the temperature and moisture content of the wood, the larval stage can be as short as a few months or as long as a few years. Just prior to emerging, the newly formed adults chew small round exit holes in the wood surface ($\frac{1}{32}$ to $\frac{1}{8}$ of an inch). In the process of emerging, finely powdered wood called "frass" is usually pushed out in front of the body. This is often the first external sign of infestation. Shortly after emerging, the beetles mate and lay eggs. They occasionally deposit the eggs in the mouth of an old exit hole, thereby reinfesting the same piece of wood. Some wood members have shown signs of extensive damage as a result of infestation by several generations of beetles. (See Figure 8-8.)

On occasion, the homeowner may be the one responsible for the powder post beetle infestation in his house. Under natural conditions, the beetles breed in the dead branches and limbs of trees. When gathering wood for the fireplace, it is possible to pick up infested pieces and store them in the basement or under the stairs for later use. If wood is left in storage through the following spring and summer, the emerging beetles may attack the unfinished lumber such as girders, joists, studs, sill plates, and/or subflooring.

### Inspection

The inspection for powder post beetles should be performed along with the inspection for termites. When probing the exposed wood-framing members, look for the small, round emergence holes of the beetles. Since it is possible for the beetles to emerge without reinfesting the wood, the fact that there are emergence holes does not mean that the wood member is currently infested. Newly formed flight holes are light and clean in appearance, like a fresh saw cut, whereas older holes are darker in color. If the infestation is well established, there will usually be more than thirty exit holes per square foot of surface. Even though the wood may no longer be infested, small amounts of larvae frass may continue to sift through the holes for many years as a result of normal vibrations of the wood. Look at the frass. If the infestation is no longer active, it will have a yellowish appearance or will be caked.

If there is any doubt about whether or not the infestation is active, call a professional pest control operator for an evaluation. An infestation in a single wood-framing member can often be controlled

FIGURE 8-8 Wood post with extensive deterioration caused by powder post beetle infestation. Note beetle exit holes (*arrow*) at the lower section of the post.

by replacing that particular piece of wood or by coating it with an appropriate insecticide. However, if the infestation is widespread, chemical treatment by a professional is considered necessary.

## ROT

Wood products used in construction are susceptible to decay (rot). However, if properly maintained, they could easily last for hundreds of years. There are three basic types of fungi that attack wood: stain, mold, and decay. Wood rot is caused by an attack of the decay fungi. Stain and mold fungi mainly grow on the wood surface, causing discoloration. By themselves, they do not weaken the wood. Their presence, however, does indicate a moisture problem and should serve as a warning that conditions exist that are favorable to the growth of the decay fungi. The decay fungi are microscopic, threadlike plants that grow within the wood and attack its thick cell walls. They break down the walls and feed on the contents of the cells. With the destruction of the cells, the wood disintegrates and decay becomes evident.

In the early stages, it is difficult to recognize that a section of wood has been attacked by the decay fungus. The wood may merely be discolored. However, the advanced stages of decay are easily recognizable because the wood undergoes changes in properties and appearance. The affected wood may be brownish in color and crumbly, or bleached white and spongy. In either case, the decay greatly reduces the strength and structural value of the wood member. The brown, crumbly, rotted sections readily break into small cubes and in their final stage of deterioration are often quite dry. Most people, when seeing this condition, refer to it as "dry rot." This is really a misnomer. The actual decay occurred when the wood was quite wet since decay fungi cannot survive in dry wood.

Sometimes the physical changes in the wood are not apparent on the surface. They can be easily detected, however, by probing the wood with an ice pick or a screwdriver. If the wood is in good condition, the probe will not penetrate much beyond the surface. However, if the wood has deteriorated, the probe will easily penetrate into the wood. The conditions that promote the growth of the decay fungi also promote subterranean termite and carpenter ant activity. Consequently, when probing wood-framing members, you may find deteriorated sections that are caused by a combination of insect damage and decay. Under suitable conditions of temperature and humidity, the decay fungus gives rise to a fruiting body that contains enormous numbers of microscopic spores. The spores are the seeds of a new generation of decay fungi and are readily distributed by air currents. The spores are always

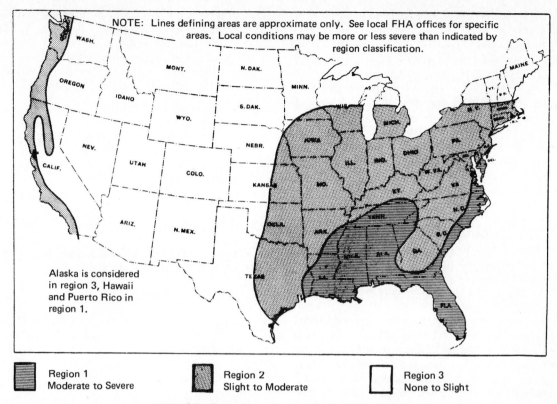

FIGURE 8-9   Decay hazard regions in the United States.

present in the air and, under normal conditions, cannot be kept away from wood. The presence of decay fungi spores on wood is of no concern unless the moisture content of the wood and the temperature are such that the spores will germinate and grow. Figure 8-9 shows the decay hazard zones in the United States.

Decay fungi will only grow and develop when the moisture content of the wood is in excess of 20 percent and the temperature is in a range of from 40° F. to 115° F. Temperatures above the upper limit will kill the decay fungi, whereas temperatures below the lower limit will merely cause the fungi to become dormant. The latter is a condition that readily occurs in the northern states during the winter months. In the spring when the temperature rises, the decay fungi in infested lumber resumes growth—assuming the moisture content of the wood has not changed. The moisture content of wood is defined as the weight of water in the wood expressed as a percentage of the weight of the wood when oven-dry. The decay fungi will thrive when the moisture content is about 25 percent. However, when the wood is saturated with moisture, the decay fungi will be inhibited from growing because of the lack of oxygen.

The moisture content of green lumber can be as high as 200 percent; whereas, after the lumber is kiln-dried, its moisture content may be as low as 7

to 10 percent. Wood in a house that has been properly constructed and maintained will seldom have a moisture content over 15 percent. However, once the moisture content exceeds 20 percent, the wood becomes vulnerable to deterioration by the decay fungi. If the building design is such that some of the wood must be subjected to damp or wet conditions, then those sections of wood should either be treated with toxic chemicals to prevent decay or be made from the heartwood of certain species (cypress, cedar, or redwood) that are resistant to rot.

## Inspection

As with the inspection for wood-destroying insects, the inspection for rot should be conducted on the exterior and interior of the structure. It can be performed concurrently with the inspection for termites. Areas that are vulnerable to attack by subterranean termites or carpenter ants are also conducive to the growth of the decay fungi. During the exterior inspection, in addition to probing the wood that is located near, or is in contact with, the ground, you should also check wood members having cracks and/or open joints that are subjected to periodic wetting from rain. One area that is particularly vulnerable to decay is the end cut of exterior wood framing, trim, or siding. An exposed end cut (across the grain) will absorb water much more readily than a section that has been cut parallel with the grain.

During the interior inspection, you should check the unfinished attic and basement or crawl space for evidence of rot. In the attic, the wood members can rot as a result of water intrusion through the roof because of a faulty roof covering or because of leakage around the joints of roof projections. Conditions conducive to rot can also result from condensation due to inadequate attic ventilation. In the basement or crawl space, the decay fungi will thrive in the wood members if the humidity is constantly high. Check the overhead wood framing and subflooring for signs of rot. Probe the wood members above and around the top of the foundation wall, and also probe the base of wood posts. Vulnerable locations for decay are the wood members through which plumbing pipes pass because of the possibility of leakage or condensation. Specifically, probe the joists and the subflooring below kitchen or bathroom fixtures.

When inspecting for rot, note on your worksheet all wood-framing members that have decayed to a point where they can no longer provide structural support. These sections should be replaced or rehabilitated. If in doubt, consult a professional. If natural decay-resistant wood or preservative-treated wood is not used for the replacement of rotted sections and the source of the moisture has not been eliminated, then it will only be a matter of time before the new sections begin to decay. Rotted wood trim that serves no structural function need not be replaced except for cosmetic reasons. Once the infected wood has been dried out and the source of the wetting has been eliminated, the decay will be permanently arrested.

## CHECKPOINT SUMMARY

### SUBTERRANEAN TERMITES

**Exterior Inspection**
- Check all exterior areas of the structure that have wood in contact with, or close proximity to, the ground.
- Note any termite shelter tubes on the foundation walls.
- Probe vulnerable areas such as garage door frames, basement windowsills and frames, deck posts, step stringers, and entry door risers.
- Probe wood-frame members adjacent to concrete covered, earth-filled porches.

- Inspect crawl areas under steps, porches, and so on.
- Probe sills and headers.
- Check wood fencing, dead tree stumps, wood debris, or stored firewood in close proximity to the house for infestation and/or rot.

**Interior Inspection**
- Inspect for shelter tubes on foundation walls and piers and around all plumbing pipes that pass through the foundation.
- Pay particular attention to areas around the heating system.
- Probe exposed sill plates, headers, joists, and girders.
- Inspect wood support posts for infestation and/or rot.
- If the house is build on a slab, note any soft spots in the baseboard trim.

### DRYWOOD TERMITES

- Inspect property fencing for infestation.
- Probe exposed wood framing throughout the house, from attic to crawl space.

### CARPENTER ANTS

- Look for small piles of sawdust below or around any wood members.
- Did you see any ants walking around in the rooms, particularly the kitchen?
- Probe the sections of wood framing, siding, and trim that show evidence of decay or past wetting.

### POWDER POST BEETLES

- Inspect wood framing for clusters of small round holes.
- Newly formed holes are the color of a fresh saw cut and indicate an active infestation.
- Probe these wood sections for deterioration.

### ROT

- Probe the vulnerable areas such as wood members that are subject to periodic wetting from rain or garden sprinklers.
- Inspect roof sheathing from the attic for decaying sections around chimney, vents, and so on.
- Check subflooring and support joists below kitchen and bathroom fixtures and around various plumbing pipes.
- Probe sill plates, headers, and the ends of joists and girders.

Insulation
Violations
Leakage
Fire Hazards
Ventilation
Attic Fans
Checkpoint Summary

Once inside the house, if there is an accessible attic, it should be the first area inspected. There are basically two types of attic, full and crawl.

A *full attic* is one in which a person can easily walk around. Usually there is a floor in this type of attic, although the walls and ceilings are unfinished. In some cases, there may be partition walls forming finished rooms with sloping or horizontal ceilings. Access to a full attic is usually through a finished staircase.

In a *crawl attic*, which is completely unfinished, the roof is sufficiently close to the floor so that, in order to get around, it is necessary to crawl or stoop over. The crawl attic usually does not have a floor. The ceiling joists from the level below are exposed. When getting around in this type of attic, be careful to walk only on the exposed joists. If you accidentally step between the joists, you will probably frighten the pants off of anyone in the room below because your foot will go right through the ceiling. Access to a crawl attic is usually through a ceiling hatch located in a closet or hallway or through hidden folding or sliding steps.

Inspecting an attic can reveal problems of which most homeowners are not aware and some of which may be potentially dangerous or costly to repair. It is not uncommon for a homeowner to say that he has lived in his house for over ten years and has never gone into the attic. Incidentally, if the homeowner does say this, you can be sure that, at the very least, the attic is inadequately insulated by current energy standards.

Insulation and roof leakage are probably the only items most people consider when thinking about the attic. However, there are other items of importance and concern such as ventilation and its associated problems, fire hazards, electrical and plumbing violations, improperly discharging vents, and open duct joints.

## INSULATION

The attic area should be adequately insulated in order to minimize heat loss. The amount of insula-

tion needed in the attic will, of course, depend on the geographic location of the structure. (See Chapter 18 to determine the proper amount of insulation for your area and for a general description of the various types of insulation.) In both crawl and unfinished full attics, the insulation should be located in the floor (between the floor joists) and *not* between the roof rafters. (See Figure 9-1.) Otherwise, heat from the habitable rooms below will escape into the attic.

The insulation should be installed with a vapor barrier facing the heated portion of the structure and not the unfinished attic area. A vapor barrier is basically aluminum foil, a plastic sheet, or an asphalt-impregnated paper that will prevent moisture movement from the heated portion of the house into the unfinished attic area. If the vapor barrier is incorrectly positioned (facing the unheated, unfinished attic), condensation problems can develop during cool weather. Moisture rising from the heated areas below the attic will condense upon contacting the cool vapor barrier. Depending

FIGURE 9-1   The proper installation of insulation in the attic, between the floor joists and not the roof rafters. Note plumbing vent stack terminating in the attic—a violation of the plumbing code.

FIGURE 9-2   Open joint in duct from kitchen exhaust fan.

on the amount of vapor, the resulting condensation buildup can reduce the effectiveness of the insulation and can cause peeling and flaking of the painted ceilings and walls in the rooms below the attic.

On many occasions, a homeowner will add additional insulation to the attic in order to bring the total amount of insulation up to current energy standards. The insulation that is added should not have a vapor barrier if the existing insulation has one. All too often, the homeowner will add insulation with a vapor barrier, which can then cause condensation problems. Look at the insulation in the floor. If there are two layers of insulation and both have vapor barriers, then the upper barrier should be slit with a razor blade in order to allow moisture movement.

If there is a full attic with partition walls forming rooms, then the insulation should be located on the unfinished sides of the partition walls and on the ceiling of the various rooms. Occasionally, insulation is placed between the roof rafters and not between the floor joists and the partition walls. This is an inefficient installation in that the heat will escape into the unfinished areas. This installation is wasteful of energy.

## VIOLATIONS

When inspecting the attic, look for vent stacks that terminate in the attic area. (See Figure 9-1.) This is a violation of the plumbing code and is a condition that should be corrected. The vent stack should extend through the roof so that the sewer gases can discharge to the outside. While in the attic, also look for ducts. Whether they are air-conditioning ducts or ducts from an exhaust fan, they should not have any open joints. (See Figure 9-2.) All open joints should be resecured. Sometimes the exhaust fan from a bathroom discharges its moisture-laden air into the attic. This is undesirable because the moisture can cause condensation problems. The duct from such an exhaust fan should be extended above the roof line so that the exhaust is discharged into the atmosphere. Also look for open electrical junction boxes and makeshift electrical wiring such as lamp-cord-type extension wiring and "pigtailed" hanging light fixtures. These are electrical violations that should be corrected.

## LEAKAGE

In addition to the above items, it is important to check the underside of the roof for signs of past water leakage and, if the structure is inspected during a rain, current water leakage. Water stains can show up on the sheathing or roof rafters and will appear as dark streak discolorations on the wood. Sometimes there is a separate masonry chimney for the fireplace and a prefabricated chimney for the heating system. Joints vulnerable to water leakage are those between the chimney and the roof and

FIGURE 9-3   Open joint between chimney and attic floor, a potential fire hazard.

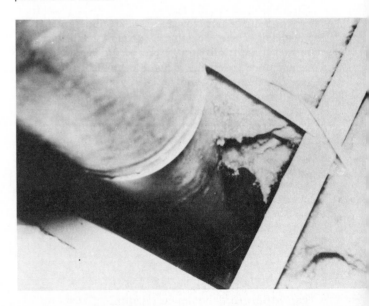

FIGURE 9-4   Partially blocked gable louvers. Louvers are used for ventilating the attic.

FIGURE 9-5   Frost on roofing nails projecting through underside of roof due to inadequate attic ventilation.

between vent stacks and the roof. These joints should be checked for leakage. Water leakage through joints is a relatively minor problem and can usually be corrected by sealing the joints with an asphalt cement.

## FIRE HAZARDS

Of particular concern is the joint between a prefabricated chimney and the attic floor. (See Figure 9-3.) If your house has a prefabricated chimney, look down the joint. On some occasions, it is possible to see the boiler/furnace room from the attic. If light is visible, then the open area is a definite fire hazard. If a fire should develop in the boiler/furnace room, the open area around the chimney will act as a flue and draw the flames up into the attic, where they can very rapidly consume the structure. Fortunately, the condition can easily and inexpensively be corrected by blocking (fire stopping) the opening with a noncombustible material such as sheetmetal.

## VENTILATION

Ventilation in an attic is very important. It allows moisture that accumulates in the area to dissipate and also helps to reduce the heat buildup that normally develops during the summer months. Some of the moisture generated in the structure by bathing and cooking works its way up into the attic. If the area is inadequately ventilated, this moisture can eventually cause problems such as delaminating roof sheathing, water streaks on interior walls, peeling and flaking paint, and, in severe cases, some rotting of the wood framing. When walking around the attic, make sure that all vents are completely unblocked. Sometimes the homeowner will block a

vent opening (see Figure 9-4) in order to cut down on the amount of cold air entering the attic and to reduce the heat loss through that opening. What he doesn't realize is that he is creating a problem for himself. If the attic is properly insulated, the heat loss through the vent openings will be minimal. Of greater importance is the need for vent openings so that moisture can escape. Look around; you'll be able to tell whether the attic is adequately ventilated.

Look at the roofing nails that are projecting through the sheathing. If you happen to be in the attic on a winter day when the temperature is around 20° F. and the area is inadequately ventilated, you will find frost on the roofing nails. (See Figure 9-5.) The frost that forms on the nails will melt and drip onto the floor during the warmer periods of the day. Many droplets of water will show up as circular stains on the floorboards and on top of the insulation. If you are in the attic during the warmer months, there will be rust stains on the sheathing near the nails.

When inspecting the attic, pay particular attention to the north slope of the roof. If the area is inadequately ventilated and plywood is used for the roof sheathing, then delamination of the sheathing may be a problem. The northerly slope will begin to delaminate before the southerly slope. Figure 9-6 shows an advanced stage of delamination as a result of the moisture buildup in the attic. At this stage, the entire roof sheathing and shingles must be replaced. The condition could have been avoided if the attic area had been adequately ventilated. Correcting an inadequately ventilated attic is relatively easy. All that is required is to increase the size of the existing vent openings (if there are any) or to provide additional openings such as roof vents,

FIGURE 9-6 Delamination of roof sheathing, resulting from inadequate ventilation of attic.

FIGURE 9-7 Thermostatically controlled power ventilator mounted between the roof rafters.

ridge vents, soffit vents, or a power ventilator. These vent openings can be used individually or in combination. The exact number of vent openings needed should be determined by a professional.

A power ventilator in an attic is a very desirable feature. (See Figure 9-7.) Because of trapped air, an attic area can reach 150° F. on a hot summer day. A power ventilator that is thermostatically controlled will greatly reduce the heat load on the building. Usually the thermostat is set to activate the fan in the ventilator when the attic temperature is about 100° F. A power ventilator provides two additional benefits regarding air conditioning. By reducing the heat load on the structure, less electrical energy is required for air-conditioning units. And, for those homes with a central air-conditioning blower coil located in the attic, the unit operates more efficiently at lower surrounding temperatures.

## ATTIC FANS

Some structures have attic fans. Check the fan before you go up into the attic. If the fan is turned on while you are in the attic, be careful when walking around. In some homes, the area of the vent openings for the attic fan is too small for the size of the fan. Consequently, the air that is moved by the fan is partially blocked from leaving the structure. As a result, pressure is built up in the attic, which decreases the efficiency of the attic fan. If the fan is turned on before you go up into the attic, put your hand over any electrical outlet box located on the level just below the attic. If you feel air rushing onto your hand, the attic vent openings are inadequate and should be increased. Some attic fans are controlled by manual snap switches. From a convenience point of view, this is not as desirable as a timer switch or a thermostat switch. If this is the case in your house, consider its replacement.

In some houses, there is no access to the attic area. If such is the case in your home, then the probability is very great that the area is inadequately insulated by current energy standards. The amount of ventilation in the area is also questionable. Installing an access hatch to the attic is recommended.

## CHECKPOINT SUMMARY

- Is attic insulated?
- Is additional insulation needed?
- Does existing insulation contain a vapor barrier?
- Is insulation properly installed?
- Is ventilation provided?
- Are vent openings blocked?
- Check operation of attic fan or power ventilator.
- If attic is poorly ventilated, look particularly at northerly slope for delaminating plywood or warped roofing boards.
- Look for signs of past/current roof leakage.
- Pay particular attention to area around the chimney and plumbing vent stacks.
- Are air-conditioning/heating ducts insulated?
- Look for open joints in the duct work.
- Do any plumbing vent stacks discharge into the attic?
- Are there kitchen/bathroom exhaust fans discharging into the attic?
- Are there open electrical junction boxes or makeshift electrical wiring?
- If house has a prefabricated chimney, is there a need for fire stopping around the joint between the chimney and the attic floor?

After inspecting the attic, you should inspect every room and closet in the house. Don't pass a door without opening it and looking inside. If a door is open, close it to see if it operates properly. Start your inspection of the rooms at the upper level and work your way down to the basement. As you walk from one floor to another, inspect the hallways and connecting staircase.

The problems normally encountered during an interior room inspection are usually of a cosmetic nature, and are not costly to correct. Occasionally, however, you may see cracks or uneven floors or walls that are symptomatic of structural problems—but that is rare. Usually, cracks and uneven floors are caused by shrinkage, warpage, or slight movement of the house. Slight movement of a house is considered quite normal. Few people realize that a house is constantly in motion. As the outdoor temperature and humidity vary with the season and time of day, they cause differential expansion, swelling, and contraction of the various structural and nonstructural elements. This movement, although slight, is very often enough to cause cracks at points of stress concentration, such as over windows or doors.

When you walk into a room, try to look beyond the cosmetics. Don't dwell on the position of the furniture or the pictures on the walls. Look at the walls, the floor, ceiling, and trim, but do not be concerned about minor cosmetic problems. Hairline cracks, small holes, chipped sections, dirty and marked-up areas can all be corrected easily by spackle, wood filler, paint, or stain, depending on the finished surface.

## WALLS AND CEILINGS

The materials most often used for covering walls and ceilings are plaster and Sheetrock (gypsum board). Plaster is usually made from a mixture of gypsum (a common mineral), sand, and water. Plaster has qualities that are very desirable for a wall finish: structural rigidity, durability, resistance to sound transmissions, and high fire resistance. In addition, it can readily be applied to curved or irregularly shaped surfaces. A plaster wall is usually applied in two or three coats to a backing called "lath." Depending on the type of lath, the thickness of the plaster will usually vary between ½ and ¾ of an inch.

Sheetrock is a sheet material that basically consists of a gypsum mixture surfaced with a treated paper. Depending on the application, the thickness of the Sheetrock can range from ¼ to ⅝ of an inch. The sheets are usually 4 feet wide and are available in lengths up to 12 feet. When constructing walls using this material, the Sheetrock is fastened directly to the studs, and the joints are covered with a tape. The edges of the Sheetrock are recessed slightly, so that when the tape is applied, it is level with the surface. This type of construction requires that the wood framing be perfectly straight and true. Otherwise, the wall surface will be uneven and there will be visible joint lines. If the moisture content of the wood used in construction is not very nearly that which will be attained in service, there may be nail pops and joint cracks. Popping nails (Figure 10-1) is a condition most often found with Sheetrock construction. It can be easily corrected. It often does, however, indicate a less-than-quality installation.

When you inspect a room, look specifically for areas that need major cosmetic rehabilitation, such as broken walls or ceiling, loose and bulging sections of plaster, and disintegrating plaster. Very often, major cosmetic damage is the result of a water condition. As you look at these areas, also look for water stains. Stains often show up as discolorations circled by a light brownish ring. If you see water stains, try to determine the source of the water, as all stains do not indicate a current problem condition. You may be looking at the results of a problem that has since been corrected.

Water stains on a ceiling may be caused by several types of problems, such as water leaking between the tile joints around a shower or tub located in a bathroom above the ceiling, an ice dam on the roof, an open joint between a plumbing vent stack or chimney and the roof, leaky plumbing, or condensation on cold water pipes located above the ceiling. Sometimes the cause is very obvious, such as a faulty roof. However, you should be aware of the fact that leaks that originate in the roof can stain ceilings two or more levels below. The stains are not limited to ceilings just beneath the roof.

FIGURE 10-1 Popping nails on a gypsum board (Sheetrock) wall—a cosmetic problem. The covering for the bottom nail has "popped" completely off, exposing the nail head.

Sometimes the source of a stain cannot be explained by any of the above. On one inspection, I noticed that the ceiling of one room had several stains that were still damp. I knew that there were no plumbing pipes above the ceiling and the roof was in good shape. Frankly, I couldn't figure out why the ceiling was damp. All of a sudden, I noticed that water was dripping from one section of the ceiling. I then went upstairs to the room above and found out what was causing the leak. Apparently, the owner kept a puppy that was not housebroken in the room. Whenever the puppy missed the newspapers that were placed there for training purposes, the urine seeped through the floor joints, wetting the ceiling below.

In addition to plaster and Sheetrock, ceilings can also be covered with composition tiles. These tiles are generally made from asbestos, glass fiber, or fiberboard. They can be applied directly over plaster or Sheetrock ceilings or over furring strips and are usually interconnected with tongue-and-groove joints. If you are inspecting an older home with plaster walls and ceilings and find yourself in a room that has a tile ceiling, the probability is high that the tiles were installed to cover broken and cracked sections in the original ceiling. It is becoming increasingly difficult to find a good plasterer. As a result, when renovating an older home, many people cover a ceiling with tiles or Sheetrock rather

than have it replastered. When looking at a tile ceiling, look specifically for loose and sagging sections. These sections must be resecured. Otherwise, they can cause adjacent tiles to loosen, which can eventually result in a "domino" effect causing most of the tiles to come down. (See Figure 10-2.) I inspected a house the day after two thirds of the ceiling tiles in one room came thundering down. The owner told me that there always had been a few loose tiles.

Water stains on walls facing the exterior may be an indication of water seepage through open joints in the exterior siding. In particular, this condition has been found in older homes with an exterior brick or stone siding and is usually caused by wind-driven rain penetrating cracked and deteriorating mortar joints. When water stains and peeling and flaking paint are found on walls just below windows, it is usually an indication of leakage through open exterior joints around the window.

Cracks in walls are normally merely of cosmetic concern. However, when walls are cracked and the windows and/or door frames in that room are not level, the condition may be indicative of a structural problem and should be evaluated by a professional.

When the walls are covered with wood or hardboard panels, cracks will not be visible. In quality homes, panels are normally installed over a Sheetrock wall. This type of backing provides added rigidity and, when applied on exterior walls, added insulation. If the room that you are inspecting has a panel wall, push on the panel at a point between the studs. The studs are usually located every 16 inches. However, in some houses, they are 24 inches apart. If the wall panel yields under your push, then there is no Sheetrock backing. I inspected a new

FIGURE 10-2 Ceiling that had been covered with tiles, which came loose and fell down. Note that the tiles had been installed to cover a cracked, broken, and peeling ceiling.

house just after construction and prior to occupancy. The buyer specifically asked me to check the Sheetrock because he was paying extra for ⅝-inch thick rather than ½-inch thick Sheetrock. The builder did install the thicker Sheetrock. However, in those rooms that were paneled, the builder completely omitted the Sheetrock behind the panels because it was not visible to the buyer.

The trim around the various joints in the room should be inspected and checked for missing, loose, cracked, and broken sections. Although a minor element, trim in this condition is an indication of shoddy workmanship in new construction and neglect in a resale.

## FLOORS

When walking around the house, you may notice that some of the floor squeaks on one or more sections. This condition is found in both new and older homes and indicates slightly loose floorboards. It is usually difficult to eliminate. One corrective procedure is to wedge the floor from below. However, the underside is usually not accessible. If a hardwood floor is nailed from above, the nail holes can ruin the finish. With regard to the structural integrity of the house, squeaking floors are not a concerning factor although if excessive, they may be annoying.

If the floors in a portion of the house are finished hardwood and the remaining floors (other than the bathrooms and kitchen) are covered with wall-to-wall carpet, do not assume that there is a hardwood floor below the carpeting. There may be, but quite often there isn't. It is not uncommon for a builder to give a buyer the option of either having hardwood floors or having the floors covered with carpeting. When the buyer selects carpeting, it is laid over a plywood floor. If you are inspecting a room and see a hardwood floor in a closet, while the floor in the main portion of the room is carpeted, do not assume that there is a hardwood floor beneath the carpeting. If you cannot see it, then you really cannot be sure what it is. If a hardwood floor is important to you, get a representation in writing from the owner that the floors beneath the carpets are hardwood.

If you walk into a room and notice that the floor is not level, do not be alarmed. In all probability, it is a condition caused by past shrinkage, warpage, and/or settlement of the wood framing and is not a concerning factor. If the floor is sagging in one section, it may indicate that that portion of the floor is or was improperly supported. Go down to the level below to check the ceiling to see if it too is sagging. If it is, have a professional evaluate the condition. Occasionally, this condition occurs in a kitchen floor when the refrigerator is placed in a location other than that intended by the builder.

Depending on the moisture content in the wood used for framing, you may see a large, open joint between the floor and the partition walls. The joint may be open as much as 1 inch and may run the entire length of the partition wall. When you see this condition for the first time, it is quite unnerving. The trim that normally covers the joint between the floor and the wall is about an inch above the floor and the joint is wide open. The condition is caused by excessive shrinkage of the wood framing and is only a cosmetic problem. By covering the open joint with trim or lowering the existing trim, the room will look almost as good as new.

The floors of some homes such as ranches or those on the lower level of bilevels may be resilient tiles laid over a concrete slab. Depending on the quality of construction, the concrete floor slab occasionally settles to a point where there is also a large, open joint between the floor and the walls. (See Figure 10-3.) During construction, if the ground below the floor slab is not properly compacted, the slab may eventually settle, resulting in open joints. The foundation walls all have support footings and are independent of the floor slab. Consequently, settlement of the floor slab usually does not indicate a structural problem. However, if the floor settlement is accompanied by cracked and settled sections of the foundation wall, a severe problem exists that must be evaluated by a professional.

Sometimes, the concrete floor slab has a raised wood floor that may be covered with carpeting or resilient floor tiling. When walking on this floor, test for soft or spongy sections. This condition can be caused by inadequate spacing of the wood framing. However, more often than not, it is caused by rotting wood. If water seeps into the area between the wood floor and the concrete slab, it eventually causes the framing to rot and the subflooring to delaminate. (See Figure 10-4.) (See Chapter 11 for a discussion of water seepage into the basement level.)

FIGURE 10-3 Settled concrete floor slab (tile covered). Note open joint between floor and partition walls.

## HEAT

With the exception of the homes in the sun belt, all the finished rooms in the house should have provisions for heating. Depending on the type of heating (see Chapter 14), look for a radiator or heat register. If you don't see any, ask the owner how the room is heated. It may be heated by radiant panels in the floor, walls, or ceiling that would not be visible. If there is no source of heat, record the fact on your worksheet. Adding heat to a room by extending the existing heating system can be costly. If there is a means of heat supply, is it properly located? For maximum efficiency, radiators and heat-supply registers should be located on an exterior wall, preferably below a window. This will allow the heat to mix with the cooler outside air that normally infiltrates into the interior from around the windows.

## WINDOWS

Although the condition of most of the windows is checked during the exterior inspection (see Chapter 5), the condition of the windows on the upper levels and the operation of the windows should be checked during an interior inspection. Also, if the windows are the casement or awning type, the storms and screens are often not visible from the exterior and should be looked for during the interior room inspection.

The cost of repairing a broken window frame or replacing a broken pane is usually not high on an individual basis unless the window is one of unusual design or a large thermal pane (double or triple glazing). Keep track of the number of windows that need repair or rehabilitation. It is surprising how

FIGURE 10-4   Rotting and delaminating sections of raised wood floor (over concrete slab) in finished basement. Condition is caused by constant wetting as a result of water seepage into the basement.

fast the dollars add up when you multiply the cost for one repair by the number of windows that are faulty.

Specifically, check the windows for cracked and broken panes that require replacement. BB holes or small cracks in the corner of a pane can be overlooked providing that the window is covered by a storm pane. Is the putty around the pane cracked, dry, chipped, or missing? If so, the window joints must be reputtied. Look at wood window frames and exterior sills for cracked and rotting sections. Some windows have metal frames. Metal frames get quite cold during the winter in the northern part of the United States and, as such, have a tendency toward excessive condensation. This, in turn, may cause peeling and flaking paint or disintegrating sections of plaster near the window frame.

Pay particular attention to steel casement windows. These windows are usually a problem. They rust easily and must be painted every few years to prevent deterioration. In many cases, they do not close properly—a condition often caused by a sprung frame or excessive layers of paint around the joints. Also, almost invariably, you will find cracked panes. Usually, although not always, casement windows are crank operated. Check the hardware. Sometimes the cranking mechanism is not operational.

Open and close the windows. They should operate relatively easily without sticking or binding. Double-hung windows should not rattle in the channel and should stay in a fixed position when opened fully or partially. Many older double-hung windows use a counterweight to hold the sash in a fixed open position. The weight is usually tied to a sash by a cord or a chain. If a cord is used, check to see if it is broken. Broken cords are not uncommon and should be replaced. If the cord is frayed, you can anticipate its early replacement.

When looking at the windows, check to see if the glazing is a single pane or a thermal pane. You can tell by looking at the thickness of the joint between the pane and the frame. A single pane is usually no more than $\frac{3}{16}$ of an inch thick; a thermal pane is about $\frac{3}{8}$ of an inch to 1 inch thick. You can also tell by looking very closely at the pane. Usually, you can see dust or dirty spots on the opposite side that reveals the thickness of the pane. Sometimes fixed-pane windows and sliding glass doors have thermal panes, even though the openable windows throughout the house have only a single pane. One of the well-known trade names for thermal glass is Thermopane. If the window pane is made by Thermopane, you will see the name in the corner.

Thermal-pane windows are fabricated by hermetically sealing dry air between the panes. This is done to eliminate the possibility of future condensation problems between the panes. When the seal breaks, accidentally or otherwise, water vapor can enter the space between the panes. Look at the windows for signs of a faulty seal. If a portion of the window appears cloudy (see Figure 10-5) or if there are water droplets between the panes, the seal has been broken. Although the insulating characteristics of a thermal-pane window with a faulty seal are at least as good as a storm window, the pane is not desirable from a visibility and a cosmetic point of view. If you see a thermal-pane window with a faulty seal, record it on your worksheet. The window requires replacement.

## ELECTRICAL OUTLETS

While inspecting the interior rooms, look for electrical hazards and violations and whether or not there are an adequate number of electrical outlets on the walls. These items are discussed in Chapter 12. According to the electrical code, the outlets in a new house must be located such that no point on the wall is more than 6 feet horizontally from an outlet. However, the actual number of outlets needed for a specific room will depend on the room's usage and the position of the furniture.

Look at the electrical outlets. In new homes and in recently rewired older homes, the receptacles will have three slots rather than the older type with two slots. The third slot is a ground connection that is used in conjunction with the three-prong plugs found on most modern appliances. It is a safety feature and is used for grounding the casing of electrical appliances and equipment. Should an internal short develop between the wiring and the equipment/appliance casing, the ground connection will direct the leakage current harmlessly to the ground rather than through the user.

Not all electrical appliances and equipment have a grounding wire (three-prong plug). Some of them are made with double-insulated plastic cases that prevent the user from touching anything electrically charged, even if an internal short should develop. This type of equipment does not require a ground connection and can, therefore, be used with the older type, two-slot receptacles. As a safety precaution, you should only use electrical appliances and equipment that have been approved by Underwriters' Laboratories, Inc., or some other nationally recognized testing agency.

The two-slot outlet receptacles can be used for the grounding of appliances with three-prong plugs. Adapters are available at hardware and electrical supply stores to enable two-slot receptacles to accept the three-prong plugs. In order to complete the ground connection when using the adapter, remember that the small wire (pigtail) must be secured to the center screw on the receptacle cover plate.

FIGURE 10-5   Faulty seal in the thermal-pane windows adjacent to the sliding glass door. Restricted visibility is caused by condensation between the glass panes.

Check the receptacles (two- and three-slot) to determine if they are electrically hot and whether or not they are properly grounded. This can be done using a simple plug-in tester that is available at all electrical supply stores. It is particularly important to check the integrity of the electrical grounding for the receptacles located in the bathroom and kitchen. Receptacles that are not properly grounded are potential hazards and should be corrected or, at the very least, not used with appliances that require grounding.

## FIREPLACE

If a house has a fireplace, it is most often located in the living room or family room, although you may find a fireplace in a bedroom or kitchen. When inspecting the fireplace, look at the front face just above the firebox. If this area has a blackish tint or color, it is usually an indication of a smoky fireplace. The blackness is called "carbonization" and is the result of a buildup over the years of layers of soot and/or creosote. This problem can usually be corrected.

A smoky fireplace may be the result of too small a flue for the size of the firebox opening. If this is the case, reducing the size of the opening by raising the hearth or installing a canopy on the top portion of the opening very often corrects the problem. However, determining the amount to raise the hearth or the size and shape of canopy to use requires experimentation. Sometimes the carbonization is caused by backsmoking as a result of downdrafts. This is the result of wind currents bouncing off the side of the building or tall trees and then down the chimney. If the fireplace smoking is caused by downdrafts, the problem can usually be corrected by installing a concrete, stone, or metal cap on top of the chimney.

Look inside the firebox for a damper. The damper is used to close the flue when the fireplace is not in use. It prevents heat loss through the flue in the winter and also prevents small animals, such as squirrels and racoons, from entering the room through the flue. On many older fireplaces, dampers were omitted. If the fireplace that you are inspecting does not have a damper, record that fact on your worksheet. A damper or equivalent is considered necessary and one should be installed.

The bricks or stones lining the firebox should be checked for cracked, chipped, broken, and disintegrating sections. Are the mortar joints intact or are they in need of repointing? Cracked and/or open sections inside the firebox are a potential fire hazard and must be repaired.

Look up at the flue from inside the firebox. Normally, this area will be coated with a layer of soot and/or creosote. If the layer is thick, have the chimney cleaned. This will minimize the possibility of a chimney fire. Is there an obstruction in the flue such as a bird's nest? If the flue has a slight offset and you can see daylight, then there is no obstruction. When the flue is offset so that you cannot see straight up, determining whether or not there is an obstruction is difficult, without lighting a fire. One trick is to blow up at the flue to dislodge fine particles of soot. If the flue is not obstructed, they will float up the chimney.

In some homes you may find a prefabricated fireplace. These units are usually available with chimneys and have a specially insulated firebox shell. They are light in weight, do not require a special foundation, and may be wall-mounted or free-standing. The fireplace can be located in practically any part of a house, depending on local codes. If you find such a fireplace, check to see if it has been approved by Underwriters' Laboratories, Inc., or some other nationally recognized testing agency.

## BEDROOMS

Every habitable room in the house must have at least one openable window. Sometimes "do-it-yourself" homeowners finish off an area in the basement or attic for use as an extra bedroom, even though there is no window in the room. If you find such a room, be advised that it is a potential fire hazard.

When a room is used as a bedroom, certain items are necessary as a fire safety measure. As a means of escaping in the event of a fire, each bedroom should have at least one outside window where the sill height is not more than 42 inches above the floor. The window should also have a minimum openable area of 4 square feet with no dimension less than 18 inches. If a bedroom is located two stories above the ground, a rope ladder or an equivalent device should be provided in the room to enable the inhabitants to escape unhurt once they climb through the window. Some municipalities have local ordinances against converting a third-level attic into bedrooms without adequate fire protection. If you find bedrooms in a converted attic during your inspection, you should check with the local Building Department to see if a Certificate of Occupancy had been issued for those rooms.

Last, from a fire safety point of view, every bedroom must have an entry door. This door should be closed when the occupant goes to sleep. A closed door reduces drafts, thus reducing flame-spread time, and drastically reduces smoke infiltration. Smoke detectors are usually not necessary in bedrooms if there is a detector in the hallway leading to the bedrooms.

Don't forget to look for a closet. In some homes where bedrooms have been added, closets are occasionally omitted in the renovation.

## BATHROOMS

Because of the nature of the room, the bathroom must be well ventilated. Ventilation can be provided naturally through an openable window or mechanically through an exhaust fan. If there is an exhaust fan, try to determine where it discharges. The air drawn through the fan should discharge into the atmosphere. This can be accomplished through the use of a duct that terminates on the side of the building or one that extends up through the attic and terminates on the roof. When the bathroom is located on the level just beneath the attic, the exhaust fan very often discharges directly into the attic. This is undesirable because the moisture-laden air can cause condensation problems in the attic. From a convenience point of view, many builders often connect the exhaust fan to the lighting circuit, so that both are controlled by the same switch. This is not an energy-efficient installation, as the exhaust fan is not always needed. If you see such a setup, you may want to consider rewiring the fan so that it can be controlled by a separate switch.

A recurring problem in bathrooms is water leakage through cracked and open tile joints around the tub and/or shower. This is a condition that requires periodic maintenance and, if neglected, can cause a considerable amount of cosmetic damage. Check the tiles for cracked and open joints. Lean over the tub or go into the shower and press on the tiles, particularly at the lower portion of the walls. Loose tiles will move slightly or may even come out. If the tiles yield, it is usually an indication that the plaster or Sheetrock backing has suffered some deterioration as a result of water seepage. Depending on the severity of the deterioration, it may be necessary to rehabilitate that portion of the wall.

If the integrity of the walls around the tub and

shower is not kept watertight, water can leak around open areas, wet the ceiling below, and eventually rot the wood framing and cause the ceiling to deteriorate. Missing tiles must be replaced, loose tiles must be resecured, and cracked and open joints must be regrouted or caulked. Caulking is the procedure most often used for making repairs. A tube of caulking compound is available at any hardware store.

If the walls around the tub or shower have a panel finish rather than a tile finish, check the joints for cracked and/or open sections. Sometimes the tub or shower and its associated walls are an integral unit made of molded plastic. In this case, the possibility of leaks through open joints is not a problem. Many homes have showers and tubs with doors to prevent water from splashing onto the floor. The doors must be made with safety glass or plastic and should be checked for cracked panes and for ease of operation.

When the shower base is covered with ceramic tiles rather than molded plastic or is terrazzo constructed, there is the potential for a problem as a result of a faulty shower pan. A large lead sheet (lead pan) is normally installed below the tiles at the base of the shower to collect water that seeps through cracked and open tile joints. If the lead pan is intact, it will direct the water down the drain without incident. However, as the shower pan ages, the joints very often deteriorate, resulting in water leakage through those joints. If you notice large water stains on or damage to the ceiling of an area below the shower, you should suspect a shower pan problem.

If you have the seller's permission, you can test for a faulty shower pan by covering the shower drain and filling the shower base with about an inch of water. Let the water stand in the base for about forty-five minutes. If the shower pan is faulty and there are cracks in the base tile joints, water will seep through and wet the ceiling below. When the tile joints at the base of the shower are all sealed, even if the lead pan is faulty, there will not be any leakage. As a result, instead of replacing a faulty shower pan, many homeowners simply recaulk the tile joints at the base of the shower. This is considered a makeshift fix. If you find a heavy layer of caulking in the shower base, even if you do not find water stains on the ceiling below (the ceiling could have been repainted after the makeshift fix), you should suspect shower pan problems.

## Water Pressure/Flow

The water pressure in a house is an item of concern to most home buyers, and rightly so. However, water pressure per se is not usually the problem. If you see water trickling out of a faucet, it does not

necessarily mean that the pressure is low. It does mean that the water *flow* is low. Low water flow can be caused by low pressure. However, more often than not, the low flow is caused by a constriction in the supply pipes. The constriction can be the result of mineral or corrosive deposits on the inside diameter of the pipes, a kink in the pipe, or small-diameter distribution piping. Quite often, low flow at a fixture is caused by a partially clogged faucet aerator, which requires only cleaning for correction. Water flow is measured in gallons per minute, and a sink faucet should be able to deliver 4 to 5 gallons per minute.

The water pressure available to a house at the meter will vary, but it is usually in a range of 20 to 60 pounds per square inch (psi). I inspected a house recently that had a pressure gauge on the house side of the water meter. (A pressure gauge in the plumbing system is desirable but is not very common.) The gauge indicated that the available water pressure was 110 psi. Yet when three faucets were turned on at the same time, the water flow from each faucet was just a trickle. Regardless of how high the pressure is, if there is a constriction inside the water pipes that limits the water flow, the amount of water discharging from the faucet will be noticeably low. In this particular case, the pipes were made of galvanized iron. Over the years, corrosion and deposits had coated the inside of the distribution piping to a point where the pipes required replacement.

When you inspect the bathroom, check the water flow by simultaneously turning on the faucets in the sink and tub and flushing the bowl. There will usually be a drop in flow when the second faucet is turned on. If it is not very noticeable, do not worry about it—it is normal. You can trust your eye. If the water flow from the faucets looks good, then for all practical purposes, it is good. If the flow is noticeably low, record it on your worksheet. The condition will require correction.

Check the flow for both the hot water and the cold water, but not at the same time. It is possible for the cold water flow to be good and the hot water flow to be fair or poor. Occasionally, when the domestic hot water is generated through the heating system, deposits form in the tankless coil that restrict the flow. If the hot water flow is poor, you will probably have to replace the tankless coil. (See Chapter 16.)

Open and close the faucets rapidly. Do you hear a hammering and vibrating noise? You should not. But if you do, you are hearing "water hammer." Water hammer comes about when the water flowing in the pipe comes to an abrupt stop. It introduces hydraulic shock and vibrations that can, in extreme cases, damage the pipe or fittings. The condition can be easily corrected by installing an air

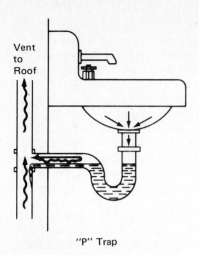

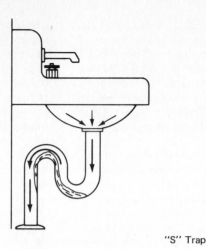

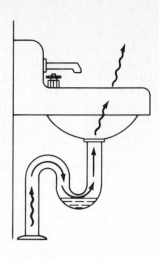

"P" Trap

"S" Trap

When the sink trap is properly vented, the trap holds enough water to form a seal against the entry of sewer gases. The gases vent harmlessly through the vent stack to the outside.

When the sink trap is not properly vented, the rush of the waste water can siphon the water seal out of the trap.

With no water seal, sewer gases can escape into the house.

A

B

FIGURE 10-6   Sink traps: A. Properly vented P-type trap and B. S-type trap, usually not properly vented.

chamber or anti-knock coil. These units provide a cushion of air to absorb the shock when the water flow stops.

While you are checking the water flow, look for water leakage around the faucets, the joint between the bowl and the floor, and in the drainage trap below the sink. If you notice that a portion of the trap is taped over, it is usually a makeshift correction for a previous leak. The drainage trap is not installed below the sink to catch rings or other valuables that fall down the drain, although very often this is the case. The purpose of the trap is to provide a water seal that blocks noxious gases from seeping back up into the room. If a sink trap is not properly vented, it can lose its seal as a result of a siphoning action when the water is draining. (See Figure 10-6.)

Usually, the P-type sink trap is vented properly. However, the S-type trap is often not vented properly. You can tell by making the following test, although it is not foolproof. Fill the sink until the water is almost at the rim and then let the water drain. When most of the water has drained, if you hear a sucking and gurgling noise, the trap is not vented and the water seal has been lost. When all the water has drained, if you let the water run freely for about five seconds, you will reestablish the water seal. If the main plumbing waste line has a house trap, the above problem is minimized.

Check the drainage in the sink, tub, and bowl. Wrinkle up some toilet paper into a ball and throw it into the bowl. When the bowl is flushed, the paper should be carried down the drain. If the water in the bowl starts to rise to the top and then settles down without flushing, there is a blockage in the drain line that must be checked further and corrected. If the house has a septic system for waste disposal, this condition may indicate a problem with the septic system. If the water in the sink and tub does not readily drain away or drains sluggishly, there is a blockage in those drains that must also be corrected. In this case, the correction may be as simple as removing hair that has accumulated around the pop-up drain plug.

Look at the sink and tub faucets. When the tub and sink are filled to the flood rim, there should be an air gap between the top of the water and the bottom of the faucet spout. (See Figure 10-7.) If there isn't, the faucet is vulnerable to back siphonage (the flowing back of dirty water from the sink or tub into the potable water supply because of a negative pressure in the line). This condition is a violation of the plumbing code and is found periodically in old homes. It is, however, not limited to old homes. The "do-it-yourself" homeowner could have installed the faucet without being aware that it is a potential problem. Are there shutoff valves below the sink and bowl for the water supply pipes? Although not a necessary feature, they are very convenient when making minor repairs.

After you flush the bowl, if the toilet is the tank type, lift the tank lid and look inside. If the lid has a cloth cover, be careful when lifting it. It may be cracked or chipped. If water is spurting out of the fill valve, maintenance is needed. You may even find the trip lever connected to the flush valve by a string rather than a metal chain or strip. Repair or replacement of the flushing mechanism is not costly.

Occasionally the seller, not being the original

owner, inadvertently misrepresents the age of the house. Depending on the manufacturer of the toilet bowl, you may be able to verify the house's age by looking on the underside of the tank lid. There may be a date stamped on the underside that can be a clue, assuming the toilet is the original and was not installed during a later renovation. The date is the date of manufacture, which is usually within a few months of installation.

## KITCHEN

When inspecting the kitchen, in addition to the items mentioned above, the condition of the cabinets and counters should be checked. The appliances, although important, need not be inspected at this time. Because appliances can break down at any time, it is recommended that on the day of, but prior to, the contract closing, you come back to the house and operationally check every appliance that is included in the purchase. If one or more appliance is not operational, you can have your attorney request an adjustment at the contract closing for the cost of repairs.

Cabinets should be inspected for missing, cracked, and loose-fitting doors and drawers. Missing hardware for doors and drawers should be noted. The shelves should be checked to see if they are adequately supported. The counters should be inspected for cracked, burned, blistered, and loose sections. If there is a cutting board or hotplate on the counter, lift it up or move it aside. You might find that it is concealing a damaged section of the counter.

When inspecting the sink, in addition to checking the water flow and drainage, look for a sprayer. If there is one, see if it is operational. On many occasions, I have seen sprayers with a disconnected hose mounted in the sink fitting. The sprayers were not functional and served only as a decoration to cover the opening in the sink.

Is there a garbage disposal unit connected to the sink drain? If there is and the house has a septic tank for waste disposal rather than a sewer, there may be a problem. A garbage disposal unit introduces solid wastes into the septic system at a greater rate than would normally occur. In order to avoid overloading the system, some states have a design criteria calling for a larger capacity septic tank when there is a garbage disposal unit. Other states recommend that the tank be cleaned at more frequent intervals. (See Chapter 13 for a discussion of septic systems.)

If the disposal unit was added after the house was constructed and provisions were not made for a larger septic tank or more frequent cleaning, then the disposal unit may have been overloading the septic system. This can result in premature failure

of the system. If the house that you are inspecting has a garbage disposal unit and a septic system, check with the local municipal Building Department to determine if the system was designed to accommodate the wastes from the disposal unit. Also, check with the owner to find out when the septic tank was last cleaned. If it was not cleaned or at least inspected for sludge buildup within the last three years, record the fact on your worksheet. The tank should be cleaned after you move in.

## HALLWAY AND STAIRCASE

The remaining rooms in the house that you are inspecting should be checked as described above. In addition, the connecting hallway should be inspected as you walk from one part of the house to another. The hallway should be treated as an interior room, and, as such, the walls, floor, ceiling, and trim should be inspected. Look for an overhead light in the hall. Is it controlled by three-way switches located at both ends of the hall? It should be. As a fire safety measure, a smoke detector or equivalent should be mounted on the ceiling of the hallway leading to the bedrooms. Several states have enacted legislation requiring the installation of smoke detectors in new construction prior to the issuance of a Certificate of Occupancy. If there is a smoke detector, is it properly located? The corners of a hallway where the walls and ceiling meet is considered dead-air space. This means that even though smoke will circulate and accumulate near the ceiling, it will not penetrate into those corners until the hall is completely filled with smoke.

FIGURE 10-7 Air gap between bottom of faucet spout and flood rim of sink prevents the backflow of nonpotable water into the potable water supply.

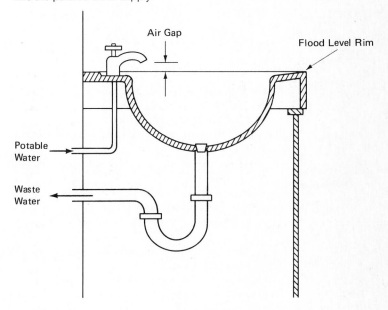

According to the National Fire Code: "Spot-type smoke detectors shall be located on the ceiling not less than six inches from a side wall, or if on the side wall, between six to twelve inches from the ceiling." If you see an incorrectly located smoke detector, you should alert the seller and record it on your worksheet.

As you proceed from one level to another, check the connecting staircase. Squeaky treads, as with squeaky floors, indicate loose sections. They are not a concerning factor, but if excessive, they are annoying. Correcting the problem is often difficult because the underside is usually concealed. The steps should all be uniformly spaced without any dimensional variation. It is not uncommon finding basement steps with uneven risers for the bottom and top steps. This condition is a potential hazard, as someone can easily trip.

As a safety precaution, all steps should have handrails. Loose handrails must be resecured. Sometimes the handrail is secured in such a manner that there is little finger room. This is a hazardous condition, especially for children. Is there a window at the base of the staircase or on the landing? If there is, its sill should be at least 36 inches above the floor. This will prevent someone from falling through the window in the event of a fall down the stairs. If the sill is less than 36 inches high, a window guard should be installed as a precautionary measure.

Lighting the stairway is essential, especially for areas that are often neglected, such as basement steps. The location of the light fixture is unimportant, as long as the light provides sufficient illumination for the entire staircase. The light should be controlled by three-way switches, one at the top and the other at the bottom of the staircase.

### CHECKPOINT SUMMARY

#### WALLS AND CEILINGS

- Do not be concerned with minor cosmetic problems. Specifically check for:
  broken walls and ceilings.
  loose, missing, and bulging areas of plaster and/or Sheetrock.
  missing, loose, and sagging sections of ceiling tile.
  water stains on ceilings, particularly below roofs, bathrooms, and kitchens.
  disintegrating plaster, peeling and flaking paint, and water stains on walls facing the exterior (usually caused by open/exposed exterior joints).
- Note rooms that have cracked walls in which the windows and/or door frames are not level

(professional evaluation is recommended).
- Check paneled walls for Sheetrock backing (often omitted).
- Check trim for missing, loose, cracked, or broken sections.

#### FLOORS

- Inspect for floors that are not level, have loose floorboards, or have sagging areas. Sagging floors that are also noted in the ceilings below should be evaluated by a professional.
- Inspect for large, open joints between floor and partition walls (usually caused by excessive shrinkage).
- Note floors that have wall-to-wall carpeting. Do not assume that there is a hardwood floor beneath the carpeting. Request that owner make this representation in writing.
- Inspect concrete floor slabs for cracked and settled areas. Note areas that have large, open joints between the floor slab and the walls.
- Check raised wood floors over concrete slabs for soft, spongy, and delaminated sections. Often, these conditions are a result of water seepage with associated rot in wood framing.

#### HEAT

- Check interior rooms for missing radiators or heat registers.
- If rooms are heated by other means (radiant panels), verify this with the owner.
- Are radiators and heat supply registers efficiently located (preferably on an exterior wall and below a window)?

#### WINDOWS

- Check windows for ease of operation.
- Inspect for cracked and broken panes; chipped, cracked, and missing putty.
- Check exterior sills for cracked and rotting sections.
- Inspect double-hung windows for broken/missing sash cords, loose or binding sashes, and missing hardware.
- Inspect steel casement-type windows for cracked panes, rusting and sprung frames, loose, missing, and/or inoperative hardware.
- Check thermal-pane-type windows for faulty seals (water droplets and/or cloudy areas between the glass panes).
- Check casement and awning windows for interior-type storm windows and screens.

#### ELECTRICAL OUTLETS

- Inspect rooms, stairways, and hallways for

electrical hazards and violations (see Chapter 12 summary).
- Note all rooms in which there are insufficient outlets and outlets that are loose and/or have missing cover plates.
- Check/test if outlets are electrically "hot" and properly grounded (particularly those in the kitchen and bathrooms).

## FIREPLACE

- Inspect brick/stone firebox lining for cracked, chipped, broken, or deteriorating sections.
- Check for cracked, loose, or disintegrating mortar joints.
- Check top of firebox for an operational damper.
- Inspect area for obstructions.
- Is the chimney flue lined?
- Check for heavy layers of soot and/or creosote. (Heavy layers indicate the need for chimney cleaning.)

## BEDROOMS

- Check that all bedrooms have at *least* one openable window with the following criteria:
  The sill height is not *more* than 42 inches above the floor.
  A minimum openable area of 4 square feet with no dimension less than 18 inches.
- Do all bedrooms have entry doors and closets?
- If a portion of the attic or basement has been converted to a bedroom, is there a Certificate of Occupancy for the room?

## BATHROOMS

- Check bathrooms for adequate ventilation.
- If there is an exhaust fan:
  Is it operational?
  Does it have a separate on/off switch?
  Can you determine where the fan exhaust discharges?
- Inspect tiled areas particularly around the tub and/or shower for open joints, cracked, loose, and missing tiles.
- Note wall areas in the tub and/or shower that show evidence of deterioration (spongy/loose sections).
- Check shower door(s) for cracked panes (should be safety glass) and for ease of operation.
- Check sinks, bowl, and tub/shower for cracks, chipped, and stained areas. Check that sink(s) and bowl are properly secured.
- Inspect sink and tub faucets for proper air gap (potential back siphonage).

- Check fixtures for individual shutoff valves.
- Inspect fixture plumbing for leaks, kinked lines, patched and makeshift corrections (taped joints and rubber-hose connections).
- Inspect sink drain lines for improper venting (S-type traps).

### Water Pressure/Flow
- Check cold water flow by simultaneously turning on the faucets in the sink(s) and tub or shower and flushing the bowl.
- Perform a similar check for hot water flow.
- Check for "water hammer" when faucets are opened and closed rapidly.

## KITCHEN

- Check sink for low water flow and proper drainage.
- If sink contains a sprayer, check operation (often this unit is disconnected).
- If sink drain contains a garbage disposal unit and house has a septic tank, you should know the following:
  Was disposal unit added after the house was constructed? (Septic tank may be undersized.)
  When was septic tank last cleaned? (If over three years, the tank should be cleaned.)
- Inspect cabinets for missing, cracked, or loose-fitting doors and drawers.
- Check for missing hardware on cabinet doors and drawers.
- Check shelving for adequate support, cracked, warped, or missing sections.
- Inspect counter and countertops for cracked, burned, blistered, or loose sections.
- Check all appliances for operational integrity on the day of, but prior to, contract closing.

## HALLWAY AND STAIRCASE

- Check for properly located smoke detectors in hallway areas leading to the bedrooms.
- Check hallways/staircases for adequate lighting. Are three-way switches located at both ends of the hallway?
- Check walls, floor, ceiling, trim, and so on, as you would for interior rooms.
- Inspect stairways for uneven risers, loose treads, missing handrails, and handrails with tight finger room.
- If there is a window at the base of the stairway/landing, is the sill *less* than 36 inches above the floor? (If this condition exists, you should install a window guard.)

# 11. BASEMENT / CRAWL SPACE

The problems that can be detected in a basement or crawl space are often among the most costly to correct. While inspecting these areas, look specifically for signs of water penetration, structural deterioration of the wood support members, and structural deficiencies of the foundation wall.

## FOUNDATION

The purpose of the foundation is to support the main portion of the house and transmit its load to the ground. The foundation of most residential structures consists of walls that rest on an enlarged base called a "footing." The footing spreads the transmitted load directly to the supporting soil and is usually resting on undisturbed earth. In areas where there are freezing temperatures during the winter months, the footings must be located below the frost line. Otherwise, the footings become vulnerable to frost heaving resulting from the freezing of soil moisture. In addition to foundation walls, pilasters, piers, and columns are also used to support the main structure. (See Figure 11-1.)

Foundation walls are normally designed to support the vertical loads from the house and to resist the horizontal forces resulting from the earth's pressure. In most parts of the country, the house must be anchored to the foundation in order to provide resistance to wind forces. High wind forces can cause a structure that is not properly anchored to lift, shift, or rotate slightly. When the house is properly anchored, the resistance to this movement produces stresses within the foundation wall. Consequently, the foundation wall must also be designed to withstand these forces. In some cases, the combined vertical and horizontal forces acting on the foundation wall is great enough to require additional bracing and stiffening of the walls. In these cases, pilasters are often used to provide the additional support.

### Settlement

All soils compress to some extent and, if the footing is not resting on bedrock, the foundation is subject to settlement. When the settlement is slight, uniform, or was anticipated in the design, it is of little concern. However, when the foundation settles unevenly (differential settlement), there is generally some cause for concern. Differential settlement introduces stresses that may seriously weaken the building. It often results in cracks in the foundation walls, unsightly cracks in the finished walls and ceilings, sloping floors and windows, and doors that bind. When the differential settlement is excessive, it can result in a structural failure of that portion of the foundation wall—a condition that may be quite costly to correct.

The principal cause of foundation settlement is a reduction of the volume of the voids in the soil supporting the foundation. The voids are the spaces between the soil particles and contain air and/or water. Sandy soil contains large, granular particles with a relatively small volume of voids; clay-type soil contains fine-grained particles with a large volume of voids. As a result, the settlement of foundations built on a sandy soil will tend to be quick and slight, whereas the settlement of foundations built

FIGURE 11-1   Elements of a building foundation.

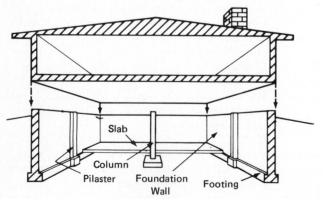

Slab

Column

Pilaster   Foundation   Footing
         Wall

on a clay-type soil will tend to be greater and may occur over many years.

Usually you do not have to worry about foundation settlement in older homes because by the time you are considering buying the house, the settlement has already occurred along with the accompanying problems (if any). And, what you see is what you get. However, if what you see is a house out of plumb with sagging sections, there may be structural problems and, as a precautionary measure, you should have the house evaluated by a professional.

Some soils are considered poor for building construction purposes. Homes built on a highly organic soil are vulnerable to excessive settlement when the soil dries out. Organic soil acts like a sponge, and, as the soil dries, the organic matter shrinks. Depending on the amount of organic matter in the soil, the condition can cause differential foundation settlement.

Some soils on steep hillsides are subject to severe slippage. When the amount of buildable soil above an impervious subsoil layer is shallow, the possibility exists that, if the soil becomes saturated (because of an extended heavy rain), the entire upper layer of the hillside can slip to the bottom—along with any houses built on the side of the hill.

Some soils with a high clay content can swell or shrink up to 50 percent between wet and dry conditions. These soils are considered unstable, and, unless special provisions are made during construction, the condition can cause excessive differential settlement cracks in the foundation.

If you have any questions about the soil on which the house that you are inspecting is built, you can usually get them answered at the local office of the U.S. Department of Agriculture—Soil Conservation Service or at the office of the local county Soil and Water Conservation District.

### Inspection

Most houses built in the last forty years have foundation walls that are constructed of poured concrete, concrete blocks, or cinder blocks, whereas older homes generally have stone and/or brick foundation walls. When inspecting stone and/or brick foundations, especially in homes built before or around the turn of the century, pay particular attention to the mortar joints. I have found that in homes of this vintage, many of the mortar joints in the foundation walls have deteriorated to a point where they are no longer functional. Some of the joints may have holes and some may be filled with soft, crumbling mortar that can easily be raked out. In some cases, the joints between the foundation

FIGURE 11-2　Deteriorated mortar joints in foundation wall. Note water seeping through the wall at base (*arrow*).

stones may have been filled with earth/mud rather than mortar.

Deteriorated mortar joints in foundation walls should be repointed, not so much because they represent a weakened structural condition (they do, but this is usually not a severe problem), but because they can allow water to penetrate into the basement (see Figure 11-2) and also enable mice and other household pests to enter the area.

In some older homes with brick foundation walls, you may find areas where there are soft, crumbled, and flaking bricks that are so badly deteriorated that they should be replaced. This condition is usually the result of using underburned bricks in the construction of the wall. Bricks that are underburned during the manufacturing process are softer and absorb water more readily. If you see this condition, it should be recorded on your worksheet, as masonry rehabilitation is needed.

#### Cracks

Cracks in poured concrete or concrete block foundation walls can be the result of shrinkage, differential settlement, lateral pressure being exerted on the wall by the soil, or poor-quality workmanship. It is not uncommon to find short cracks in foundation walls. These cracks may be vertical, horizontal, inclined, stepped, smooth, and/or irregular and are usually of no structural concern. All cracks, however, should be sealed as a precautionary measure against water penetration into the basement. Otherwise, if there should be a hydrostatic pressure buildup in the soil against the foundation, water will seep through the cracks.

If there are long, narrow cracks in the wall and both sides of the cracks line up so that there is no noticeable differential settlement, it is usually not a serious condition and can be controlled by sealing the cracks. However, when both sides of the cracks do not line up and/or there are long, open cracks, a more serious condition of differential settlement exists. Since it is not possible to determine, from a single inspection, whether the differential settlement is active or dormant, if a section of the foundation wall is suspect, it should be checked for incremental movement over a period of time—usually several months. In most cases, after some time, the differential settlement stabilizes with little effect on the house, other than functional annoyances such as binding windows or a floor that may not be level. It is possible, however, that because of excessive settlement, an unstable condition can occur either in the foundation wall or the wood framing being supported by the wall. If there is any doubt in your mind about the condition of the foundation wall, you should have it checked out by a professional.

Another type of crack that is of concern is a long, open, horizontal crack in the foundation wall, especially if the wall shows signs of bowing. This condition is principally caused by an excessive horizontal pressure being exerted on the foundation wall by the earth backfill and indicates that the wall cannot adequately withstand these external lateral forces. If you see this condition, it should be recorded on your worksheet as a condition that requires further investigation and/or repair.

### Structural Support Framing

Because of the vulnerability to deterioration as a result of rot and/or wood-destroying insects, all exposed wooden support members (i.e., girders, joists, posts, and sill plates) should be checked for structural integrity. Steel beams and columns, on the other hand, need only be checked for degree of rust or corrosion. Usually the rusting is only a surface defect that can be corrected by scraping, priming, and painting.

Wooden support members should be probed with a screwdriver or an ice pick, as described in Chapter 8. If the wood is in good condition and has not deteriorated, the probe will not penetrate much below the surface. The portions of the joists and girders that are most vulnerable to deterioration are those sections that are resting on, or are adjacent to, the foundation wall. While probing these areas, you should also check the sill plate (which is anchored to the top of the foundation) for structural integrity. Many older houses have wood support posts rather than steel columns. If there are wood posts, check their bases for decay. The base has a tendency to rot because of periodic wetting resulting from dampness or, possibly, from seepage through the floor. If a post is found with a rotted base, it should be replaced. Joists with deteriorated end sections, however, need not be replaced. They can be rehabilitated. In most cases, all that is needed is to place a similar sized wood member alongside the affected joist and secure it to the portion of the joist that has not deteriorated.

Girders (which are the main support beams) are often supported at both ends by the foundation wall. If the girder is wood constructed, then the notch in the foundation wall in which the girder rests should be large enough to allow the sides and end of the girder to be ventilated. Otherwise, there can be a moisture buildup, which will promote decay. There should normally be at least ½-inch clearance around the sides and end of the girder. For adequate support, there should be a minimum of a 4-inch end bearing of the girder in the foundation notch. (See Figure 11-3.)

If you find that the end of the girder has deteriorated so that it is no longer providing adequate support, do not be overly concerned. The condition can be corrected at a reasonable cost without replacing the girder. In many cases, all that is needed to correct the condition is to support the girder by a column or pier located near the foundation wall. This repair, however, should be performed by a professional, as the column or pier must have an adequately sized footing to spread the load.

When girders or joists have sagging sections, it is usually noticeable on the floors above. During your interior inspection, if you find floors that are not level, you should be alerted to the possibility of sagging support beams. Sagging sections can be braced with adjustable screw-type columns to prevent further sag. The adjustable columns can also

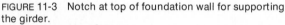

FIGURE 11-3 Notch at top of foundation wall for supporting the girder.

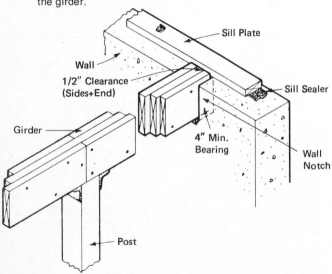

Sill Plate

Wall

1/2" Clearance (Sides+End)

Sill Sealer

Girder

4" Min. Bearing

Wall Notch

Post

FIGURE 11-4 Hole in center of beam width does not effectively reduce beam strength.

be used for releveling sagging sections. This procedure, however, should be approached with caution, as the leveling process will introduce new stresses that, in turn, can cause cracking.

During the wood-framing inspection, you may find joists or girders that have been notched at the top and/or bottom to accommodate the passage of pipes. Notching a beam at the top or bottom will reduce its strength. Just as a chain is as strong as its weakest link, a beam is as strong as its narrowest section. As an example, if a 2 × 8-inch joist is notched to a depth of 2 inches, its strength will be reduced to that of a 2 × 6-inch joist. When a beam deflects, the top of the beam is in compression and the bottom is in tension. At a point approximately midway between the depth, the stresses change from one to the other so that, at this point, there is no compression or tension. Consequently, if a hole is cut midway between the top and bottom of a beam (as long as the hole is less than one fourth of the depth), there will be no effective reduction in strength. (See Figure 11-4.) Using the above example, if a 2 × 8-inch joist has a 2-inch hole in its center, it will still be as strong as it was without the hole. If you find any notched beams, look specifically for signs of excessive deflection. This is an indication that reinforcement or bracing of the beam is necessary.

Most building codes require cross or solid bridging between the floor joists. (See Figure 11-5.) The purpose of bridging is to hold the joists in a vertical position and to transfer the floor load from one joist to another. Cross bridging consists of pieces of wood or steel set in a diagonal position between the joists to form an X. Solid bridging consists of solid blocks set between the joists. While inspecting the overhead floor joists for rot, insect damage, notching

and/or sagging sections, you should also check for the presence of bridging. If it is missing, record the fact on your worksheet for later installation.

## DAMPNESS

In many parts of the country, the basement or lower level will be damp during portions of the late spring and summer months. Dampness in a basement is a normal phenomenon that occurs because cool air cannot hold as much moisture as warm air. It does not necessarily indicate that there is a water problem in the basement. The temperature of the air in the basement or crawl space during the late spring and summer months will always be cooler than the outside air. Consequently, when outside air infiltrates into the basement through open windows, doors, cracks, or joints, the temperature of the air will drop. This lower-temperature air cannot hold as much moisture and results in a higher relative humidity of the volume of air that entered the basement. Depending on the temperature and the amount of moisture present in the air, some moisture may condense on cool surfaces such as foundations walls and cold water pipes.

FIGURE 11-5 Bridging. Cross and solid bridging between the floor joists.

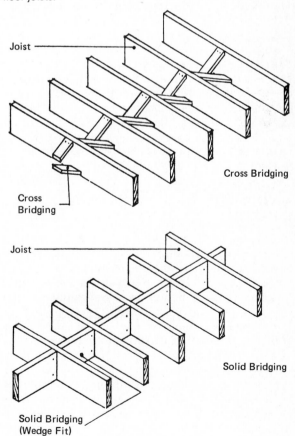

Sometimes, water droplets on the foundation wall caused by condensation are erroneously diagnosed as being caused by seepage through the wall. If you see a damp/wet foundation wall during your inspection, you can easily check whether the condition is caused by seepage or condensation. Simply fasten a small piece (4 × 8 inches) of aluminum foil to the foundation wall. Using wide strips of an adhesive tape, seal all the edges of the foil to the wall. After the foil has been on the wall for at least twenty-four hours, examine its surface. If it is moist, the condition is caused by condensation. However, if the foil surface is dry and the area behind the foil is damp, the condition is caused by moisture seeping through the foundation wall from the outside. Of course, it is possible for both the foil and the wall to be damp, indicating that both seepage and condensation exist.

Dampness in a basement or crawl space should be controlled. Otherwise, it can produce conditions that are conducive to the growth of mold and decay fungi. Dampness can often be detected during an inspection by musty odors and/or a clammy, close feeling. In the drier portions of the country, normal dampness (not caused by seepage) in the basement can be controlled by opening the windows and ventilating the area. However, in areas where the climate is hot and humid during the summer months, the benefit gained by ventilating the area is lost by the introduction of moist air into the basement. In these areas, the dampness in the lower level can be controlled with one or more electric dehumidifiers. Most of these units have a humidity control that will automatically shut the dehumidifier off when the moisture content in the air reaches a preset amount. Depending on the weather and on the size of the dehumidifier, the unit may have to run for many hours during each day in order to "wring" out a sufficient amount of moisture from the air so that it is not uncomfortably damp.

## WATER SEEPAGE—CAUSES AND CONTROL

Depending on the topography, drainage conditions of the soil, and groundwater level (water table), the basement and/or crawl space of the house that you inspect may be vulnerable to water seepage. Water seepage, as used herein, is a general term that refers to water intrusion into the lower level of the structure. It may manifest itself as a small wet area or puddle or, possibly, as a layer of water completely covering the floor. If the ground under and around the house is wet, water can seep into the basement through cracks and open joints in the foundation walls and/or floor slab. Since water seepage can be caused by a number of factors and water can leak into the basement at any number of locations, it is important to determine the cause and source of the seepage so that the proper corrective action can be taken.

As an example, if water is entering the basement through the foundation walls, then installing a sump pit and pump below the floor slab will not correct the problem. Similarly, if water is seeping into the basement through the floor slab, sealing the walls will not correct the water infiltration problem. All too often, the unsuspecting homeowner is talked into a full waterproofing job, which can cost several thousand dollars, when all that may really be needed is to redirect the water discharging from the roof drainage system (gutters and downspouts) so that the water does not accumulate around the foundation.

### High Groundwater Level

If water is entering the basement through the floor slab, it is an indication that water pressure is being exerted on the underside of the floor. When the level of the water below the house is sufficiently high (due to a seasonal high water table or improper drainage) so that it pushes on the underside of the floor slab, it will seep into the basement through cracks, open joints, or porous sections of the slab. If the pressure is great enough, it can cause the floor to crack and heave.

If the amount of seepage is minor, it can often be controlled by sealing cracks and open joints with a hydraulic cement and coating porous areas of the slab (if any) with a cement-base or epoxy sealant. However, a better solution to this problem would be to lower the level of the water below the floor slab. This can be done by installing a sump pump below the slab. Subsurface water will then flow into the sump pit in the manner of water flowing into a hole dug at the seashore. The water is then removed by the pump and discharged either into a storm drain or at a point sufficiently far from the house so that it will not be absorbed by the ground and flow back under the basement floor slab.

Depending on how the floor slab was constructed, a single sump pump may or may not be adequate to lower the level of the subsurface water so that it does not press on the underside of the slab. In areas where there is a seasonal high water table, a concrete floor slab should be installed over a gravel base. Water that accumulates below the slab can then flow through the voids between the gravel and drain away or flow into a sump pit. However, in many houses the floor slab has been installed directly over soil with poor drainage characteristics or over an inadequate gravel bed. In this case, water in the saturated area below the slab will not readily flow into a sump pit and, in order to control the water buildup, it is necessary to install a series of perforated drain pipes below the floor slab that will terminate in the sump pit. Caution should be observed when lowering the level of the groundwater below the basement floor. With some slow-draining soils such as silts and clays, the possibility exists that some soil can wash out from around the foundation footing. This can result in unequal settlement, which could crack the walls. Whether or not a sump pump and/or drain pipes are needed below the floor slab is an evaluation that should be determined by a professional.

If the house that you are inspecting is located in an area where there is a high incidence of power failures, you should not depend solely on an electrically driven sump pump to control groundwater seepage. It is possible for the power to be "knocked out" at a time when the water level below the floor slab is rising. As a precautionary measure, there should be an auxiliary water-actuated (nonelectrical) ejector-type pump in the sump pit. The pump is connected to the house water supply and is activated by a float control. (See Figure 11-6.) This type of auxiliary control is particularly helpful in vacation homes, where the house will be vacant for extended periods. However, it will be of no help if the water to the house is supplied by an electrically driven well pump.

### Hydrostatic Pressure—Walls

If water is seeping or leaking through the foundation walls into the basement, it is because there is a hydrostatic pressure being exerted on the walls by saturated soil. This condition is the result of water accumulation around the foundation. The best way to control this type of problem is to minimize the amount of water that accumulates around the foundation. The following are some of the more common causes of water accumulation around the foundation, which can easily be detected and corrected by the homeowner.

1. Missing or defective gutters and/or downspouts to handle the rain runoff from the roof: The downspouts must discharge the water away from the structure. All too often, an elbow or splash plate at the base of a downspout is missing, so that the water is discharged directly around the foundation.
2. Improper grading: The ground immediately adjacent to the structure should be pitched so that it slopes away from the building. Around many homes this area is incorrectly pitched, resulting in surface water (rain and/or melting snow) collecting around the foundation.
3. Unprotected basement window wells: The areaway around basement windows, if not shielded from rain or serviced with a drain,

FIGURE 11-6   Water-actuated sump pump. *(Courtesy Penberthy, Houdaille Industries, Inc.)*

can easily accumulate water that can leak through window joints or seep down around the foundation.
4. Uneven settlement of walkways or patio: Occasionally, I find that the walkways around the house or the patio have settled and are sloping toward the house. As with improper grading, this condition can cause surface water to collect around the foundation.
5. Leaky garden spigots: Most homes have exterior-mounted spigots for connection to a garden hose. If the valve is faulty or is not tightened properly, water will drip or leak around the foundation. Water dripping at a rate that will fill one cup per minute will result in 90 gallons of water per day accumulating around the foundation. This water can enter the basement through cracks and/or open joints in the foundation wall.

When the house is located on an inclined lot, surface and subsurface water will flow toward the house from the higher portions of the lot. In this case, depending on the incline and the amount of water involved, water-flow control measures will include grading the lot on the high side so that there is a swale to collect and redirect surface water around the house and installing a French drain (curtain drain) below the ground to intercept subsurface water and direct it away from the house.

If the amount of water that accumulates around the foundation walls is not excessive, it can be prevented from penetrating into the interior by sealing cracks and open joints on the inside walls with a hydraulic cement and then coating the walls with a cement-base or epoxy sealant. Coating the wall is particularly helpful when the wall is porous, as in the case of a cinderblock wall. However, when an excessive amount of water accumulates around the foundation wall, as can occur with a poorly drained soil such as clay, then waterproofing the exterior surface of the basement walls may be more effective than treating the interior surface. In addition, a perforated drain pipe is normally installed near to, and parallel with, the foundation footing. (See Figure 6-5, page 39.) The purpose of this footing drain is to carry away water that is accumulating around the foundation and thereby reduce the hydrostatic pressure.

In order for the footing drain to operate properly, it must have a free-flowing outlet. I know of several cases where builders installed faulty footing drains around houses during construction. The problem was that the drains completely encircled the houses like a doughnut and did not have any free-flowing outlets. In these cases, the footing drains were of absolutely no value. Even though initially a footing drain may function properly, over the years it can malfunction because the perforations in the drain pipe or the outlet can become clogged. Also, many a footing drain has been damaged during a later modification or addition to the structure. If the house that you are inspecting has a footing drain, you should ask the owner to show you the location of the outlet. The drain outlet should be kept clear and should be checked occasionally during a heavy rain to ensure that it is operating properly.

Even though waterproofing the exterior surface of the foundation wall is more effective than treating the interior surface, quite often an interior treatment is chosen because of the costs involved in

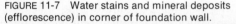

FIGURE 11-7 Water stains and mineral deposits (efflorescence) in corner of foundation wall.

excavating around the foundation and temporarily relocating trees and/or shrubbery. For excessive water accumulation around the foundation, an interior treatment would include sealing the cracks and coating the walls to make them watertight and also installing a drain pipe along the foundation footing below the floor slab that discharges into a sump pit.

Just a word about waterproofing the exterior surface of the foundation wall using a pressure-pumping process that requires no digging or relocation of plantings—CAUTION. In this process, a sealant, pumped through tubes that are inserted into the ground, is supposed to coat the wall and render it watertight. The effectiveness of this treatment depends on the condition and porosity of the ground around the foundation. Since contractors doing this work do not always take test borings and analyze the soil, the process is usually not effective and additional measures are invariably necessary.

### Inspection

The inspection for water seepage into the basement or crawl space should begin during your exterior inspection. As you walk around the house, record on your worksheet the location of those conditions that can cause water to accumulate around the foundation: faulty gutters and downspouts, improper grading, settlement of walkways, and so on. When you go into the basement, if there are problem conditions on the exterior, the walls and floor opposite those areas should be checked first for signs of water penetration. Figure 11-7 shows water stains and deposits in the corner of a foundation wall as a result of a faulty downspout. Even if there are no indications of past or current water seepage, the exterior problem conditions should be corrected.

A basement can have a water seepage problem and can be *dry* when you look at it. I have had many clients tell me that there were no seepage problems in the basement. After all, they looked at the basement during a heavy rain and found it to be "bone dry." So how could there be a problem? Well, as previously discussed, there are many causes for water seepage and, depending on the cause, a single rain may or may not result in seepage. As an example, if water penetrates into the basement through the floor slab as a result of a seasonally high water table and the basement is inspected when the water table is 1 or 2 feet below the high level, then a heavy rain will *not* raise the groundwater level sufficiently to cause water to seep through the floor slab. It takes time for rainwater to percolate into the ground and raise the water table.

Water puddles or flooded areas in the basement are very obvious signs of a water problem. In most cases, however, you will not see standing water, and you must then make an evaluation as to whether or not there is a condition of water intrusion based on other, more subtle signs. Water seepage signs only indicate that water has seeped into the basement in the past. They will not indicate the frequency with which the seepage has occurred or the exact extent to which it has occurred. Consequently, if you see indications of water seepage during your inspection, you should not engage a contractor to waterproof the house immediately upon taking possession. If you do, it could prove to be quite costly.

First, talk with the homeowner about the condition. It is possible that whatever it was that caused the past seepage has already been corrected. (If the problem was corrected by installing buried drain pipes or by coating the outside surface of the foundation wall, the correction would not be visible.) If the homeowner indicates that the problem has been corrected, you should ask to see a copy of the paid bill. Or, get the name of the contractor so that you can call to find out exactly what corrective steps were taken. Quite often, a contractor will provide a guarantee against water seepage. If there is such a guarantee, you should find out whether it is transferrable.

The possibility exists that, even though there are signs of water seepage, the actual seepage may occur very infrequently—such as only after an excessively heavy rain as might occur every few years. In this case, depending on the extent of the seepage and the projected usage of the basement, costly waterproofing measures may not be justified. The best approach to take when considering the correction of water seepage is to immediately correct any obvious problem conditions, such as faulty gutters and downspouts, improper grading, cracks through which water is actively leaking, and so on. However, before undertaking any major water seepage control measures, such as excavating and coating the exterior surface of the foundation wall, inserting perforated drain pipes below the floor slab, or trenching and installing buried drain pipes in the yard, you should live in the house for at least one full year. This will enable you to evaluate the degree and extent of the seepage over a full weather cycle. If it turns out that the year is particularly dry so that there is no seepage, well and good. Wait another year. By not taking a "shotgun" approach and waterproofing everything, as is recommended by many contractors, you may be able to resolve the problem at a cost that truly reflects the work needed to stop the seepage.

### Seepage Indications in an Unfinished Basement

When looking for indications of water seepage, you should check the walls, the floor, the joint between the walls and the floor, and the base of all the items stored or standing on the floor. Specifically, look for white powdery deposits on masonry foundation walls and floor. (See Figure 11-8.) The deposits, called "efflorescence," are mineral salts in the masonry that dissolve in the water as it passes through the wall and/or floor. When the water evaporates from the surface of the walls and/or floor, it deposits these salts. A thick layer of efflorescence is usually an indication of considerable seepage.

**Walls** Look for efflorescence, peeling and flaking paint, and scaling sections (surface deterioration) on the foundation wall. Any one of these items can indicate some degree of seepage. Porous walls, such as those made of cinder blocks, may have damp spots. Masonry block walls are constructed with interior voids. When the hydrostatic pressure on the exterior portion of the wall is high, the voids often fill with water. As a result, the wall may be quite wet to the touch. (Caution: This may also be caused by condensation.) Vulnerable areas for seepage are cracks and the joints around pipes passing through the wall, such as the inlet water pipe and the drain pipe leading to the sewer. Look closely at these areas for water streak stains and/or efflorescence.

A poured concrete foundation wall is supposed to be more watertight than a concrete block wall. This, however, assumes that the poured concrete wall is properly constructed. Quite often, it isn't. If the entire wall is not constructed with a single pouring, then the joints between the sections constructed with each pour are vulnerable to water leakage. I inspected a new house just after construction was completed. The inspection was performed during a heavy rain, which was opportune, although not

FIGURE 11-8 Efflorescence and water stains on foundation wall.

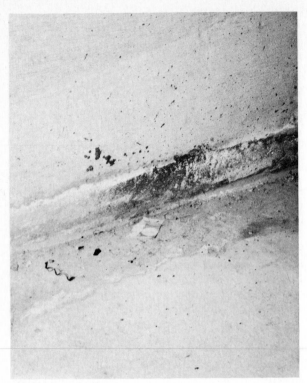

FIGURE 11-9   Signs of water seepage (stains and efflorescence) at joint between the floor slab and the foundation wall.

planned. While inspecting the basement, I found water leaking out of the joint at the seam between the individually poured sections of the foundation wall. The builder's mason apparently had not prop-

FIGURE 11-10   The house trap is often used to drain the water in a wet basement. Cleanout plug has been removed from top of trap. Note water stains on floor around pit. If sewer line becomes overloaded, sewage can back up and flood the basement.

erly prepared the joint for a new pour and, consequently, a cold joint with a poor bond was formed.

Another area to look for seepage in a poured concrete wall is around the tie rod holes. These are holes in the concrete wall around the small-diameter metal rods that are used to hold (tie) the forms together when the wall is being poured. More often than not, these holes have been patched over. Also, these tie rods can corrode away over a period of time and, when below grade, are vulnerable areas for water intrusion. Sometimes, you will see efflorescence and water streaks just under the hole or patched sections. Occasionally, I find these holes plugged with corks. This is not considered a permanent patch, and, if seepage should develop, they should be plugged with hydraulic cement.

**Floors and Floor Joints**   A vulnerable joint for water seepage is the joint between the foundation wall and the floor. Look closely at this joint as you walk around the entire basement. Water stains and efflorescence are an indication of seepage. (See Figure 11-9.) In some cases, you may find silt deposits at the joint. This also is an indication of some degree of seepage. The fine silt is in suspension in the water as the water seeps in from the exterior. When the water evaporates, the silt is deposited. If you find evidence of water seepage through the joint between the floor slab and the foundation wall, you should record it on your worksheet for later correction. The joint should be sealed either with hot tar or a hydraulic cement.

Cracks tend to develop in the floor slab near the base of metal columns. Look at these cracks (if any) and/or any other cracks in the floor slab. Specifically look for water stains, efflorescence, and/or silt deposits. Cracks in basement floors are a common phenomenon and are generally caused by slight settlement or shrinkage in the concrete. Usually they are of no concern other than the fact that water can seep through them. Therefore, they should be sealed. However, if the cracks are extremely wide or show evidence of heaving, they are of concern and should be checked further. In all probability, a cracked and heaved floor slab is the result of water pressure being exerted on the underside of the slab by a high water table.

Some homes have a cleanout and trap for the house waste line located in a pit below the basement floor slab. The bottom of the pit should be dry. If it is wet, it is an indication of a high groundwater level or, possibly, a crack in the drain line. Occasionally, I find that the top of the cleanout is open. (See Figure 11-10.) It should normally be plugged. Some homeowners remove the plug so that the open cleanout can function as a drain in the event that the basement becomes flooded. Note the water stains on the floor leading to the cleanout pit in Figure 11-10. This is definitely not the way to eliminate the water in a flooded basement. If the basement periodically floods and there is no drain in the floor, a sump pump can be installed in the lowest section of the floor. The water can then be pumped out of the basement. With the cleanout plug removed from the top of the house trap, the possibility exists that, if the sewer line becomes overloaded (as is the case in some communities), sewage can back up and flood the basement. I know of several homes where this has happened; it was quite unpleasant.

Some people lose interest in a house when they find a sump pump in the basement. They feel that the house has water problems. That is not necessarily so. There may have been periodic problems resulting from a seasonal high water table, but the sump pump may have controlled the water level. Or, the pump may have been installed when the house was built in order to prevent a problem. In order to determine whether or not there still are problems, you must look beyond the sump pump. Look for signs of water seepage.

If the house has a sump pump, look down into the pit. If there is water in the pit and you are inspecting it during the "dry" season (the water table is usually highest during the spring), then the probability is high that the sump pump will be operating continuously during the spring. If possible, try to check the sump pump operation. However, do not actuate a pump unless there is water in the pit. When you do actuate the pump, watch the water level to see if it drops. You may find that the motor that drives the pump is operational, but the coupling between the pump and the motor is broken. In this case, it will sound as if the pump is working, but it is not and the water level will not drop. A sump pump is relatively inexpensive and can be easily repaired or replaced.

Although a sump pump is sometimes located in the low section of the floor (when it is being used to collect surface water), it should not be located where it will present a tripping hazard. (See Figure 11-11.) The pump can be placed in a corner where it will not take up valuable floor space and can be connected to the low spot in the floor by a drain pipe placed below the floor slab and that discharges into the sump pit.

After inspecting the walls and the floor for signs of water seepage, you should check the bases of the items stored or standing on the floor for water stains and/or rust. On occasion you may find that the walls and the floor of the basement appear to be freshly painted. If you see this, you should be suspicious because the new layer of paint will cover almost all of the signs of a water seepage problem. There are some areas, however, that are often omitted when painting the basement. These areas should be checked for water stains and/or rust. Spe-

FIGURE 11-11  Sump pit in center of basement floor—a tripping hazard.

cifically, look at the base of the steps leading to the basement and, in particular, the back of the bottom step. Also look at the base of columns. Wood columns may have stains or may be rotting and metal columns may be rusting. The base of the inside portion of a furnace sheetmetal casing is often overlooked when painting. Look inside. Is there extensive rust? If there is, it may have been caused by a past flood. However, it could also have been caused by a faulty humidifier, so do not jump to a quick conclusion.

### Seepage Indications in a Finished Basement

Usually, the finished walls in a basement are a few inches or more away from the foundation walls. Therefore, seepage indications on the foundation wall will not be reflected in the middle and upper portions of the finished wall. Look at the bottom portion of the wall for signs of water intrusion. If the wall is paneled, look for rotted and warped sections and water stains. Sometimes, there are grayish mold spots or mold fungi on the walls—a condition brought on by excessive dampness. With a Sheetrock wall, look for water stains and blackened areas and spots. The latter is mold and mildew. In some cases, the lower portion of the Sheetrock wall may have deteriorated.

Next, look at the floor. If the floor is raised above the level of the concrete floor slab, the wood flooring and the wood-framing members used to raise the floor are vulnerable to rot in the event of seepage. The wood framing below the floor should be pressure-treated but often is not. Try to walk all over the floor, especially around the perimeter. If there are any rotting sections, they will feel soft and spongy beneath your feet. If the floor is covered with resilient tiles, the rotting sections may be visible, as the dampness in the wood tends to loosen the tiles. (See Figure 10-4, page 72.)

An area that is particularly vulnerable to water seepage is the portion of the basement that faces a yard where the overall topography is inclined toward the house. Even if the ground adjacent to the house is graded properly, there will still be sub-surface water moving toward the house. The walls and the floor of the vulnerable section should always be checked for signs of seepage. Sometimes, this is quite difficult, as some homeowners may inadvertently—or intentionally—block the area with furniture. If the area is blocked, ask the home-owner if it is all right to move the furniture.

If the floor slab is covered with resilient tiles and there is a problem with heavy seepage through the floor, it is usually noticeable by looking at the tiles. The joints between the tiles become swollen and filled with a white crusting of mineral deposits (efflorescence). Some tiles become loose and efflores-cence is noted below them. Occasionally, the tiles are covered with wall-to-wall carpeting. In this case, the tiles cannot be examined for signs of seepage. However, some checking for seepage can be done. Ask the homeowner for permission to lift the edge of the carpet off the tacking strip along a section of the exterior wall. If there is seepage in this area, the tacks will be rusted and the wood strips water stained and/or rotted.

If the basement is heated with baseboard con-vectors mounted on an exterior wall, another place to look for signs of seepage is below the convector. If there is some seepage in that area (the joint between the floor slab and the wall), the base of the convector will be rusted.

On occasion, a portion of the basement may become flooded as a result of faulty plumbing, an overflowing sink or tub, a malfunctioning water

FIGURE 11-12  Exposed wood joists above heating system boiler—a potential fire hazard. They should be covered with fire code Sheetrock.

heater, and so on. Flooding from the above is basi-cally a one-time affair and will not cause the type of damage that results from repeated wetting. There will be water stains, but there usually will not be rot, peeling or flaking paint, efflorescence, or heavy rusting.

## FURNACE ROOM

The heating plant in a house will normally be a fur-nace or a boiler. (See Chapter 14.) For the purpose of this chapter, the heating plant will be called a furnace and the room in which it is located will be called the furnace room.

In most homes, the furnace is located in the basement or lower level. It can be located in a large, open area or confined in a relatively small room. In either case, the area around the furnace is consid-ered a potential fire hazard. Consequently, there should not be any exposed wood framing in the ceil-ing or partition walls that are in close proximity to the heating plant. (See Figure 11-12.) Exposed over-head floor joists or wall studs that are near the fur-nace should be covered with Type X fire code Sheet-rock as a fire safety precaution. Sometimes, I find that wood paneling has been installed around the furnace to make the area more attractive. However, it also makes the area more of a fire hazard—espe-cially the portion of the wall around the chimney. (See Figure 11-13.) If you find wood paneling near the furnace, you might consider covering it with fire code Sheetrock. There should be a minimum of a 2-inch clearance between the chimney and any wood framing or paneling. Note that the area around the furnace should *not* be used for storage purposes. On many occasions, I have seen combus-tible items actually stored against the furnace. For-tunately for the families involved, the items never ignited—but they could have!

Many heating systems have prefabricated chim-neys that extend from the furnace room up through the interior portion of the structure, terminating above the roof. If the house that you are inspecting has such a chimney, look at the joint between the chimney and the ceiling of the furnace room. If there are large openings, they represent a potential fire hazard and should be covered with a noncom-bustible material such as sheetmetal. The open area around the chimney, if not properly blocked, can act as a flue and, in the event of a fire in the furnace room, will draw the flames up to the attic.

### Ventilation

All fuel-burning heating systems must have adequate ventilation for proper operation. If the furnace is located in an unconfined space, the nor-mal air infiltration into the area will provide the needed ventilation. However, when the furnace is located in a confined space such as a small room, inlet and outlet ventilation openings must be provided. The vent openings can lead directly to the outside or to a large, unconfined area within the structure. The size of the openings will depend on the total input (BTU/hour) rating of all the fuel-burning equipment in the enclosure. For most residential structures, an unobstructed inlet and outlet opening of 15 inches by 15 inches is sufficient.

If you would like to calculate the size of the vent openings needed, a safe formula to use is 1 square inch per 1,000 BTU/hour of input rating for both the inlet and outlet vents. The input rating will usually be found on a data plate that is mounted directly on the equipment. If the vent opening is covered by louvers, remember that metal louvers will reduce the effective opening by about 25 percent and wood louvers by about 50 percent. In addition, an insect screen covering the louvers will reduce the effective opening by another 25 percent.

Some homes have louvered entry doors to the furnace room, which provide the means for ventilation. Occasionally, I find that for decorative reasons, the louvers have been covered over, blocking the effective ventilation opening. If the louvers have been covered in the house that you are inspecting, look for additional vent openings.

## CRAWL SPACE

The foundation walls, piers, posts, and wood-support framing in a crawl space should be inspected (as described in the section on the unfinished basement) for deterioration, structural deficiencies, and evidence of water seepage. During the inspection, pay particular attention to the wood-framing members that, because of the damp conditions that often exist, are very vulnerable to decay and/or termite infestation. (See Figure 11-14.)

FIGURE 11-13  Wood paneling near furnace—a potential fire hazard.

Many homes, however, have crawl spaces that are inaccessible and cannot be inspected. These homes were built in accordance with the Federal Housing Administration (FHA) Minimum Property Standards, which permit the ground level to be 18 inches below the bottom of the floor joists and 12 inches below the bottom of the girders. Even if there is an access opening to the area (see Figure 11-15), the clearance in the crawl space is too low for a person to maneuver around easily and perform a detailed inspection. However, you should look into

FIGURE 11-14  Cracked and rotting wood-frame members in crawl space.

FIGURE 11-15  Access hatch to crawl area.

FIGURE 11-16   Loose, hanging insulation in crawl space.

the area from the access opening (using your flashlight) to determine if any obvious problems or problem conditions exist.

In most parts of the country, the crawl space will be quite damp even though there are no problems with water seepage. The dampness is the result of the capillary rise of ground moisture. Unlike a basement where the ground is usually covered with a concrete floor slab, the floor in a crawl space is often bare earth. Even though the soil may appear to be dry and dusty, there can be moisture present. In some soils, the capillary rise is more than 11 feet above the water table.

Dampness associated with capillary moisture can be effectively reduced by covering the ground with a vapor barrier, such as 4 to 6-mil thickness polyethylene. Roll roofing is also a good vapor bar-

FIGURE 11-17   Water stains on back side of entry door leading to a crawl area.

rier, but it tends to deteriorate from fungi. If you do not notice a vapor barrier ground cover during your inspection of the crawl space, you should consider its installation.

To help minimize the dampness, the crawl space must be ventilated. There should be at least two vent openings on opposite sides of the foundation with a total free area of 1 square foot for each 1,500 square feet of crawl space area, providing there is a ground cover. When no vapor barrier is used, there should be at least four vent openings (one on each side) with ten times the total free area. Look for vent openings. If you do not see any, or if they have been permanently blocked, put a note on your worksheet to that effect.

Crawl spaces are usually not heated. Consequently, unless there is insulation between the floor joists, there will be a heat loss between the heated room above and the unheated crawl area. Since moisture from the house can travel down through the floor, the insulation should have a vapor barrier on one side in order to further reduce moisture entry into the crawl space. The vapor barrier should be located above the insulation, facing the heated room rather than below, facing the crawl area. If this vapor barrier is located below the insulation, the vapor will condense on its surface during cool weather. Depending on the amount of vapor, the resulting condensation buildup can reduce the effectiveness of the insulation. During your inspection, look for insulation. You may find missing, loose, or hanging sections, which should be replaced and/or resecured. (See Figure 11-16.) If you find uninsulated heating ducts or pipes in the crawl space, record this fact on your worksheet as a reminder to insulate the exposed sections.

Some homes are constructed with both a basement and a crawl space. In this case, the crawl space need not be vented to the outside, but can be vented to the basement. Look for evidence of water seepage in the crawl space. Even though there may be no signs of seepage in the basement, there may be in the crawl area. I recently inspected a home that had a combination basement/crawl space. The basement had been painted and there were no visible signs of a past water condition. The crawl space was separated from the basement by plywood doors that were painted on the basement side and looked good. However, when I inspected the crawl space, I found evidence of a previous water condition. Apparently, the back of the plywood doors (facing the crawl area) had not been painted over. There were water stains on the lower section. (See Figure 11-17.)

While in the crawl space, check subflooring and support joists below kitchen and bathroom fixtures for evidence of decay and/or plumbing leaks.

## CHECKPOINT SUMMARY

### FOUNDATION

- Note foundation wall construction type: poured concrete, concrete block, brick, stone, and so on.
- Check for cracked areas of concrete; crumbled and flaking bricks; cracked, loose, missing, and eroding mortar joints.
- Check for long, open cracks that do not line up and have shifted sections.
- Note long, open, horizontal cracks and signs of bowing in the foundation wall.
- Are sections of the structure sagging and no longer vertical? (Consult a professional.)

#### Wood-Support Framing

- Inspect/probe all vulnerable wood-support members (sill plates, girders, joists) resting on the foundation wall for rot and/or insect damage.
- Note floor joists or girders that sag or have notched sections.
- Is there bridging/blocking between the floor joists?
- Inspect wood columns, support joists, and subflooring for cracked sections and evidence of rot.

### WATER SEEPAGE

#### General

- Is the ground adjacent to the house pitched so that it slopes away from the structure?
- Are there concrete patios and paths that are improperly pitched (toward the house)?
- Are there basement windows or stairwells that are vulnerable to flooding?
- Do downspouts
  have extensions?
  discharge against the foundation?
  terminate in the ground?
- Is there a sump pump present?
- Is there water in the sump pit?
- Is the water being discharged away from the house or to a dry well?
- If the structure has been waterproofed, is there a guarantee or warranty available? Did you request a copy?

#### Basement Walls

- Check for areas of scaling, peeling and flaking paint, damp spots, and signs of efflorescence.
- Check construction joints, tie rod holes, and pipe openings for signs of seepage.
- Inspect wall paneling and base trim for stains, warped sections, and rot.
- Check underside of basement steps for water marks.
- Note areas of rust at base of metal columns and sheetmetal furnace casing.
- Check for dampness, noting musty odors and signs of mildew.

#### Basement Floors

- Check for extensively cracked and heaved floor sections (usually the result of a high water table).
- Record all areas of active seepage and puddling.
- Check joint between foundation wall and floor slab for silt deposits.
- Check for porous areas and signs of efflorescence on floor and around perimeter.
- If floor is covered with tiles, are there swollen floor tile joints?
- Is there efflorescence between joints?
- Inspect the house trap pit. Is it dry? Is the cleanout plug secure or loose?

### FURNACE ROOM

- Check for exposed wood-frame members (wall studs, ceiling joists) that are in close proximity to the boiler/furnace.
- Check for large openings between the ceiling and the chimney.
- Is the room adequately ventilated?

### CRAWL SPACE

- Inspect foundation walls, posts, and wood-support framing for deterioration and signs of water seepage.
- Check subflooring and support joists for insect damage and/or rot.
- Check area for adequate ventilation.
- Is this area damp?
- Is there a dirt floor? Is it covered with a vapor barrier?
- Is area insulated? Is insulation loose or incorrectly placed?
- Are there water supply pipes that are vulnerable to freezing?
- Are there heat supply ducts or pipes that should be insulated?

# 12. ELECTRICAL SYSTEM

The electrical system of a house can be compared to the nervous system of the human body. Just as every part of the body is supplied by nerves that are connected to the brain, so every part of a house is (or at least should be) supplied by electrical wires that are connected to the inlet service panel box. These wires are called "branch circuits." A properly sized and functioning electrical system is essential for a healthy house.

## INLET ELECTRICAL SERVICE

The electrical service is provided to a house either through overhead wires or underground cables. If

FIGURE 12-1 Two-wire inlet service provides 110 volts.

there are overhead wires, they can be seen when walking around the outside of the house. These wires will usually run from a utility pole to the house and are fastened to the structure at a point which is at least 10 feet above the ground level. Count the number of wires coming into the house. If there are two wires (see Figure 12-1), then the electrical service for the house is *inadequate*. Two-wire service provides only 110 volts, not 110/220 volts. There should be three wires coming into the house from the electrical service entry. (See Figure 12-2.) Three-wire service will provide 110/220 volts. In some cases, there may be four wires. Four-wire service will also provide 110/220 volts, but is unusual in a residential structure. It is usually found on a structure with heavy electrical demands such as an industrial or commercial building. The inlet service voltage may vary slightly so that in some areas, it may be 120/240 rather than 110/220 volts. The difference is of no concern to the homeowner.

Before going into the house, look to see if there are any tree branches overhanging or hitting the inlet service wires. If there are, they should be pruned. Otherwise, the wire's outer insulation can be worn away, exposing the electrically hot conductors. This could be potentially dangerous if that section of conductors is within reach, as from an upper-level porch.

While looking at the inlet service wires, check to see if they are securely fastened to the house and whether there are any frayed sections of the outer insulation. In many communities, the inlet service wire (from the attachment to the house to the electrical meter) is the responsibility of the homeowner, not the utility company. Service entry wires that are badly frayed should be replaced because they can eventually result in a hazardous condition.

The inlet service wires, whether they are overhead or underground, terminate at the electrical meter, which can be mounted on the exterior or interior of the structure. The wires then run from the meter to a panel box, which is sometimes called the "service switch." The panel box is basically a distribution center. The electrical branch circuits throughout the house terminate in this box. See Figure 12-3 for a generalized residential wiring diagram.

## ELECTRICAL CAPACITY

The unit of electrical power is called a "watt." Watts are equivalent to volts times amps (W = V × A). The electrical service that I have found in houses and the corresponding equivalent power capacity is shown in the following table.

| Amps | Volts | Watts | Evaluation |
|------|-------|-------|------------|
| 30 | 110 | 3,300 | Inadequate |
| 30 | 110/220 | 6,600 | Inadequate |
| 60 | 110 | 6,600 | Inadequate |
| 60 | 110/220 | 13,200 | Marginal (small house only and no major appliances) |
| 100 | 110/220 | 22,000 | Minimum |
| 150 | 110/220 | 33,000 | Good |
| 200 | 110/220 | 44,000 | Very Good |

In older houses, unless the electrical service has been upgraded, you are likely to find 30 and 60 amps at 110 or 110/220 volts. Any service less than 60 amps at 110/220 volts is considered inadequate. Homeowners with such electrical service may indicate that they have lived in the house for twenty or thirty years and have found the service to be totally acceptable. That may be true—for them—because they have adjusted to the lower electrical capacity by not using any major electrical appliances. Nevertheless, if you buy a house with low electrical service, you will probably have to upgrade the service after you move in.

The capacity of the electrical service provided to a house should be great enough to satisfy the power requirements of the various electrical appliances to be used. The following table shows some typical electrical appliances and their associated power requirements.

| Appliance | Power Requirement (Watts) |
|-----------|---------------------------|
| Attic fan | 400w |
| Central air conditioning | 6,000w |
| Clothes dryer | 4,500w |
| Dishwasher | 1,500w |
| Forced air furnace (electric heat) | 28,000w |
| Freezer | 575w |
| Garbage disposal | 900w |
| Hand iron | 1,000w |
| Instant hot water dispenser | 1,000w |
| Lamp (each bulb) | 25w–150w |
| Microwave oven | 500w |
| Range, electric | 8,000w |
| Portable room heater | 1,600w |
| Room air conditioner | 1,100w |
| Sauna | 8,000w |
| Steam bath generator | 7,500w |
| Television (color) | 150w–450w |
| Water heater | 2,500w–4,500w |

FIGURE 12-2    Three-wire inlet service provides 110/220 volts.

Considering the many electrical appliances that are available to the homeowner, the *minimum* electrical service that a home should have is 100 amps at 110/220 volts. However, if the house is small and the intention is not to use many electrical appliances, then 60 amps at 110/220 volts will probably suffice. When a house is equipped with an electric water heater, electric range, electric clothes dryer, and a central air-conditioning system, it should have at least 150-amp service. If electric heat is used in addition to the above appliances, the house should have 200-amp service.

## FUSES/CIRCUIT BREAKERS

The panel box will contain either circuit breakers or fuses to protect individual branch circuits from an overload. Overloaded circuits are one of the chief causes of home electrical fires, and proper protection of branch circuits is essential. Figure 12-4 shows a circuit breaker panel box, and Figure 12-5 shows a fuse panel box. There are advantages and disadvantages to circuit breakers and fuses. Circuit breakers are more convenient than fuses. Once they have been tripped, they can be reset like a switch; whereas once a fuse has blown, it must be replaced. On the other hand, circuit breakers are somewhat less reliable than fuses. Circuit breakers have been known to "freeze" in the on position and should be manually tripped periodically to assure operational integrity.

It is important that the capacity of a fuse be matched up with the current-carrying capacity of a branch circuit. When a fuse has been blown, it must be replaced by a new fuse with the same current-carrying capacity. Too often, a homeowner will replace a 15-amp fuse with a 20- or 30-amp fuse, not realizing that all three are physically (but not elec-

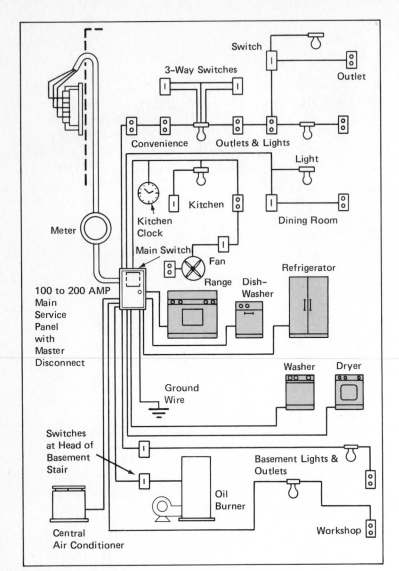

FIGURE 12-3   Generalized wiring diagram for a residential structure.

hazard. Replacing the exterior box with a new box mounted in the interior of the structure is recommended.

Some panel box covers have a door. If there is a door on the panel box that you are inspecting, lift or swing it open. DO NOT REMOVE THE PANEL COVER. The cover should only be removed by a professional inspector or electrician because of the danger involved with exposed electrically "hot" wires. Some homeowners remove the panel cover when doing home wiring and then forget to replace it. Others remove the cover and then cover the panel box with a picture. They think this provides easy access. It does—for children too, and is very dangerous. Panel box covers should be mounted and securely in place at all times.

When looking at the panel box cover, note whether or not there are any missing knockout plates or missing fuses. If there are, they represent a potential hazard in that it is possible for a child to stick his or her finger in these openings and be electrocuted. If there are openings, they must be permanently blocked off. Check the size and number of the fuses and/or circuit breakers. There should be at least two 20-amp appliance circuits and one 15-amp lighting circuit for each 500 square feet of floor area. Anything less than this is not considered adequate. Also, if the branch circuits are protected by fuses, note if there are many blown fuses in the area. If there are, it may indicate that one or more of the circuits is often overloaded, a condition that may require installing additional branch circuits.

## Panel Box Interior

Because of the hazards involved, certain items should not be checked by the home buyer/owner,

FIGURE 12-4   Circuit breaker panel box with master disconnect.

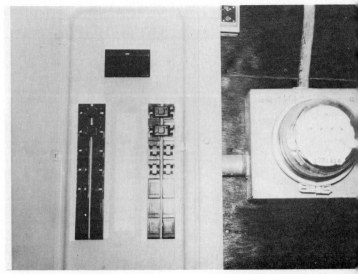

trically) interchangeable. In this case, if there is an overload on that branch circuit, the fuse will not blow, but rather the wires will become excessively hot and possibly cause a fire. This type of problem can be circumvented by replacing the fuse with a Fustat. (See Figure 12-6.) A Fustat is basically a fuse with an adapter that fits into the fuse holder in the panel box. Once the adapter is inserted, it usually cannot be removed. The adapters are sized so that they can only accept fuses of a specific current capacity and, as such, are not interchangeable.

## INLET SERVICE PANEL BOX

In older, rural-type homes, the main panel box may be mounted on the outside of the building. These boxes are often not watertight and are a potential

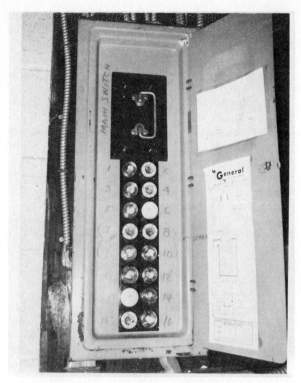

FIGURE 12-5  Fuse panel box with master disconnect.

specifically those items found inside the main panel box. A professional home inspector or licensed electrical contractor checking the interior of the panel box should tell you whether the fuses or circuit breakers are properly sized for their respective branch circuits. Improperly protected branch circuits are found fairly often during inspections.

Once the panel cover has been removed, the actual inlet electrical service capacity can be determined. It depends on the size of the inlet service wire only and not on the rated capacity of the panel box or the size of the fuse or circuit breaker used for the master disconnect, if there is one. Figure 12-4 shows a circuit breaker panel box with a 200-amp master disconnect. A home buyer seeing this would normally believe that the house is supplied with 200-amp electrical service, and rightly so. In this case, however, the inlet service wire is too small to supply 200 amps. When the cover was removed, it was determined that the inlet service was 100 amps and that the master disconnect circuit breaker did not provide the overload protection.

## ALUMINUM WIRING

Inspecting the interior of a panel box will also reveal whether aluminum wiring was used for the branch circuits rather than copper wiring. Aluminum wiring is considered a potential fire hazard if

not installed properly. If aluminum wiring was used, then the electrical connections to the receptacles and switches throughout the structure should be checked by a competent electrical contractor to determine if they have been properly made or whether they show evidence of possible problems. If the house that you are inspecting does have aluminum branch circuits, you should be aware of the following trouble signs:

Unusually warm cover plates on switches and outlet receptacles
A distinctive or strange odor in the vicinity of a receptacle or switch
Sparks or arcing at switches and outlets
Periodic flickering of lights (sometimes traceable to faulty appliances or fixtures)

As recommended by Underwriters' Laboratories, Inc., problems associated with aluminum wiring can usually be corrected by pigtailing a copper conductor to the aluminum conductor or by properly connecting the aluminum conductor to a receptacle or switch marked "CO/ALR." The home buyer/owner should not attempt to correct this condition.

## GROUNDING

The electrical system must be grounded as a safety precaution. This means that a portion of the wiring in the main panel box must be deliberately connected to the ground. This is done by connecting the wiring to a grounding wire that, in turn, is clamped to a metallic inlet water pipe or, if none is available, to a rod driven into the ground.

Check to see if the electrical ground has been properly connected. There should be a wire coming out of the main panel box that runs to the inlet water pipe. Sometimes the wire is not visible, so go directly to the inlet water pipe. This pipe is located by the water meter (if there is one) and usually protrudes through the foundation wall or lower-level floor slab. The electrical ground wire should be clamped to the water pipe on the street side of the water meter. (See Figure 12-7.) It may also be connected on the house side, but in such cases, there

FIGURE 12-6  A. Fustat with adapter. B. Plug fuse. *(Courtesy Bussman Manufacturing)*

(A)  (B)

FIGURE 12-7  Electrical ground wire clamped to inlet water pipe.

*must* be a jumper cable running around the meter to the street side.

### Improper Ground Connections

It is surprising how many houses have loose clamps on the water pipes, resulting in an improperly grounded electrical system. Many homeowners do not realize that the wire clamped to the water pipe is a grounding wire for the electrical system and they loosen the clamp when making a repair or finishing the basement, often forgetting to reclamp the wire because nothing "apparent" happened when it was disconnected.

Look at the clamp. Is it loose? If it is, it *must* be resecured. This can usually be done with a screwdriver. Sometimes the clamp or screws have corroded and must be replaced. If there is no clamp or ground wire visible, then you should question the integrity of the ground system. Sometimes the ground wire is clamped to a water pipe other than the inlet pipe. This procedure provides a false sense of security because the possibility exists that a section of the pipe can be removed, causing an open circuit in the electrical ground.

The inlet pipe to which the electrical ground is connected *must* be a functioning water pipe. This ensures that the pipe extends a considerable distance into the ground. According to the electrical code, the pipe should extend at least 8 feet into the ground. If a new inlet water pipe has been installed, then the ground wire should be moved to the new pipe. Otherwise, there is no way of knowing how far the old pipe extends into the ground. Often, when replacing an old water pipe, the portion outside of

the structure is cut off at the foundation wall. This cannot be determined when looking at the pipe from inside the house.

When the inlet water pipe is plastic, as is often the case with a well, the electrical system is grounded by connecting the grounding wire to a rod that has been driven into the ground. If this is the case in the house that you are inspecting, check the clamp connection and the rod. If either the clamp or rod is loose, the integrity of the electrical ground should be questioned.

## INTERIOR ELECTRICAL INSPECTION

Now that the basic system has been checked, walk around the interior portion of the house looking at the adequacy of the electrical distribution and for possible violations.

### Electrical Outlets

While walking through the house, check each room for electrical outlets. You may feel that the number of outlets in each room is not very important. This is not so. If there is an insufficient number of outlets, the homeowner will tend to use extension cords. Most extension cords have a lower electrical current capacity than the outlet and an overload on the extension cord can result in a fire rather than a blown fuse. Figure 12-8 shows one arrangement that is a potential hazard. The convenience outlet in the kitchen is capable of carrying 20 amps, whereas the extension cord can only safely carry 10 amps. Kitchens, ideally, should have 20-amp appliance outlets that are conveniently located (about every 24 inches) above a working counter.

The actual number of outlets needed for each room will depend on the room's usage and the position of the furniture. Generally speaking, one receptacle outlet per wall for an average-size room (10 feet by 12 feet) is adequate. The outlets in larger rooms should be spaced so that no point along the wall is more than 6 feet (measured horizontally) from an outlet.

In addition to checking whether there are a sufficient number of outlets in each room, you should inspect the outlets to determine if they are functional and whether or not they are grounded properly. You can check the outlets with a simple plug-in tester that is available at electrical supply stores. Do the outlet receptacles have two or three slots? The newer type outlets have three slots and are intended for use with appliances that have three-prong plugs, although two-prong plugs can also be used. The third slot is a grounding connection used for grounding appliances. This is particularly important for appliances that are not double-insulated or that have a metal casing. (See discussion on

FIGURE 12-8 The home wiring "octopus"—a potential fire hazard.

electrical outlets in Chapter 10.) Even though an appliance has a three-prong plug and requires grounding, it can be used with a properly grounded two-slot receptacle with an adapter. There are, however, many electrical appliances that are double-insulated against shock hazards and, thus, do not require a grounding connection. These appliances can be safely used with outlets that have only two slots.

Bathrooms should have at least one, and preferably two, outlets that are readily accessible. Often, there is only a single outlet in the wall-mounted light fixture located above the medicine chest, which usually cannot be conveniently reached by anyone less than 6 feet tall. As a safety feature, the outlets and switches in the bathroom must not be reachable from the tub or shower.

According to the National Electrical Code, all receptacle outlets in bathrooms of new construction must have ground-fault circuit protection. The protection can be achieved by using a special receptacle or circuit breaker that has been equipped with a ground-fault interrupter (GFI). A GFI is an electronic device that will trip (open) the circuit when it senses a potentially hazardous condition. It is very sensitive and operates very quickly. The GFI will interrupt the power in less than 1/50 of a second if it senses an imbalance in the electrical current of as little as 0.005 amps. The quick response time in interrupting the power is fast enough to prevent injury to anyone in normal health. Ground-fault protection, however, is not a retroactive requirement and, as such, will probably not be found in most existing homes. If there is a GFI circuit breaker or receptacle, it should be tested to see if

the fault-sensing function is operational. These units are equipped with manually operated test buttons that, if pushed, will trip the circuit when they are operating properly. The GFI should then be reset. Underwriter's Laboratories, Inc., recommends that all GFIs be tested monthly.

When walking through the hallways, rooms, and up and down steps, it should be possible to light the path ahead and to turn off the light without retracing one's steps. This can be done with three-way switches. Also, there should be a convenience outlet in hall areas for nightlights and cleaning equipment.

### Knob-and-Tube Wiring

Knob-and-tube wiring is no longer used in new construction. However, since you may be considering an older house, there is the possibility that the building may have knob-and-tube wiring throughout or in portions of the structure. A knob-and-tube wiring system uses porcelain insulating knobs, tubes, and flexible nonmetallic tubing for the protection and support of single-insulated conductors. (See Figure 12-9.)

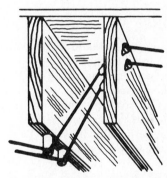

FIGURE 12-9 Knob-and-tube wiring, which is obsolete.

Obviously, you cannot see the type of wiring behind the walls. However, very often there are exposed wires in the unfinished attic or basement. If there are exposed sections of knob-and-tube wiring, then the outer insulation covering should be checked for broken and open sections. The insulation often is dry and brittle and chips easily. If there are exposed conductors, the exposed areas must be covered with electrical tape as a safety measure. Knob-and-tube wiring, although obsolete, is considered safe providing that no modifications are made to that portion of the electrical system. If any changes or extensions are made, rewiring of that particular branch circuit may be necessary. All modifications to knob-and-tube wiring must be made by a licensed electrician. In addition, the outlet receptacles of a knob-and-tube wired system are not grounded. Consequently, as a precautionary measure, they should only be used with appliances that do not require grounding.

### Low-Voltage Switching Systems

Ceiling and wall light fixtures are normally controlled by switches that interrupt the electrical flow in a 110-volt circuit. However, in some houses, the light switches operate at about 24 volts. This type of wiring is generally installed so that the lights can be controlled from three or more locations. With this system, it is possible to control all the lights in the house from a master panel located anywhere in the house. The circuit for a low-voltage system includes a transformer and an electrically operated switch (relay) that is usually mounted near the fixture. If your house has this type of system, make sure that there are replacement relays. Many electrical supply houses do not stock these relays, and they would have to be specially ordered from the supplier. If you do not have replacement relays and a relay breaks down, you may be without light from that fixture for several weeks before the condition can be repaired.

## VIOLATIONS

Electrical violations should be of concern to the home buyer/owner because they represent potential safety or fire hazards. As you walk around the interior and exterior of the structure, keep in mind those items that are considered common electrical violations. If there is an outside pole lamp, are the wires leading to the lamp buried? They should be. If a portion of the wire is exposed, is it stamped "UF— Sunlight Resistant"? This indicates that it can be used as exterior wire. Many times, homeowners unknowingly use interior-type wire as exterior wire. This is quite dangerous as the sun, rain, or soil conditions can cause the insulation covering the wire to deteriorate, exposing the conductors. Incidentally, if there is an outside pole lamp, it should be turned on to see whether or not it is operational. If it is not, the problem may be as simple to correct as changing the bulb or replacing the switch. However, it is also possible that there may be faulty underground wiring. Do all of the outside electrical outlets have exterior-type covers that provide protection against water penetration? Although it is not required in many municipalities, it is recommended that all outside lights and outlets be protected with ground-fault interrupters.

Inside the house, particularly in the basement, look for open junction boxes, loose, hanging wires, and exposed wiring and splices (except if the wires are low voltage). Recently, an inspection of a four-story, multifamily, brownstone walkup in New York City revealed several violations in one circuit located in the basement. The wire coming from the panel box was rated at 15 amps. However, it was protected in the panel box by a 30-amp fuse. The wire was hanging in loops from the basement ceiling and had open splices with exposed conductors (splices in a branch circuit should be contained in a closed junction box). One of the hanging loops with exposed conductors was resting on the inlet water pipe leading to the heating system boiler, while the floor below the pipe was wet. You seldom run into a more dangerous condition. Yet, there were ten families living in that house.

If the wiring in a house looks makeshift or appears to have been modified by a nonprofessional, you should request that the seller provide you, at contract closing, with the Board of Fire Underwriters' Certificate of Approval for the electrical wiring *currently* in the house. In your area, the Board of Fire Underwriters may be called by a different name or a private, commercial service may be used.

Finally, when walking through the house, look to see if all of the receptacle outlets and switches have cover plates. They should. Also, the homeowner, when using an extension cord, will sometimes run the cord through the inside of a partition wall. This is a violation of the electrical code. If an outlet is needed, a permanent one should be installed.

## CHECKPOINT SUMMARY

### EXTERIOR

- Is electrical service provided by underground cables or overhead wires?
- Are overhead service wires securely fastened to the house?
- Count the number of house service wires. Note that a two-wire service will provide only 110 volts, *not* 220 volts.
- Inspect inlet service wires for cracked, missing, and frayed sections of insulation.
- Note overhanging dead tree limbs or branches in contact with service wires.
- Inspect for exterior-mounted main panel boxes. (Replacement on the interior is recommended.)
- Check outside electrical outlets for weather protection.
- Inspect exterior wiring for proper type. It should be marked "UF—Sunlight Resistant."
- Inspect/check exterior lights and outlets for operation.
- Note inoperative fixtures and/or fixtures that are missing, loose, or hanging by wires.

## INTERIOR

- Inspect main panel box. Is it a fuse or circuit-breaker type?
- Does system contain a main disconnect?
- Note the following: (*Do not remove the panel cover.*)
    Loose or missing cover.
    Missing knockout plates or fuses.
    Are there at least two 20-amp appliance circuits?
    Is there at least one 15-amp lighting circuit for each 500 square feet of floor area?
    Are there many spare or burned-out fuses present?
- If panel box cover is removed by an electrician or an inspector, he should inform you of:
    the amount of service.
    circuits that are improperly protected (overfused).
    circuits that have aluminum wiring.
    evidence of water leakage or corrosion deposits.

## GROUNDING

- Check/inspect electrical system for proper ground protection.
- If there is a municipal water supply, is the ground wire from the main panel box fastened on the street side of the water meter?
- Inspect the connection for tightness of fit and corrosion.
- If the inlet water pipe is plastic (often in a well-pumping system), check on the exterior for a rod or pipe to which the ground wire should be clamped.
- Note if the ground wire is missing or has a loose or corroding section.

## INTERIOR WIRING—OUTLETS/SWITCHES—VIOLATIONS

- Does house contain old/obsolete wiring (i.e., knob-and-tube-type wiring)?
- Inspect for cracked and open sections of insulation.
- Inspect/check wiring in basement and attic areas for:
    loose and hanging sections.
    extension-cord-type outlets.
    open junction boxes.
    exposed splices.
    makeshift/nonprofessional alterations.
- Inspect each room for electrical outlets:
    at least one outlet in the bathroom.
    at least one outlet per wall for an average-size room (10 × 12 feet).
- Are outlets functioning (electrically hot)?
- Check for loose outlets, switches, and missing cover plates.
- Are stairways and hallways adequately lit?
- Are there three-way switches?
- Are there outlets in the hallways for night-lights and/or cleaning equipment?
- Note violations such as:
    open splices.
    fixtures hanging by wires.
    extension-cord wiring that passes through partitions or around door openings.

# 13. PLUMBING

As with the electrical system, the major portion of the plumbing system is concealed behind the walls and below the floors. Nevertheless, the part of the plumbing system that is accessible for inspection is sufficient for you to make a meaningful evaluation of its condition. A basic plumbing system consists of a water supply source, distribution piping, fixtures, drainage piping, and a waste disposal system. Figure 13-1 shows the layout of a plumbing system for a typical one-family, two-story house.

## WATER SUPPLY AND DISTRIBUTION

The system functions as follows: Water is supplied to the property line from the street water mains of the local utility company. At the property line, there is a shutoff valve called a "curb valve" that can be used to control the water supply to the house. If you do not pay your water bill on time, the water company may close this valve. The pipe that actually delivers the water to the house is called the "house service main." It runs from the curb valve to just inside the house and is the responsibility of the homeowner. Should this pipe be in need of repair or replacement, it is at the homeowner's expense. If water is not supplied by a utility company, then it will be supplied by a well-pumping system.

Once inside the house, the cold water is distributed to the various fixtures located throughout the house. At the house inlet, there is a shutoff valve that the homeowner can use to close the water supply for the entire house. If there is a water meter in the system, it will usually be located inside the house near the inlet before any branch connections. Sometimes, it is located near the curb valve. The cold water pipe will have a branch connection (usually near the inlet, although not necessarily) that directs a portion of the water to a heater for generating the domestic hot water. The water heater can be a separate stand-alone unit or part of the heating system and is discussed in Chapter 16. Distribution piping for the hot water will run from the heater to the various fixtures. The hot water pipes are very often near and parallel to the cold water pipes. They should, however, be at least 6 inches apart so that the heat from the hot water pipes will not affect the temperature of the cold water supply system.

## FIXTURES

Plumbing fixtures are located at the end of the water supply and the beginning of the drainage system. They provide a means by which the water brought into the house can be used. Depending on their purposes, the fixtures will have either hot water, cold water, or both. They will also have a drain for the removal of the waste water. This waste water is channeled away from the fixtures through drain pipes to either a sanitary sewer or to a private sewage disposal system such as a septic tank or cesspool.

## DRAINAGE SYSTEM

The drainage system is more complex than the water distribution system, as it consists of three parts—traps, drain pipes, and vents. The drainage

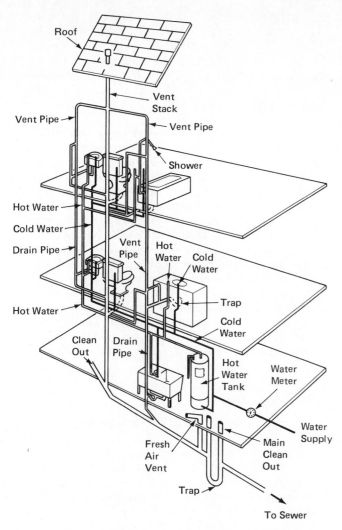

FIGURE 13-1 Plumbing system layout showing water supply, drain and vent pipes for a typical one-family, two-story house.

prevent the gases that occur in the sanitary sewer from circulating back through the plumbing system. When there is a house trap, there should also be a fresh air inlet pipe connected to the main drain. This air inlet pipe is located on the house side of the drain approximately 1 foot from the trap. (See Figure 13-2.) In cold climates, it is located about 5 feet from the house trap in order to prevent the water seal from freezing during the winter. When the outer end of the fresh air inlet terminates on the outside of the foundation wall, it should be covered with a perforated metal plate that admits the air and prevents obstruction. When it is freestanding, it should be covered with a cowl or gooseneck. (See Figure 13-3.) The function of the fresh air inlet is to maintain atmospheric pressure at the house trap and to ensure complete air movement within the drainage system. When there is a private sewage disposal system (septic tank), there should not be a house trap on the drain line. The gases that are generated within septic tanks are usually discharged to the atmosphere through the house drainage/vent system.

Venting is needed within the drainage system, as it provides a means to discharge to the atmosphere gases that develop within the system. It equalizes the air pressure in the drainage system by allowing air to flow into and out of the drain

FIGURE 13-2 House trap on main drain line leading to a sewer. Fresh air inlet pipe on house side of the trap terminates on the outside of the foundation wall.

system begins just below the fixture with a water-filled trap. The trap is generally U-shaped and should have water at the bottom portion. The water in the trap forms a seal to block sewer gases that are usually in the drain line from entering the room.

The wastes flow from the fixture trap, down the drain line, and out to the sewer or private sewage disposal system. Unlike the water distribution system where the flow is under pressure, the drainage system flow is entirely by gravity. Consequently, the drain pipes are larger in diameter than the water pipes, varying from 1½ inches to 4 inches as compared to ⅜ of an inch to 1 inch for the water pipes. In some communities, the house drain line leading to the sewer must have a house trap. The trap is usually located inside of the house near the foundation wall. Its purpose is to provide a seal and

pipes. This free air movement maintains atmospheric pressure at the various fixture traps, which prevents the waste water from siphoning the water seal out of the drain trap. See discussion on fixture traps in Chapter 10 (page 76). Venting in the drainage system is achieved by vent pipes that are connected to the drain line near each fixture trap and to a pipe that terminates above the roof line. This pipe is called the "vent stack" and is visible from the outside. Vent pipes must be unobstructed. They carry no water or wastes.

## WASTE DISPOSAL SYSTEM

Waste disposal from a residential structure will be either through sewers connected to a municipal or community waste treatment plant or through a private disposal system, such as a septic tank or cesspool. When all other items are equal, a house with a sewer is more desirable than one with a private disposal system. Sewers are relatively maintenance-free. On occasion, there may be a blockage, which can usually be cleared at a low cost by using a drain auger ("plumber's snake"). Maintaining a private disposal system, on the other hand, can be quite costly, although not necessarily so.

Whether or not the house is serviced by a sewer or is connected to a septic tank usually cannot be determined during an inspection. The house drain line passing through the foundation wall is the same, regardless of whether there is an exterior connection to a sewer or to a septic tank. Since not all municipalities require a house trap on the main drain, the absence of a trap does not mean that there are no sewers. And just because there is a sanitary sewer in the street, it should not be assumed that the house is connected to the sewer line. Tying into the sanitary sewer (if the connection is permitted) is at the homeowner's expense. I know several instances where homeowners elected to stay with their functioning septic systems rather than go to the expense of tying into the sewer. In some communities, however, once a sewer line is installed in the street, all the homes on that street are legally obliged to connect. Your best bet, so that you will know for sure, is to contact the local municipal Building Department and ask them if this specific house is connected to the sanitary sewer system. It may save you a lot of aggravation later on.

### Cesspool

A cesspool is basically a hole in the ground that has been lined with stone, brick, or some other material. It is constructed in such a manner so as to allow raw contaminated liquid sewage to leach into the soil while retaining the organic matter and solids. Because of environmental and health considerations, most communities no longer allow cesspools in new construction. The existing older homes that do have cesspool disposal systems are not required to upgrade them to septic systems, as long as they are functioning properly. However, when problems do develop, the homeowner is often legally obligated to replace the cesspool with a septic system rather than repair it. Depending on the soil conditions, topography, and available space, the installation of a new septic system may cost several thousand dollars.

### Septic System

A septic system consists of a watertight container that functions as a detention tank for sewage sludge and a disposal field for the absorption of the liquid wastes. A septic tank is usually made of concrete, but may also be made of steel or fiberglass. Raw sewage from the house is discharged into the septic tank through the house drain line. (See Figure 13-4.) After the sewage in the tank settles, the solids are decomposed by bacterial action and are converted into a liquid and a sludge that accumulates at the bottom of the tank. Several types of gases are also a byproduct of the decomposition process, the most common of which is methane, an odorless and highly inflammable gas. The gases that are generated in the septic tank usually flow back through the house drain and are discharged

FIGURE 13-3 Termination of house fresh air vent. *Left:* Perforated plate covers opening in foundation wall. *Center:* Perforated cover plate for vent opening is missing—a not uncommon condition. *Right:* A freestanding "gooseneck" cover.

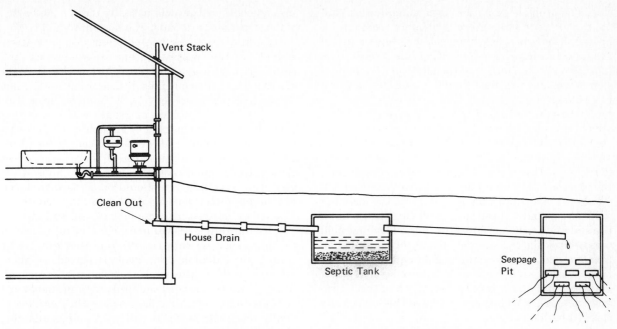

FIGURE 13-4  Typical septic system with seepage pit. Depending on the topography and amount of available land, the pit may be replaced by a leaching field.

harmlessly to the atmosphere at the roof-mounted vent stack.

When the level of the liquid (effluent) in the septic tank rises to the outlet port, the effluent flows through the outlet pipe to a drainage field. The drainage field, also called the "leaching field," consists of a series of perforated pipes that have been set into a bed of gravel. As the effluent flows through these pipes, it trickles through the perforations and is absorbed into the ground. The rate at which the ground absorbs the effluent (percolation rate) will determine the size of the leaching field. When the topography changes abruptly or when the area available for a leaching field is too small for adequate absorption, a seepage pit is used. It is basically a covered pit with an open jointed or perforated lining through which the effluent will seep or leach into the surrounding soil.

In order to determine the size of the leaching area needed for a particular house, percolation tests are taken in the area of the proposed sewage disposal system. The rate of water absorption will depend upon, among other things, the type of soil and the level of the water table in that area. If the percolation tests are taken during a drought or when the water table is low (the water table rises and drops during the year), the concluding data may result in designing an undersized leaching field that, in turn, will cause premature failure of the septic system. I know of a village just northwest of New York City where the septic systems in hundreds of homes failed within eight years of

installation. Some of them failed within two years. A properly designed and maintained septic system should last between twenty and thirty years; indeed, fifty or more years are not uncommon.

Failure of the septic system will usually show up in the area of the leaching field and not necessarily over the septic tank, although there may be indications in both areas. Look for wet spots and/or a lush growth of grass. Both can be accompanied by an objectionable odor. When the ground in the seepage field becomes saturated and can no longer absorb the effluent, the liquid will build up and accumulate on the surface. The effluent contains nitrogen and other compounds that are natural fertilizers. When the effluent surfaces, it causes vegetation in the area, particularly grass, to thrive and have a lush green color. However, a healthy-looking patch of green grass over the leaching field by itself is not necessarily an indication of a septic failure. During dry weather, when grass is apt to grow very slowly and turn brownish, the ground over the leaching field (depending on the depth of the field) often contains sufficient moisture to promote the growth of the grass and maintain the green color.

In order for the leaching field to function properly, there must be sufficient voids in the soil so that the effluent will be absorbed by the ground. Over the years, the voids can be filled with suspended solids, reducing the rate at which the effluent is absorbed into the soil to the point where the effluent surfaces. When this occurs, it is necessary to install a new leaching field. Aside from the cost, a serious problem can arise concerning how to handle the effluent when there is no more room on the property for a new leaching field or seepage pit. If the house that you are inspecting has a septic system, find out if there is sufficient room for expansion of the leaching field should it be necessary at a later date.

Premature failure of the septic system can also occur as a result of neglect and abuse on the part of the homeowner. A septic tank should be cleaned or, at least, inspected for sludge buildup every two to four years. If the tank is not cleaned periodically, the sludge will build up to such a level that the solids are carried out of the tank and into the leaching field. Eventually, these solids will clog the voids in the soil and/or the perforations in the leaching field pipes, blocking the normal flow of effluent. When this happens, the leaching field requires replacement. This type of problem could have been avoided. Unfortunately, it is very common to find homeowners who neglect to inspect and have the septic tank cleaned periodically.

On many occasions, I have been told by an owner that the septic tank has never been cleaned. The owner knew from experience that, if the septic system functioned properly, it was best not to disturb it. After all, his neighbor across the street had had his septic tank cleaned after fifteen years and two weeks later, the system failed and had to be replaced. If he had not touched the system, it would have been all right, wouldn't it? No! That system apparently had been on the verge of failure before the cleaning. The cleaning had nothing to do with the failure.

There are some rare instances in which septic systems can operate satisfactorily for many years without the tank ever being cleaned. In those cases, the tank may have been grossly oversized for the number of people living in the house or, possibly, the house was used as a vacation home and occupied only part of the time. One method of extending the life of a septic system is to reduce the volume of water that passes through the tank and leaching field. This is often done by installing a separate drain line for the waste water from fixtures such as the washing machine and connecting it to a dry well or seepage pit that is located away from the leaching field.

Sometimes the homeowner indicates that he has not cleaned the septic tank because he has been using a chemical compound or septic tank cleaner that he pours down the drain. This cleaner is supposed to improve bacterial activity and eliminate the need for periodic cleaning. The advertising claims of these cleaners are not well founded, as there will always be a sludge buildup that *must* be removed. In addition, some of the cleaners may contain compounds that will actually reduce the bacterial process and can cause the system to fail.

In order to reduce the possibility of premature failure of the septic system, some homes are equipped with a grease trap in the waste disposal system. The trap separates grease from the kitchen waste line, thus preventing it from entering the septic system. A buildup of grease within the system can result in clogging or reducing the porosity of the leaching field and can also affect the bacterial action within the septic tank. If there is a grease trap in the waste disposal system of the house that you are inspecting, you should be advised that, for maximum effectiveness, it should be frequently cleaned or, at least inspected for grease buildup.

Discharging large volumes of water into the septic tank, such as rain runoff from roof gutters or from storm drains can, over a period of time, adversely affect the tank's operation. Large volumes of water can flood the tank, forcing suspended solids into the leaching field where they can eventually block the perforations in the pipes and clog the voids in the soil.

Depending on the soil condition, a water softener can be detrimental to a septic system. If the seepage field consists of a clay-type soil, the waste water from the water softener regeneration process must not be discharged into the septic tank. The salt brine in the water softener waste water is not broken down by bacterial action as it passes through the septic tank to the leaching field and can clog the voids in the finely textured clay soil.

Even though a septic system may be faulty, there may not be any visual indications of a problem when you inspect the house. Whether or not there is a water (effluent) accumulation over the leaching area or septic tank will depend upon the dryness of the season, the amount of usage of the plumbing system prior to the inspection, and the degree of deterioration of the septic system. One way to check the operation of the system is to "push" it by turning on the water in the tub and letting it run for about one hour. (Before you do this test, ask the owner for permission.) The tub drain must be open so that the water will flow into the septic tank. Assuming an adequate water supply, this "pushing" should introduce about 275 gallons into the septic system which, very often, is enough to cause the effluent in a faulty system to surface and be visible when you reinspect the areas over the tank and leaching field.

An adequate evaluation of the plumbing system requires both an interior and an exterior inspection. Although most of the plumbing inspection is performed in the interior, an exterior inspection can reveal venting problems, violations, and septic system problems.

## EXTERIOR INSPECTION

### Vent Stack

As you walk around the house looking at the roof, look for a plumbing vent stack. If you do not see one, it indicates either that the plumbing system is not properly vented or possibly that the vent stack terminates in the attic. Both possibilities are violations of the plumbing code. If the construction of the roof is such that there are sections that are not visible from the ground, then a vent stack should be looked for during the attic inspection. If there is a vent stack, you will see a pipe coming up from the floor and going out through the roof. Sometimes it is difficult to check for the vent stack in the attic because of the restricted space and the lack of adequate lighting.

The vent stack should terminate above the roof. If you see one that terminates near a window or one that runs up along the side of the building (in the northern portion of the country), it is in violation of the National Plumbing Code (as explained in Chapter 3).

### Fresh Air Vent

When there is a fresh air vent for the house trap, if the outer end terminates on the outside of the foundation wall, the opening should be covered with a screen or perforated metal plate. The covering is needed to prevent children from stuffing toys, balls, or other objects into the opening and blocking the air movement. Technically, an unprotected fresh air vent opening is also a violation of the plumbing code. If you do not see a cover over the fresh air inlet vent, record the fact on your worksheet as a reminder for later installation. You should also use your flashlight to determine if there is any blockage.

### Lawn Sprinkler Systems

Does the house that you are inspecting have an underground lawn sprinkler system? If it does, look specifically for a vacuum breaker (anti-siphon device) on the water supply line for each zone. When the piping arrangement is such that the water is supplied to each zone through a manifold, then the vacuum breaker should be on the pipe supplying water to the manifold.

A vacuum breaker is recommended in order to prevent dirty water or foreign matter that normally accumulates around pop-up spray heads from flowing back into the potable water supply as a result of a negative pressure in the line. It is a relatively simple device and is usually no larger than a few inches in diameter and a few inches high. (See Figure 13-

FIGURE 13-5  Typical atmospheric vacuum breaker used in lawn irrigation systems. *(Courtesy Rain Bird Sprinkler Mfg. Corp.)*

5.) The vacuum breaker has an atmospheric vent that is sealed when water is flowing to the spray heads. When the water pressure drops to below atmospheric pressure (vacuum) because of a problem in the supply line, a mechanical float drops, opening the atmospheric vent. This allows air to enter the piping system upstream of the spray heads and, thereby, prevents dirty water at the spray head from being siphoned back into the supply piping.

Vacuum breakers must be located at least 6 inches above the level of the highest sprinkler head. Look for them near the foundation wall. Sometimes the piping is located in a well adjacent to the foundation, similar to a basement window well. Usually, the vacuum breaker(s) and the electric solenoid valves that control the water flow to the various zones are in the same general area.

### Septic System

If the house has a septic system, find out from the owner the location of the tank and the leaching area. As you walk around the house performing the general exterior inspection, look specifically for puddles over the leaching area and/or septic tank. If the puddles have a film on top and there is a foul odor in the area, you can be sure that there is a septic problem. If the puddle is a clear liquid and there is no odor, there may still be a septic system problem. The best way to find out whether the liquid is septic effluent or surface water as a result of a past rain is to collect a sample and have it analyzed. If no puddles are noted during your initial exterior inspection, reinspect the area after "pushing" the septic system as described on page 106.

## INTERIOR INSPECTION

### Fixtures

Since you will start your general interior inspection at the attic level and will work your way down to the basement, the interior plumbing inspection will begin in the first room that you inspect that has fixtures. (See the bathroom section of Chapter 10 for further discussion of plumbing.) The fixtures should be checked for general condition—cracked, chipped, and stained sections—and also for operation. Do the faucets function properly or are there leaks around the handles or spout? Is there an air gap between the spout and the top level of the water when the sink or tub is filled? There should be in order to prevent back siphonage. Is the sink drain leaking or does it show signs of past leakage? Occasionally, you may find a pot below the drainage trap to catch dripping water. Sometimes you may find rubber-hose-type connections on the drain, or a drain that has been taped up. These are makeshift corrections and require proper attention. Are there individual shutoff valves for the water supply to the various fixtures? Shutoff valves are not necessary, but are desirable when making repairs or replacing the faucet. When you open and close the faucet rapidly, do you hear a "water hammer" noise? You shouldn't. But if you do, it can usually be corrected with an anti-knock coil or air chamber. Are the toilet bowl flushing and fill valves operating properly? While the bowl is filling up, if you hear a whistling noise, the fill valve needs adjustment. After the water closet (tank) has been filled, do you still hear water running? If you do, minor maintenance is needed.

## Water Pressure/Flow

After inspecting the fixtures, faucets, and associated valves, pay particular attention to the water flow and drainage. When there is a considerable flow of water from a faucet, most people say the pressure is good, and when the flow is merely a trickle, they say the pressure is bad. This is a popular misuse of the word *pressure*. It is true that if the pressure is low, the water flow will be low. However, a low-flow condition is not usually caused by low pressure. It is caused by a constriction in the inside diameter of the supply pipes. Depending on the quality of the water, mineral and/or corrosion deposits can form along the inside diameter of a pipe, reducing the effective pipe opening to that of a straw. In this case, even when the source pressure is good, the flow will be less than minimal.

Check the cold and the hot water flow separately, by opening two faucets and flushing the bowl at the same time. If the flow appears to your eye to be less than adequate, record the fact on your worksheet as a reminder to check further. The low flow may be caused by a kink in the supply pipe, small-diameter distribution piping or, possibly, low water pressure at the service entry. However, the probability is greatest that the low flow is caused by a decrease in the inside diameter of one or more sections of pipe supplying the fixture(s).

Old galvanized iron piping is particularly bad for water flow. In addition to mineral deposits, there is often a buildup of rust that further constricts the flow. If you find low water flow, especially in an older house, look for galvanized piping. You may find that the house has been partially repiped. Some iron sections may have been replaced with copper and/or brass. The mixing of iron in a copper plumbing system is not desirable for two reasons. First, just as a chain is as strong as its weakest link, so is a plumbing system as good as the weakest section of pipe. Even a small section of iron pipe whose inside diameter has been reduced by a buildup of rust and mineral deposits will lower the flow of water discharging from a faucet. Second, when ferrous (iron) and nonferrous (copper) metals are in contact with one another, a galvanic action takes place between the metals that accelerates the corrosion of the plumbing system at the point of contact. Some plumbers, although not many, use an electrolytic tape to separate the dissimilar metals and avoid the galvanic corrosion.

On occasion, in those homes that have water supplied by a well-pumping system rather than by a local utility, you may find that the water discharging from the faucet has a pulsating flow. This condition is caused by a rapidly fluctuating water pressure and is the result of a waterlogged storage tank. The condition is relatively easy to correct and is discussed on page 115.

## Plumbing Wall Hatch

In many older homes, an opening in the wall of a hallway provides access to the plumbing pipes for the tub. The opening is usually no larger than 2 feet by 3 feet and often has a wooden cover that has been painted along with the rest of the wall, so that it is not very noticeable. Sometimes, this access hatch is in a closet or bedroom. If there is such a hatch in the home that you are inspecting, remove the cover. You should be able to see the water supply pipes, the overflow, and the drain pipes. (See Figure 13-6.)

## Pipes

Water distribution pipes can be made of either copper, brass, or galvanized iron. Once you become familiar with the types of pipe, you will be able to differentiate between them very easily. Here are some pointers. Brass and galvanized pipe have threaded joints, whereas copper joints are soldered. So, if the pipe joints are threaded, you will know that they are not copper pipes. Do not try to determine by its color whether the pipe is brass or galvanized. There may be a dirt film on the pipe or it may be painted. The easiest and most foolproof method is to use your magnet. If the pipe is made of galvanized iron, it will attract the magnet; if it is made of brass, it will not.

Now look to see if the piping is a mixture of copper, brass, and galvanized sections. Even if there is no noticeable drop in water flow, mixed plumbing is not desirable because the resultant galvanic corrosion at the joints will eventually cause leakage. Figure 13-7 shows such a joint. The white encrustations on the pipe are mineral deposits that were left when the water oozing out of the fitting evaporated. Although deposits on this joint self-sealed past leakage, it is only a temporary correction, for the deposits can come loose at any time. Properly correcting this conditon requires replacing the iron section with pipe made of copper or brass.

## BASEMENT INSPECTION

After inspecting all of the fixtures, associated pipes, and fittings in the various interior rooms, the rest

FIGURE 13-6   Wall hatch in hallway provides access to plumbing pipes for bathtub.

FIGURE 13-7   Mixed plumbing as seen from a hallway wall hatch. Some of the fittings are deteriorating, as noted by the rust and mineral deposits.

of the plumbing inspection is carried out in the basement. Some homes are built on ground level and do not have a basement. In those cases, this portion of the inspection will be performed as part of the interior room inspection.

### Water Supply Pipes

Look for the entry of the water supply pipe. It will be located near the foundation wall and will usually have a meter near the inlet. If you cannot find the water service entry, ask the homeowner. Sometimes it is concealed behind boxes or storage shelves. The inlet service pipe will generally be made of copper, brass, or galvanized iron. However, in some older homes, you may find that the pipe is made of lead. A lead pipe can be detected by the type of joint between the sections. Lead pipes have wiped lead joints that appear in a horizontal section as a spherical bulge. (See Figure 13-8.) There is usu-

FIGURE 13-8 Lead inlet water pipe. Note wiped joint (spherical bulge) near shutoff valve.

ally a joint near the foundation wall. If you do not see a joint, you can *gently* scratch the surface of the pipe. If the pipe is made of lead, the surface will be relatively soft and the scratch will expose an area with a silver-gray color.

Although a lead water pipe may be acceptable in a plumbing sense, it can be a potential health hazard. Depending on the quality of the water, some of the lead may dissolve out. Since the amount of lead that a person can absorb is limited and cumulative, the possibility does exist that by drinking this water over an extended period of time, the maximum tolerance level can be reached. If you find a lead inlet water pipe, you should have the water analyzed for lead content. In many communities, the local Health Department will do the analysis for free or for a very nominal charge. If the lead content is high, the pipe should be replaced. Again, remember that replacing the inlet water pipe is not the responsibility of the water company and the associated cost must be borne by the homeowner.

During my inspections, I periodically find a lead inlet water pipe. When I do, I always recommend to the prospective home buyer that, as a precautionary measure, the water should be analyzed. In one home, located in White Plains, New York, an analysis of the water revealed that it had seven times the allowable concentration of lead. Needless to say, that water pipe was replaced.

If the water flow from the plumbing fixtures is low and the piping in the house is good (all copper or brass pipes and fittings with no leaks), then the problem will either be a constriction in the inlet water supply or low pressure at the street main. On several occasions, I have inspected houses where the old water pipes were completely replaced with new copper pipes and still the water flow was low.

Further inspection revealed that even though the house had been repiped, the old galvanized inlet supply pipe had not been replaced. Under normal soil and water conditions, this pipe should last about forty years. As these pipes age, rust deposits build up on the inside restricting the flow. Also, a galvanized iron pipe will eventually corrode from the outside and leak. Replacement may cost anywhere from several hundred to several thousand dollars, depending on the length of the line and ground conditions.

When domestic water is supplied by a utility company, the inlet supply pipe will lead directly to the house distribution piping. In some areas, depending on the quality of the water, there may be a water softener and/or a filter between the supply and distribution piping. Normally, however, you will not find a storage tank (similar to that needed in a well-pumping system) between the supply and distribution piping. If you do find such a tank, you should suspect a low-pressure condition at the street main. When the water pressure in the street main is low and there are simultaneous demands for water by the houses on the street, the flow to each house may be inadequate. To compensate for this conditon, a storage tank is often installed to provide a reservoir that can supply water during these periods. Water drawn from the tank is then replaced when the plumbing fixtures in that house are not being used. If you see such a tank between the inlet supply and distribution piping, record the fact on your worksheet.

When domestic water is not supplied by a utility company, it will be supplied by a well-pumping system. Such systems are discussed in the last section of this chapter.

At the house inlet side of the water supply pipe, there will be a master shutoff valve that can close the water supply to the entire house. Sometimes there are two valves, one on each side of the water meter. See whether or not the valve(s) is operational. Close and open it. Over the years, because of lack of use, the valve often freezes in the open position.

## Distribution Piping

Water is supplied to the various fixtures throughout the house by means of distribution piping. The distribution system begins by the inlet supply pipe just after the water meter and consists of two components: supply mains and fixture risers. The supply mains are usually suspended from the basement ceiling and can be readily inspected in an unfinished basement. The fixture risers run between the supply mains and the fixtures and are usually concealed behind the walls. For the most part, the risers cannot be inspected.

In addition to copper, brass, and galvanized iron pipes, many communities also allow the use of plastic pipes for both hot and cold water distribution. Some communities, however, will only allow plastic pipe for use in cold water lines. Trace and inspect all of the exposed water pipes in the basement. You will find that there will be a branch take-off pipe that leads to the domestic hot water heater, and if the house is heated by steam or hot water, there will be a cold or hot water take-off leading to the boiler. As a point of interest, over the years, cold water copper and brass pipes take on a darker color than the hot water pipes. Sometimes you may find sections of cold water supply piping "sweating" profusely. This is not a problem condition. It is merely condensation and can easily be eliminated by insulating the pipes or reducing the amount of moisture in the air through the use of a dehumidifier.

Faulty plumbing does not necessarily mean that there is a steady stream of water leaking from a pipe or fitting, although if that is the case, immediate correction is necessary. Of particular concern are indications of aging and deterioration. When inspecting the pipes, look specifically for signs of past and current leakage around fittings and valves. Look for mineral deposits, corrosion, and patched sections. The presence of galvanized iron pipes and fittings in a copper and brass plumbing system is a potential problem, as discussed previously. If you see iron pipes, you should make an estimate as to the amount and anticipate their replacement. Copper pipes often take on a greenish cast, particularly around the fittings. Although this condition looks as if it could have been caused by water leaking from the joint, it is not. It is usually caused by the soldering flux. A leak, on the other hand, usually shows up as an encrustation of mineral deposits around the joint.

Brass pipes found in residential structures will usually be "red brass" or "yellow brass." You can often tell the difference by the color. Red brass, however, is really not red, but a yellowish brown. Yellow brass water pipes are more vulnerable to corrosion and dezincification (zinc leaching out of the brass into the water) than are red brass pipes. The projected life for yellow brass pipes is about forty years, while seventy-five years for red brass is not uncommon. The weakest part of a brass pipe is the threaded joint. With some older yellow brass pipes, the threads are paper thin. In this case, if a force is applied to one of the pipes (with a wrench during a repair or even by leaning on the pipe), the joint could easily rupture. Usually, weak joints can be detected by a slight encrustation of mineral deposits. If you find encrusted joints on yellow brass pipes, you should anticipate repair or, possibly, replacement of those sections.

Also, when the distribution pipes are brass, look along the length of the pipes for signs of leaks. Brass pipes are vulnerable to pinhole leaks along their length. Depending on its chemical quality, the water in the pipes can cause some of the zinc in the brass to dissolve. When this occurs, pinhole openings can be seen along the length of the pipe. Because of the small size of the openings, water drips from the holes very slowly. In many instances, the water will evaporate before it drips, leaving whitish mineral deposits around the opening. (See Figure 13-9.) Eventually, the deposits can self-seal the leak, although the pinhole openings will get larger.

I once inspected a house that had this problem. The owners had moved out in the beginning of the winter before they found a buyer. As a precautionary measure, water was drained from all of the pipes to keep them from freezing over the winter months. My inspection took place the following spring when the water was turned on. Well, the sudden surge of pressure in the pipes was enough to loosen all of the deposits, and water started to leak out all along the pipes, so that is looked like a sprinkler system. If you see brass pipes with mineral encrustations along their length, even though there may not be any current leakage, those pipes should be replaced.

### Drainage Pipes

The wastes discharging from toilets and sinks flow from the various fixtures down to the sewer or septic tank by means of drainage pipes. As with the

FIGURE 13-9 Brass water pipe with pinhole leaks. Condition caused by leaching zinc. Note mineral deposits on underside of pipe.

distribution piping, only the portion of the drain line that is in the basement will be visible for inspection. In those houses built on ground level or in those with finished basements, the drain pipes will probably not be visible and, as such, cannot be inspected.

Drain pipes are generally made of cast iron, galvanized iron, copper, lead, or plastic. Very often, the drainage system will consist of a combination of the different types of pipes. This is acceptable. The problems that are encountered in the distribution system when using iron and copper pipes together or when using lead pipes do not exist in the drainage system.

For most of the day, the drain pipes are empty. The wastes flow down the drain by means of gravity. Consequently, the main house drain in the basement must have a steady downward pitch leading directly to the sewer or septic tank. Look at the drain line. If there is a low point along the length of the pipe, there is a problem. (See Figure 13-10.) The low point in the pipe will allow grease and sewage solids to settle and eventually block the pipe. This condition is a violation of the plumbing code and must be corrected. When inspecting the house drain pipes, look for signs of current and past problems, such as cracked and patched sections, improper pitch, and leakage.

One question that I am asked fairly often by prospective buyers is, "Can we put a bathroom in the basement?" The only difficulty in installing a bathroom is how to handle the drainage which must flow by gravity. If the house drain is connected to the sewer at a level above the basement floor, then the wastes from the fixtures will have to be pumped up

FIGURE 13-10   Low point in drain pipe. Condition can cause solid wastes to build up and block the flow.

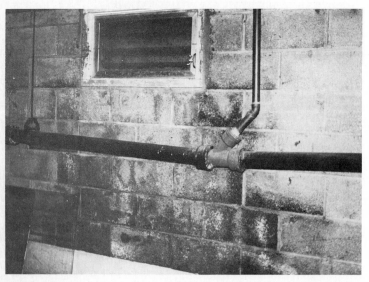

to the house drain so that they can flow out to the sewer. A pump installation alone can be quite costly. Another approach is to use a specially designed toilet that can lift the wastes about 10 feet without the use of a pump. It uses water pressure. This toilet is moderately priced. However, it is quite sensitive and if used for anything other than human wastes and toilet paper, it can become clogged. If only a sink is desired in the basement, a simple, inexpensive lift pump can be used to lift the waste water to the house drain.

When the house drain is located below the basement floor slab, then connecting the fixture drains to the house drain will require breaking up sections of the floor. In order to minimize the installation cost, the proposed bathroom should be located near the existing drain line. In some cases, when the drain line is at, or just below the basement floor surface, the toilet is located on a platform to facilitate the connection.

## WELL-PUMPING SYSTEMS

When domestic water is not supplied by a utility company, it will be supplied by a private well-pumping system that includes a well pump, storage tank, and pressure switch.

### Wells

As explained in Chapter 6, part of the water hitting the surface of the earth as a result of rain, snow, hail, or sleet seeps into the ground and percolates down until it hits an impermeable rock strata through which it cannot penetrate. The water then flows along the strata until it eventually reaches the ocean or river, which can be more than a thousand miles away. The underground flow is not like a running stream but more like a turtle climbing a rock pile. The water flows through the pores and cracks of rock formations, sometimes surfacing along the way as a river or lake. The water comprising this underground flow is known as "groundwater," the top surface of which is commonly called the "water table."

Subsurface rock formations that readily yield the groundwater to wells are called "aquifers." There are two types of wells, shallow and deep wells. A well that draws from an aquifer that is located less than 25 feet below the earth's surface is called a "shallow well." When the aquifer is more than 25 feet below the earth's surface, the well from which the water is drawn is called a "deep well." Wells over 500 feet deep are not uncommon.

Because of the proximity of the surface, shallow wells are vulnerable to contamination from cesspools, malfunctioning septic systems, barnyard manure, and industrial waste disposal. Deep wells, although less vulnerable to contamination, can also become polluted. Bacterial and chemical pollutants move downward in the soil until they reach the water table and then flow with the groundwater. To a large extent, the soil acts as a natural water purifier for bacterial contamination by filtering small suspended solids and allowing large pollutant particles to settle out. In addition, bacterial pollutants tend to die away after a period of time. Their life spans are usually short in the unfavorable conditions found in the soil.

Chemical pollution of the water source, however, can persist for years. I recently read a newspaper article about a toxic chemical solvent, trichlorethylene (TCE), that was contaminating the water supply of seventeen private wells. The solvent, which is used for thinning paint or removing grease, can cause neurological problems if inhaled or ingested in high concentrations. The source for the contamination could not be determined. The local Health Commissioner, however, indicated that he thought that it was the result of TCE being dumped in the area many years ago—prior to the homes being built.

Water that has a foul taste or odor and appears dirty may be completely potable, whereas water that is very clear and has a good taste may be polluted. You cannot tell, by looking at it or tasting it, whether or not the water is contaminated. As a precautionary measure, well water should be analyzed once a year for both bacterial and chemical pollutants. If the house that you are inspecting has a well, have the water analyzed prior to contract closing.

## Well Pumps

The purpose of the pump is to draw water from the well and push it through the distribution piping with sufficient force so that the water overcomes the frictional resistance of the pipes and provides an adequate flow at the various fixtures.

There are three basic types of well pumps used for residential structures: submersible, jet, and piston. All three can be used for shallow or deep wells. The submersible pump, however, is most frequently used for deep wells. In shallow wells, the jet or piston pumping mechanism is not located in the water. It is located on top of the well. The water is drawn up to the pump by a suction action, not unlike drinking through a straw. A suction will result in a pipe immersed in a body of water when the pressure inside of the pipe is reduced below atmospheric pressure (vacuum). Under ideal conditions, the maximum suction lift attainable is 34 feet. However, because of pump inefficiencies and frictional resistance of the pipe walls, the practical limit of suction lift is 25 feet, which is used in defining a shallow well. A deep well, therefore, is one in which water is pumped from a depth that exceeds 25 feet.

Well pumps and their accessory equipment are usually very reliable. Nevertheless, all well-pumping systems require occasional repair and/or replacement. The projected life expectancy of a pump is seven to ten years, although many pumps run without trouble for twenty to thirty years.

### Piston Pump

These pumps are no longer in general use, although they may be found in older homes. Basically, they are motorized versions of the old hand pump. A motor drives the piston that alternately sucks water into the cylinder and then discharges it on every other stroke. In a shallow well, the pump (motor-piston assembly) is above the ground. In a deep well, the motor is above the ground and the piston assembly is located in the well. Usually the motor is connected to the piston assembly by a belt and pulley. Inspect the belt for partially torn and frayed sections and for adequate tension. Also look for signs of leakage around casing joints and around the piston rod. There should not be any. An overall evaluation of any pumping system must necessarily include an inspection of the accessory equipment, which is discussed later in this chapter.

### Jet Pump

The jet pump consists of a jet assembly and a centrifugal pump. The centrifugal pump can be thought of as a small paddle wheel driven by a motor. As the wheel turns, it imparts energy to the water, increasing its velocity and pressure. A portion of the water discharging from the centrifugal pump is diverted to the jet assembly, which has no moving parts. However, it uses this recirculated water to perform two functions. It creates a suction that draws well water into the assembly and pushes this water back up to the centrifugal pump. After passing through the pump, some of the water is again rediverted to the jet assembly and the remainder directed to the plumbing system for distribution.

You can tell whether the pump is a shallow-well or deep-well jet pump by the number of pipes extending into the well. The basic difference between the two pumps is the location of the jet assembly. In a shallow-well jet pump, the jet assembly is built into the centrifugal pump casing and has only one pipe extending into the well. In a deep-well jet pump, the jet assembly must be located within the well (so that the suction lift does not exceed 25 feet). In this case, there are two pipes extending into the well. (See Figure 13-11.) In areas where the temperature drops below freezing, proper weather

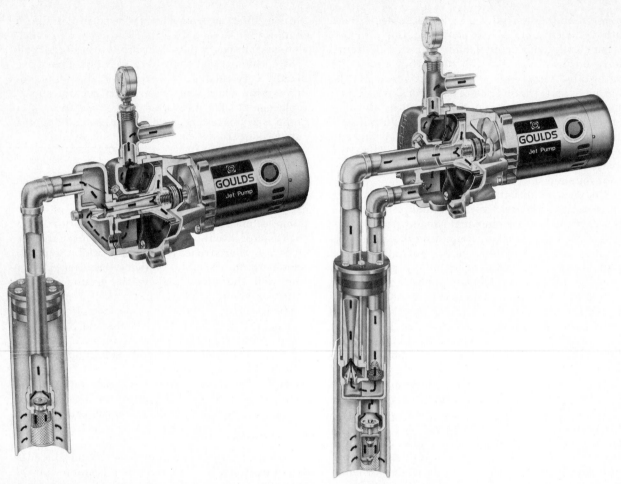

FIGURE 13-11   Jet pumps. *Left:* Shallow well jet pump—one pipe extending into well. *Right:* Deep well jet pump—two pipes extending into well. *(Courtesy Gould Pumps, Inc.)*

protection on jet pumps is important. According to Gould Pumps, Inc., frozen pumps represent one of the most common reasons for pump replacement.

### Submersible Pump

A submersible pump consists of an electrically driven centrifugal pump, designed so that both the electric motor and the pump can operate under water. This pump is intended for placement directly in the well and, as such, is used primarily for deep wells. It can, however, also be used for shallow wells. Water is drawn into the unit through screened openings located between the motor and the pump. A single discharge pipe is connected to the top of the pump and runs to the storage tank, which is usually found in the lower level of the house. In this case, when inspecting the pumping system, you will not see the pump, only the accessory equipment. (See Figure 13-12.)

Because the electric motor is located in the well, in those areas where electrical storms are frequent, it is advisable to have a lightning arrester at the motor power supply. This will conduct high-voltage surges from the line to the ground before they enter and damage the motor. Submersible pumps have the advantage of quiet dependable operation. They are relatively maintenance-free and are more efficient than jet or piston pumps. If, however, a problem should develop with the pump or motor, the entire unit must be withdrawn from the well.

### Accessory Equipment

In order for a private well-pumping system to provide water service that is comparable to that offered by a utility company, accessory equipment is needed.

### Storage Tanks

The pump discharge line must be connected to a storage tank. The tank, also called a "pressure tank," is generally located on the lower level of the house, but may also be located in an outside pump house. Water from the tank is forced into the house supply pipe whenever there is a demand at one of the plumbing fixtures. A properly functioning tank provides a water reservoir that balances the capacity of the pump against the usage demand. It prevents excessive short-cycling (too rapid starting and stopping), which can cause switch and motor trouble.

The water in the storage tank is under pressure. Since water cannot be compressed, in order for the tank to function properly, it must be partially filled with air. Over a period of time, the water in the tank absorbs the air, so that the tank eventually becomes completely filled with water. When this condition exists, the tank is "waterlogged" and the pump performs as if no tank were used. Any small request for water, such as filling up a glass, will cause the pump to cycle rapidly. This, in turn, will cause premature wear on the pump, motor, and switch.

The pressure range normally used for well-pumping systems is between 20 to 40 or 30 to 50 pounds per square inch (psi). If a waterlogged condition exists and there is a demand for water, you will hear the pump starting and stopping rapidly if the pump is the jet or piston type. However, when a submersible pump is used, you will not hear the pump. In this case, you can tell that a waterlogged condition exists because the pressure switch will be clicking on and off. Also, the pointer on the pressure gauge will be fluctuating between the high and low pressure limits. If you find a waterlogged tank during your inspection, record it on your worksheet. The condition can be easily corrected by draining and then injecting air into the tank.

Some pumping systems have an air charger apparatus that introduces air into the tank with each cycle in order to avoid waterlogging. Some pre-pressurized tanks claim to achieve a permanent separation of air and water by means of a plastic or rubber diaphragm or bag. These tanks should also be checked to determine whether or not they are waterlogged. I have found that on occasion they are, a condition that also indicates a faulty diaphragm or bag.

In most areas of the country, the storage tank should be insulated to prevent condensation during the summer months. Some tanks show signs of deterioration because of excessive rusting, a condition brought about over the years by moisture condensation on the tank. Depending on the degree of deterioration, the tank may have to be replaced or scraped, repainted, and insulated.

### Pressure Switch and Gauge

All systems must have a pressure switch and pressure gauge. The switch automatically starts and stops the pump at predetermined pressures. The pressure differential between start and stop is

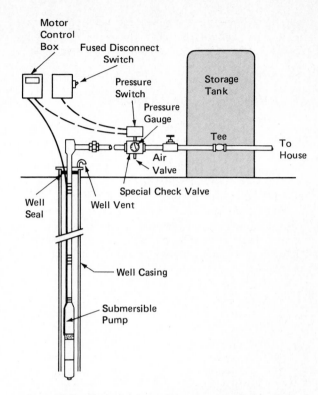

FIGURE 13-12  Typical submersible pump installation. Only the controls and storage tank are visible, as the pump is located in the well.

usually about 20 psi. The normal pressure range, as mentioned earlier, is 20 to 40 psi or 30 to 50 psi. Sometimes you will find a range of 40 to 60 psi. Pressure in excess of 65 psi is abnormal and should be checked out by a pump service company. It may be caused by a faulty pressure switch.

The switch can easily be checked by turning on a faucet. Look at the pressure gauge and watch the pressure drop until the pump is activated by the low limit. Have someone turn off the faucet while you watch the pressure building up on the pressure gauge. When the upper limit is reached, the pump should stop. If it does not or if it cuts out at too high a pressure, then there is a problem condition. If the pressure gauge is broken, this test cannot be performed. All too often, I have found inoperative pressure gauges. If you find one, it should be replaced.

Standard tanks are normally rated for a maximum pressure of 75 psi. As a precautionary measure, there should be an automatic relief valve on the storage tank or associated piping. The relief valve will prevent problems associated with excessive pressure buildup if the pressure switch malfunctions and allows the pump to continue running.

Look at the pressure gauge to see if the system will hold pressure when the pump is not running and no water is being used. If the pointer on the gauge drops, it indicates a leak. If no signs of leaks were noted during the plumbing inspection, then the leak is probably between the storage tank and the well. Note this item on your worksheet, for it must be corrected.

## GENERAL CONSIDERATIONS

When the yield of a well is less than 5 gallons per minute (gpm), some municipalities require an auxiliary storage tank from which water can be drawn during periods of peak demand. The rate at which water will be used in a home can vary from 1 gpm (rinsing hands) to a peak rate of 12 gpm or more, depending on personal habits and plumbing fixtures available. The approximate rates at which the various home fixtures use water is shown below. This assumes adequately sized distribution piping.

| | |
|---|---|
| Bathroom sink (lavatory) faucet | 3 gpm |
| Water closet (toilet) | 4 gpm |
| Bathtub | 5 gpm |
| Shower | 5 gpm |
| Dishwasher | 2 gpm |
| Washing machine (laundry) | 5 gpm |
| Garden hose | 3 gpm |
| Lawn sprinkler | 2 gpm |

The following table shows the approximate water supply requirements of home fixtures.

| | |
|---|---|
| Filling bathroom sink (lavatory) | 2 gallons |
| Filling average bathtub | 30 gallons |
| Each shower | Up to 60 gallons* |
| Flushing water closet (toilet) | 6 gallons |
| Dishwasher | 3 gallons per load |
| Washing machine (laundry) | Up to 50 gallons per load |

*This figure will, of course, vary with each individual. Also, shower heads are available that will reduce the flow rate.

Obviously, all of the fixtures will not be in operation at the same time. Nevertheless, for a home with two full bathrooms, the pumping system should be designed so that it can supply a peak of about 10 gallons per minute, even if this is greater than the yield of the well. If you find an auxiliary storage tank or the controls for a storage tank (the tank may be buried), you should try to find out the design criteria for the well-pumping system. You may find that the water flow at the design peak demand is less than you require. The design criteria may be known by the seller or may be available through local Health Department records or through the company that installed the system.

## CHECKPOINT SUMMARY

### EXTERIOR INSPECTION

- Did you note any vent stacks that:
  terminate near windows?
  run up an exterior side of the house (in northern climates)?
  have TV antennas, and so on, strapped to them?
- Is house drainage system connected to a municipal sewer, a septic tank, or a cesspool?
- Do you know where the septic system or cesspool is located?
- If house is connected to a septic tank, has the tank ever been cleaned? When?
- Did you note any wet spots or any foul odors in the area of the septic system?
- Are there any areas where liquids are oozing from the ground?
- Does property contain a lawn sprinkler system?
- Is sprinkler water supply line protected by a vacuum breaker?

### INTERIOR INSPECTION

#### Fixtures (Operation/Condition)
- Check all plumbing fixtures for operation.
- Note any cracked, chipped, or stained areas.
- Are sinks and/or bowls loose?
- Do faucets leak around handles or spouts?
- Do sinks, bowls, tubs, and/or showers drain properly or are they sluggish?
- Do sink and tub drains open and close properly?
- Are there any missing or inoperative "pop-up" units?
- Does toilet bowl fill and shut off properly?
- Do any fixture drain lines leak, have makeshift patches, or missing traps?
- Do fixtures have individual shutoff valves on supply lines?

#### Water Pressure/Flow
- Check individual fixtures for low hot or cold water flow.
- Is water flow adequate?
- Note if there are knocks (water hammer) when faucets are opened and closed rapidly.
- Note any fixtures with galvanized iron piping or kinked lines (copper).

### PIPING

#### Inlet Service
- If water is supplied by a utility company,

locate the inlet pipe and the water meter, if any.
- Is the inlet pipe made of iron, brass, copper, or lead?
- If inlet pipe is lead, take a water sample for analysis.
- Is there a master shutoff valve? Check its operation.

### Distribution Piping (Supply Mains/Fixture Risers)
- Are these pipes copper, brass, galvanized iron, plastic, or a combination?
- Are there signs of leakage, patched, or corroding pipe sections or valves?
- If system is basically brass, note any mineral deposits along the underside of pipe runs or around threaded joints.
- Pipes located in an unheated area such as a crawl space, garage, and so on, may be vulnerable to freezing and should be insulated.
- Are any pipes sweating?
- Are any pipes improperly supported?
- Are hot and cold water lines adequately spaced apart?

### Drainage Pipes
- These pipes are generally made out of cast iron, galvanized iron, copper, lead, or plastic.
- Look for low points or sagging sections where solid wastes can accumulate.
- Are any visible drainage lines improperly pitched?
- Note any signs of leaking, cracked, or patched sections.

## WELL-PUMPING SYSTEMS
- Have a water sample analyzed for possible contamination.
- Is there a deep- or shallow-type well?
- Is well pump a piston, jet, or submersible type?
- Do you know the design criteria (gallons/minute) of the system?
- Are installation records and recorded flow available?

### Accessory Equipment
- Is storage tank insulated?
- Are there signs of rust or corroding areas?
- Does tank contain a pressure-relief valve?
- Is pressure gauge operational?
- When system is active (pumping), note the pressure differential.
- Does the pressure exceed 65 psi?
- Does gauge fluctuate rapidly or does pump cycle on and off?
- Does system hold its pressure when all faucets are shut and there are no house plumbing leaks?

# 14. HEATING SYSTEMS I

**H**eating systems fall into two principal categories, central heating systems and area heaters. In a central heating system, warm air, hot water, or steam is generated in one location of the house and is distributed through ducts or pipes to heat other portions of the house. An area heater, on the other hand, is basically a space heater and is used to provide warmth to the room in which it is located—as in the case of a fireplace or potbelly stove. The area heaters of today, however, are much more sophisticated and are equipped with temperature and safety controls.

The principal fuels and energy source used in heating systems are gas, oil, and electricity. To some extent coal, wood, and solar energy are also used for heating residential structures.

## CENTRAL HEATING SYSTEMS

Most of the homes in the United States have central heating systems. The basic components of these systems are:

1. A burner for converting gas or oil to heat or a resistance coil for converting electrical energy to heat.
2. A heat exchanger for transferring this heat to the air or water. When the heat exchanger is used to produce warm air, it is called a "furnace." When it produces hot water or steam, it is called a "boiler." Because many people have unknowingly been calling a boiler a furnace, the term *furnace* is pretty much the generic name for the heat exchanger.
3. A distribution system consisting of ducts or pipes for conveying the warm air, hot water, or steam to the various parts of the house.
4. Heat outlets such as registers (vents) or radiators for transferring heat into the room.
5. Automatic safety and temperature controls.

A central heating system will provide heat to the rooms throughout the house and, in some cases, to the nonhabitable areas such as the garage and/or unfinished basement. In many cases, the system can be extended to provide heat to additions or modifications to the house such as a finished attic or a new dormer. Whether or not the heating system can be extended will depend on its heating capacity and the configuration of the distribution system. If you are thinking about extending the heating system of the house that you are inspecting, you should consult a professional to determine its feasibility.

One advantage of central heating is that the distribution system can be designed so that the house is divided into separate heating areas called "zones." A multizoned house is more economical and more efficient to heat. Zoning is used to maintain the same or different temperatures in various parts of the house. Only those rooms that require it need be heated. Zone control is automatic. Each zone has a thermostat control that opens and closes valves for hot water and steam systems or dampers for a warm air system. If the house that you are inspecting was originally designed with only one heating zone and you are considering converting it to a multizone system, have the conversion plans checked out by a professional. The configuration of the distribution system may be such that conversion to a multizone system is not economically justifiable. The breakeven point on your investment (cost versus fuel savings) can take many years.

One of the problems of a central heating system is that of distributing the heat evenly to all parts of the house. The larger the house, the more difficult it is to obtain an even distribution. Often the registers or radiators farthest from the furnace/boiler do not supply as much heat as those that are closest. Minimizing this problem is called "balancing the heating system" and requires the use of dampers for warm air systems, throttling valves for hot water systems, and certain types of air valves for steam systems. Balancing the heating system to your family's requirements is best performed after living in the house for a while. It may be that the system is already properly balanced for your needs and requires no further adjustment. Balancing is discussed in this chapter in the sections pertaining to the various systems.

## HEATING OUTLETS—REGISTERS AND RADIATORS

The most effective location in a room for forced warm air supply registers and hot water and steam radiators is along the exterior wall near windows or doors. This enables the heated air to mix with the cold air that very often infiltrates into the interior through the joints around the windows and doors. Of course, if the joints are properly caulked and weatherstripped, the air infiltration on a cold, windy day will be minimized. Most homes, however, are not adequately caulked and weatherstripped. (See section on caulking and weatherstripping in Chapter 18.) The mixing of warm air with the cold air around the exterior walls will eliminate cold spots, reduce drafts, and produce a more uniform heat distribution within the room. If the registers or radiators in the house that you are inspecting are not located along the exterior walls in any of the rooms, then the overall heat distribution in those rooms may be less than what you consider desirable.

All central heating systems have advantages and limitations. If you feel that the type of heating system is critical to your decision on whether or not to buy the house, then these advantages and limitations are important. Your decision, however, should be based on fact and not hearsay. I have had many clients tell me that they would only consider a house heated with a hot water system because a warm air system is "too dry." Well, all heating systems are "too dry" unless the air is intentionally humidified. I have been in homes heated with a hot water system where the humidity was less than 10 percent, and I have also been in homes heated with warm, humidified air where the humidity was over 30 percent. Since a hot water system does not have ducts, the house cannot be humidified from a central location as with a warm air system. The advantages and limitations of various heating systems are discussed later in this chapter.

## THERMOSTAT AND MASTER SHUTOFF

There are many types of controls for heating systems. The ones most familiar to homeowners are the thermostat and the master shutoff. The thermostat is used to automatically turn on or shut down the heating system on an as-needed basis. It is a temperature-sensitive switch that normally operates at low voltage (24 volts), although some operate at line voltage (110 volts). As the temperature drops below the thermostat setting, contacts within the thermostat close, activating the heating system. When the temperature in the room containing the thermostat rises above the setting, the contacts open, shutting down the heating system.

In some thermostats, the contacts are exposed to air and dust and should be cleaned periodically. Otherwise, a dust layer can form on the contacts that can prevent them from operating properly. Over the years, the contacts in some thermostats become worn because of cleaning and no longer close properly. In this case, the thermostats require replacement. In newer-type thermostats, the contacts are encased in a glass enclosure or have been replaced by a sealed mercury switch.

In a house with a multizoned heating system, each zone will be controlled by a thermostat. The placement of the thermostat is quite important. Since the thermostat will sense only the temperature in the surrounding area, the placement of the thermostat must be such that the temperature in that area is representative of the temperature for the entire house or for that zone. The thermostat must never be placed in a draft or in an area where air circulation is blocked.

Research has indicated that by lowering the thermostat setting five to ten degrees at night prior to going to sleep and resetting it in the morning, you can save 5 to 15 percent of your fuel bill, depending on your geographical location. If you want to take advantage of these savings but feel that you may forget to lower the thermostat setting each night, you can replace the regular thermostat with a clock thermostat. A clock thermostat will automatically lower the temperature setting each night and raise it each morning. From a convenience point of view, a clock thermostat is very worthwhile. If the house that you are inspecting does not have a clock thermostat, you should consider its installation. Some units allow for a double setback, which is useful in houses that are empty during the day.

Every heating system should have at least one master shutoff switch. Usually, the switch is located near the furnace or boiler. Sometimes the switch is located at the top of the stairs that lead to the basement. In the event of a problem with the heating system, this switch can be used as an emergency shutoff for the burner. The switch is also used by a repairman when servicing the system. By turning the master switch off, no one can inadvertently turn the heating system on by raising the thermostat.

## WARM AIR SYSTEMS

In this system, air heated in a furnace travels via supply ducts to the rooms to be heated. The warm air enters the rooms and is discharged through wall or floor registers and/or ceiling diffusers. The cooler air in the room, being displaced by the heated air, travels through return ducts back to the furnace, where it is reheated and recirculated. If the system does not have cold air return ducts, the cold air travels back to the furnace via gravity. Usually the stairway allows the cold air to travel to the first floor and grilles in the floor of the first level then allows it to recirculate to the furnace. Of course, doors must be open to permit the air movement. Where doors are closed, the heat will rise in a very restricted manner.

The air in a warm air system can be supplied to the furnace by recirculating heated air through ducts or by drawing in cool air from the basement. The latter method is seldom, if ever, used for modern warm air systems because of the heating inefficiency. Since the temperature of the basement air is lower than the temperature of the recirculated air, more fuel will be required to heat it to the desired temperature.

Although this method of supplying air to the system is, for the most part, no longer used, it will still be found in many older systems. You can easily spot it. Look for a large opening in the furnace casing. Do not confuse the opening with that belonging to the fan compartment of a forced warm air system. The fan compartment is normally covered. Sometimes, however, the cover is removed for performing minor maintenance and is not replaced. In this case, the open fan compartment will also draw in cool basement air—but that is not the design intention.

There is only one condition under which a furnace must be replaced: when the walls in the heat exchanger that separate the circulating air from the hot exhaust gases deteriorate because of age, premature corrosion, or cracks, and thus allow the exhaust gases to mix with the circulating air. Included in the exhaust gases are carbon monoxide and unburned gas (when furnace is gas-fired), which are poisonous. The mixture of air and exhaust gases circulating around the house is quite dangerous. The life expectancy of a furnace refers to the average number of years of usage that can be expected before the walls of the heat exchanger deteriorate. For many modern furnaces, the projected life is between fifteen and twenty years, although some older ones have been safely operational for well over thirty years.

## Advantages

Warm air systems have an advantage over other types of heating systems in that the air in the house can be cleaned (dust particles removed by filtering) and humidified. Most systems use either inexpensive, disposable filters or permanent-type filters that require periodic washing. Some systems utilize an electronic filter, which is very effective in removing dust and pollen from the air.

Not all warm air furnaces are equipped with a humidifier for adding moisture to the circulating air. If you do not see any during your inspection, you should consider installing one. The humidifier may be mounted in the main return or supply duct and is usually located near the furnace. Humidifiers such as the evaporative-plate or wick type add some moisture to the circulating air. However, they are not totally effective. A more positive introduction of moisture into the air stream can be achieved with a power spray humidifier that is controlled by a humidity-sensing device.

Additional advantages of a warm air system are:

1. Adaptability to a central air-conditioning system. (See Chapter 17.) The distribution ducts and the furnace blower can be used to circulate the cool air. This results in a considerable cost savings when installing a central cooling system.

2. There are no distribution pipes to freeze and burst. Consequently, if the heating system is not operational for several days during the winter months, as would be the case in the event of an extended power failure, there would be no need to worry about the distribution system freezing (a condition that can occur with a hot water heating system). Of course, regardless of the type of heating system, during an extended power failure, the domestic water pipes are vulnerable to freezing.

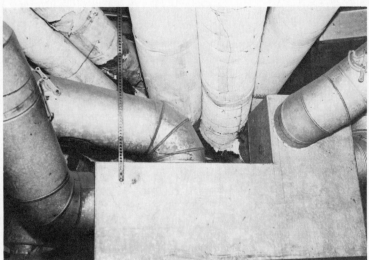

FIGURE 14-1  *Left:* Old "octopus" warm air furnace. System was converted from gravity type to forced warm air by installing a blower unit, which is located in the black casing on left side. *Right:* Heat supply ducts at top portion of "octopus" furnace.

3. The replacement cost for a new warm air furnace is less than the replacement cost for a new hot water or steam boiler.

## Disadvantages

1. The major disadvantage of a warm air system is that, in the event of a faulty heat exchanger, the exhaust gases will mix with the circulating air and be distributed around the house.
2. In a multizoned warm air heating system, the zones are not totally independent of one another. The zones are controlled by motorized dampers that are located in the ducts. When the dampers are closed, they block the air flow in their respective ducts, preventing that portion of the house from being heated. However, some air will always flow around the closed damper, decreasing the overall efficiency of operation. In quality-constructed homes, zone control is often obtained by using two separate furnaces with separate distribution systems rather than by using motorized dampers.

Warm air systems are classified by the type of air movement—gravity or forced.

## Gravity Warm Air

A gravity warm air system is a very simple system that is often found in older homes. Generally,

the furnace is quite large and often looks like a mechanical "octopus" with many ducts sticking out of the upper portion. (See Figure 14-1.) There are no moving parts, motors, or electrical connections other than those required for the thermostat and burner control. The basic principle of operation is the fact that warm air rises and, as it does, it displaces the cool air which, in turn, results in air circulation.

The heat distribution in a house heated by a warm air gravity system is often less than desirable. In order to obtain a uniform heat distribution, there must be good air circulation. And, in order to have good circulation, there must be a considerable temperature difference between the warm air entering the room and the cooler air in the room. As the room begins to warm up, the temperature difference decreases, thereby reducing the air circulation.

The cooler air returning to the furnace is drawn into the return duct by a natural draft that is the result of thermal air currents. The moving air does not have much force. Consequently, there will usually not be a filter in this system for cleaning the air. The resistance offered by a filter (especially a dirty one) is often enough to block the air flow.

Although a gravity warm air system is considered obsolete, it can be updated to a forced warm air system by installing a blower unit (fan and motor assembly). For the most part, the old gravity systems are quite rugged and can last for many years. I have seen many units that are over fifty years old. They are usually made of heavy-gauge cast iron or steel and can probably be used for many more years—assuming that efficiency of operation is not a consideration. As mentioned earlier, the only time a furnace must be replaced is when there is a crack in the heat exchanger that allows the exhaust gases to mix with the circulating air.

### Forced Warm Air

Because it is economical to install and because of its versatility, the forced warm air heating system is found in more homes than any other central heating systems. The basic difference between this system and the gravity warm air system is a blower in the heat exchanger that circulates the warm air. Since the warm air is distributed under a draft, comfort heating can be achieved at lower furnace

FIGURE 14-2   Warm air distribution systems. *Top:* Extended plenum. *Bottom:* Radial.

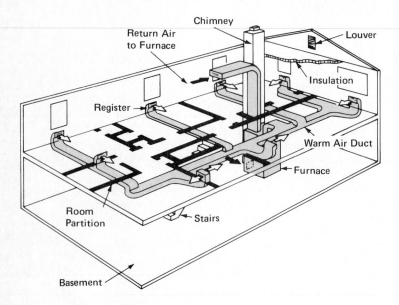

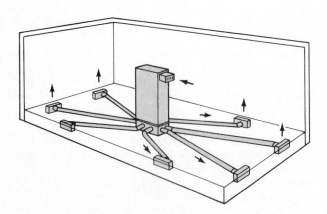

temperatures with a lower fuel consumption. In addition, the supply and return ducts need not be as large as those of a gravity system.

### Controls

There are three basic controls for this system: a thermostat, a fan control, and a high-temperature limit control. The thermostat has been discussed earlier in this chapter. The purpose of the fan controller is to prevent the fan from circulating cool air around the house. The fan control is a temperature-sensitive switch that turns on and shuts off the blower at preset air temperatures. It is independent of the thermostat. When the thermostat calls for heat, only the burners should fire. The fan should not begin to operate. If it does, the fan controller is either faulty or in need of adjustment. After the heat exchanger warms up to a temperature of about 110° F. to 120° F., the fan should begin to operate. When the temperature setting on the thermostat is satisfied, the thermostat will shut off the burner but not the fan. The fan will continue to operate until the temperature in the heat exchanger drops to about 85° F.

In the event that the heat exchanger gets too hot, the high-temperature limit control will shut off the burner. The limit control is usually set at about 175° F. For proper operation, the fan should begin to operate before the burners are shut by the limit control. Otherwise, the temperature of the air discharging from the registers will be too high for comfort heating.

### Distribution Systems

There are two basic configurations used for the distribution of a forced warm air heating system—the extended plenum and the radial configuration. (See Figure 14-2.) Regardless of the configuration, there should always be a physical separation of the furnace at the beginning of the duct. The separate sections are usually connected by a heavy canvas fabric. (See Figure 14-3.) The separation is intended to isolate the distribution system from the furnace so that blower noise will not be transmitted throughout the house.

In the extended plenum configuration, a large rectangular supply duct extends in a straight line from the plenum mounted on the furnace. From this main duct, branch ducts are taken off to supply warm air to the various rooms. The large supply duct results in less resistance to air flow and produces a more effective heat distribution for those rooms farthest from the furnace.

In the radial configuration, there is no main supply duct. Each branch duct takes off directly from the plenum and runs to the individual room registers. This system is usually found in smaller houses.

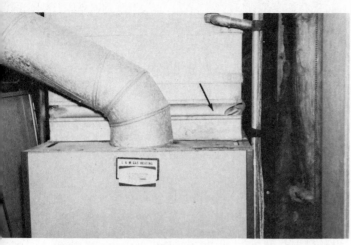

FIGURE 14-3 Canvas fabric cover (*arrow*) over the separation between the furnace and the main duct. The physical separation isolates the distribution system from noises and vibrations that may develop in the furnace.

A variation on the radial configuration is the perimeter loop duct arrangement, which is intended for basementless houses built on a slab. This configuration uses a duct that encircles the perimeter of the floor slab and is connected to the furnace by feeder ducts. (See Figure 14-4.)

The branch supply ducts for both the extended plenum and the radial configuration will either be rectangular or round. The round ducts are usually relatively small in diameter (4 to 6 inches), have a higher resistance to air flow, and are normally not used for air conditioning. (Do not confuse these ducts with the insulated flexible ducts used in many central air-conditioning systems.)

The return duct for both configurations is usually made of sheetmetal and has a rectangular cross-section. However, in some homes with basements, you may find that a portion of the return duct has been formed using a section of the overhead wood framing. This is done by covering the channel that is formed by adjacent joists with sheetmetal. (See Figure 14-5.)

### Supply Registers and Return Grille

As discussed earlier, the most effective location for the warm air supply registers is along the outside walls. If the supply register is not located along the outside wall, and often it is not, then the location of the return grille will be important for developing a uniform heat distribution. For optimum distribution, warm air entering the room from the supply register circulates around the room and then leaves through the return grille. If the return grille is located on the same wall as or on a wall adjacent to the supply register, then there will be a

short cycle of the air circulation, which reduces its effectiveness. In this case, warm air discharging from the supply register can be drawn into the return grille before it has a chance to circulate.

During your inspection, you should look for either separate return grilles for each room or a centrally located return grille for each floor. When there is a separate return for each room, the grille should be located on the wall opposite the supply register. If there is a centrally located return, the supply register should be located on the wall that is farthest from the door. This will provide a better circulation, as the air will flow through the door opening. Also, in this case, about 1 inch should be cut off the bottom of the door to allow for air movement while the door is closed.

Balancing the warm air flow for your personal needs can best be accomplished after you move into the house. The various supply ducts will have dampers that can vary the air flow. By reducing the flow to the registers closest to the furnace, more warm air will flow to the registers farthest from the furnace. In addition, each register will have dampers that can be used for further restricting and "fine tuning" the air flow.

### Heat Pump

Central heating using a heat pump is basically the same as a forced warm air system. However, the means by which the furnace is heated differs. The heating element is not a gas or oil burner, but a component of a reversed cycle air-conditioning system. The heat pump system is discussed in detail in Chapter 17.

## HOT WATER SYSTEMS

This system operates on the principle of circulation and recirculation. Water, heated in a boiler, is

FIGURE 14-4 Perimeter loop duct arrangement—a variation on the radial configuration.

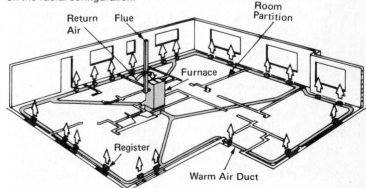

FIGURE 14-5 Return duct for warm air heating system. The duct was made by enclosing the channel formed by adjacent ceiling joists with a sheetmetal covering. Usually found in older systems.

transmitted through pipes to radiators located throughout the house. At the radiators, the hot water gives up some of its heat. The cooler water then continues to flow back to the boiler, where it is reheated and recirculated.

In this system, the boiler, distribution piping, and all of the radiators are completely filled with water. Water, when heated, will expand, increasing its overall volume. Consequently, all hot water heating systems must be equipped with an expansion tank to temporarily store the increased water volume. When the system is shut and the circulating water cools, the volume decreases, drawing the water back from the expansion tank. Without such a tank, excessive pressures could be built up in the system, which could rupture the distribution pipes and fittings.

The water circulating within the heating system operates under a pressure that normally ranges from 12 to 22 psi. Although the water is constantly recirculating and there is no need for additional water, an automatic water feed device is provided with all systems, as a precautionary measure. The automatic water feed device is a pressure-reducing valve. The water supply to the boiler is taken from the house water supply. Since the house supply pressure is normally in a range of from 30 to 60 psi, it must be reduced before being introduced into the boiler. The reducing valve is usually preset by the manufacturer to 12 psi.

There are two basic types of hot water heating systems—gravity and forced. They are classified as to the means by which the water within the system circulates.

## Gravity Hot Water

As with the gravity warm air heating system, the gravity hot water system is inefficient, not very responsive to changing demands for heat, and is no longer installed in new construction. However, it may be found in many older homes. The principle of operation is also similar to that of a gravity warm air system: As the water is heated, it becomes lighter than the cooler water and tends to rise. Since the system is filled with water, as the hot water rises, it displaces the cooler water, forcing it to return to the boiler for reheating, and thus induces circulation. In order to keep the resistance to flow at a minimum, the size of the distribution piping is relatively large—about 3 inches in diameter—as compared to the distribution piping in a forced system—which is about 1 inch in diameter.

Gravity systems may also be classified by whether they are "open" or "closed." In an open system, the expansion tank has an overflow pipe that is open to the atmosphere. The expansion tank must be located above the highest radiator in order to ensure that the radiator will be filled with water. It is usually found in the attic with the overflow pipe extending through the roof or side of the building. (See Figure 14-6.) If the attic has been partitioned off into rooms, the expansion tank may be found in a closet or corner. When the tank is located in an unfinished, unheated area, it must be insu-

FIGURE 14-6 Expansion tank for "open" gravity hot water system located in attic.

lated to minimize heat loss and also as protection against freezing should the system malfunction.

Hot water and steam heating systems are normally equipped with automatic pressure-relief valves that discharge when the pressure exceeds 30 psi and 15 psi respectively. A relief valve, however, is not needed in an open gravity hot water system because if the pressure should build up to a point where it exceeds the design pressure, the water will simply discharge through the overflow pipe in the expansion tank.

In the closed system, no portion of the expansion tank is open to the atmosphere. In this case, the expansion tank can be located anywhere in the system. It is, however, usually located near the boiler. Because the system is closed, it can operate at higher pressures and, therefore, higher temperatures without turning to steam. The higher temperatures permit the use of smaller radiators.

There are two types of expansion tanks used in closed systems—air cushion and diaphragm. In the air-cushion type, air is initially trapped in the tank to provide a cushion, which is compressed as the water in the heating system expands and enters the tank. Over the years, the air in the tank can be absorbed by the water resulting in a "waterlogged" expansion tank. In this case, when the heating system is turned on, since there is no room for expansion, the pressure will increase rapidly until the relief valve discharges. When this happens, the expansion tank must be flushed and the air cushion reinstalled.

In order to eliminate "waterlogging," the diaphragm expansion tank was developed. This tank uses a rubber diaphragm to separate the air cushion from the water. For the most part, the diaphragm does eliminate waterlogging. However, there are cases where the diaphragm is faulty and waterlogging does occur.

If the heating system in the house that you are inspecting is gravity hot water, do not fret. It can be converted into a forced hot water system by installing a centrifugal pump with the associated controls to circulate the water through the distribution pipes and radiators. If the system is the open type, the expansion tank will have to be replaced with a closed tank.

## Forced Hot Water

Quite often, my clients comment on the small size of the boiler for the forced hot water system. They apparently had been used to seeing a boiler that was originally designed for use in a gravity system or one that was converted from coal-fired to oil- or gas-fired, both of which are considerably larger—two to six times as large, depending on the

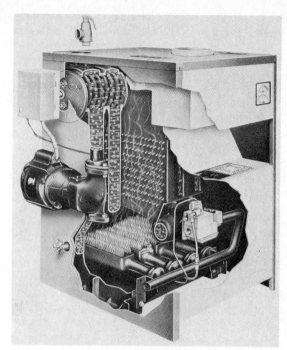

FIGURE 14-7   Boiler for forced hot water heating system. Note the circulating pump. *(Courtesy U.S. Department of Agriculture)*

manufacturer. Regardless of the size, you can easily recognize a forced hot water heating system by the presence of a circulating pump in the distribution return pipe just before the connection to the boiler. (See Figure 14-7.)

### *Boilers*

The boilers used in these systems will be made of either cast iron or steel. You can often tell the composition of the boiler by initials on the name plate. Most cast-iron boilers are stamped "IBR" (Institute of Boilers and Radiator Manufacturers) and most steel boilers are stamped "SBI" (Steel Boiler Institute). Cast-iron boilers are more resistant to corrosion than are steel boilers and thus have a longer projected life. The projected life span of a modern cast-iron boiler is about twenty-five to thirty years. However, many of the boiler manufacturers will only provide a twenty-year warranty. The older gravity-type boilers were probably made with a heavier gauge metal. I have inspected many that were over fifty years old and still going strong. (See Figure 14-8.) Steel boilers, being vulnerable to corrosion, have a shorter projected life, usually about twenty years. I have seen a number of steel boilers that required replacement after fifteen years.

Other than for reasons of efficiency and economy, the only time a boiler must be replaced is when a leak has developed that cannot be effectively patched. Sometimes, just after firing a boiler that has not been operational for a day or more, you may see a slight amount of water dripping into the firebox (assuming that the firebox is accessible for visual inspection). This is often the result of condensation caused by cold water circulating into the boiler or by some slight joint movement. As the boiler heats up, the various sections tend to move slightly. In some cases, this results in a slightly open joint that allows water to drip out. However, as the sections continue to heat up they expand, compressing the joint and sealing the leak. Although this condition is usually not a problem, if you should see water dripping into the firebox, it would be best to have the condition checked by a professional.

On occasion, I have found a regular tank type domestic water heater (the type described in Chapter 16) being used in the heating system in place of a boiler. From a safety point of view, this is acceptable because there is a high-temperature and pressure control along with a thermocouple control for the gas valve. However, water heaters have a projected life of from seven to ten years and are often

FIGURE 14-8 Old cast-iron boiler with new oil burner. Boiler had been converted from a coal burner.

guaranteed by the manufacturer for only five years. In addition, with the exception of those homes located in the sun belt, the BTU (heat) output of these units per hour is less than that needed to adequately heat most homes. This type of setup may be effective for heating an addition to a house where the existing heating system cannot be extended. The only drawback, in this case, is the short projected life of the water heater.

### Advantages and Disadvantages

Because the forced hot water heating system operates under pressure, with the water being circulated by means of a pump, it is very flexible. It can be used to heat an area below the level of the boiler. Additional, completely independent heating zones can be readily installed. Because the hot water remains in the pipes after the boiler is no longer being heated, there is less heat fluctuation and more of an even temperature distribution. Also, the operation of this system is relatively quiet.

One of the disadvantages of this system is that with water in the pipes, the distribution system is vulnerable to freezing temperatures. In the event of an extended power failure or if an oil-fired boiler runs out of oil for several days during a cold spell, the pipes can freeze and burst. I know of several cases where antifreeze was introduced into the circulating water to prevent that type of a problem. In addition, this system is not adaptable to central conditioning of the air such as cooling, humidifying, and filtering.

### Distribution Piping

There are three basic types of distribution piping arrangements for forced hot water heating systems: series loop, one-pipe, and two-pipe arrangements. The specific distribution system installed usually depends on the size and the cost of the house.

**Series Loop** This is the simplest and least expensive piping arrangement to install. It is usually used in smaller homes where room-by-room radiator adjustments are not needed for balancing the heat distribution. In a series loop, the radiators, which are usually baseboard convectors, are an integral part of the supply piping. (See Figure 14-9.) If a radiator were to be shut off, the flow throughout the system would be stopped. In this arrangement, the temperature of the water entering the last radiator will be considerably less than when it enters the first radiator. In order to minimize the difference in temperature and to produce a more uniform heat distribution, the heating system for larger homes is often designed so that the house is divided into two or more heating zones. Each zone

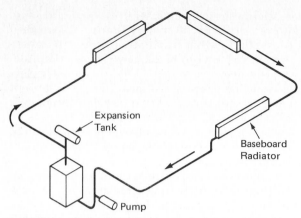

FIGURE 14-9 Series loop piping configuration for forced hot water heating system.

has a separate piping configuration and either has a separate circulating pump or it shares a common circulating pump with the other zone(s), but has a separate thermostatically controlled valve in the main supply pipe.

**One Pipe** In a one-pipe distribution configuration, as with the series loop, a single pipe makes a complete circuit from the boiler and back again, serving as both the supply and the return. In this case, however, rather than the radiators being integral with the supply pipe, they are attached to it by two risers, one connected to each end of the radiator. (See Figure 14-10.) Each radiator will also have a shutoff valve located at the inlet riser. In this case, each radiator can be shut without affecting the water flow in the supply main. Consequently, this system can provide room-by-room heat control. However, as with the series loop, there is a considerable temperature difference between the water entering the first and last radiators. To compensate for the cooler water entering the radiators downstream, larger radiators are often installed. They emit an amount of heat comparable to the smaller ones closer to the boiler.

**Two Pipe** The two-pipe distribution configuration is the most costly to install, but it overcomes the deficiencies of the other configurations. In this case, there are two main pipes—one for the supply and the other for the return. The inlet and outlet ports of the radiators are attached to the mains by risers. (See Figure 14-11.) The cool water leaving the radiator does not mix with the hot water flowing through the supply main, so the temperature difference between the water entering the first and last radiator is small.

Even though both the one- and two-pipe configurations will provide heat control for individual

rooms if the radiator shutoff valve is manually closed or partially closed, the configurations are also often used in homes with zone heating. Zone heating is automatic. All that has to be done is to set the thermostat to the desired temperature for that portion of the house.

### Radiators

As discussed previously, the optimum location for a radiator is along an outside wall, preferably near or under a window. There are three basic types of radiators found in hot-water heating systems— freestanding cast iron, freestanding convector, and baseboard convector. Freestanding cast-iron radiators are mostly found in older homes. Unless an old home is being restored, a freestanding radiator is usually considered undesirable. Many clients have asked whether or not the radiators can be replaced with the newer finned-tube baseboard radiators. Yes, they can. Baseboard convector radiators are usually preferred because they distribute the heat better than cast-iron or freestanding convector radiators and are less conspicuous. They achieve an even temperature throughout the room because they distribute the heat near the floor. Natural convection causes the heated air to rise and warm the outside wall.

### Panel Heating

Another method of heating using a forced hot water system is to imbed the distribution piping into the walls, floors, and/or ceilings and let those areas (panels) function as radiators. (See Figure 14-

FIGURE 14-10 One-pipe distribution configuration for forced hot water heating system.

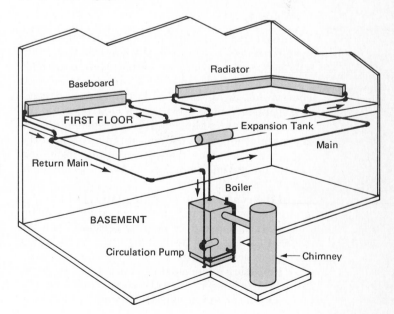

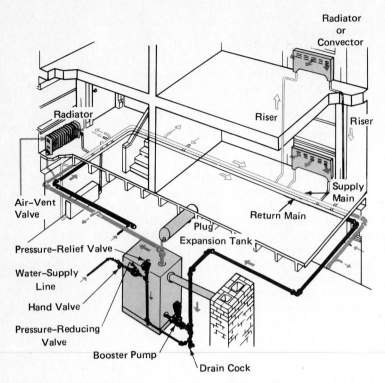

FIGURE 14-11  Two-pipe distribution configuration for forced hot water heating system.

12.) In this case, the heat from the distribution piping is conducted to the surface of the panels that, in turn, heats the room by radiation and convection. This system produces a very uniform temperature distribution and is particularly effective when the heating panel is the floor slab in a basementless house.

### Controls

In addition to the thermostat, hot water heating systems have safety and operational controls. In a simple forced hot water heating system without individual zones, there is a high-temperature limit control that prevents the boiler water from exceeding a preset temperature and a controller for the circulating pump. Depending on the system design, the circulating pump can operate in any one of the following three modes: constant-running circulator, aquastat-controlled circulator, and relay-controlled circulator.

In the constant-running circulator, the pump is energized by a manual power switch and operates continuously during the heating season. When the thermostat calls for heat, it fires the burner that heats the boiler. When the heating season is over, the circulating pump must be manually shut. Sometimes, the homeowner forgets to shut the pump and, as a result, the pump runs all summer. This type of operation is somewhat wasteful of electrical energy. However, this wastefulness must be weighed against the fact that intermittently operated circulating pumps tend to break down sooner than continuously operated pumps. The constant starting and stopping causes the bearings to wear out sooner. A constant-operating circulating pump is the least expensive to install because there is no relay or temperature controller. If desired, it can be converted to either one—the aquastat-controlled or the relay-controlled.

In the aquastat-controlled circulator mode, as with the constant-running circulator, the thermostat will only control the burner. When the boiler water reaches a preset temperature (approximately 120° F.), the circulator pump begins to operate. After the thermostat is satisfied and shuts the burner, the circulator continues to operate until the water temperature drops below the temperature setting of the circulator control. In the relay-controlled mode, the thermostat simultaneously activates the burner and the circulating pump. When the thermostat is satisfied, it will simultaneously shut the burner and the circulating pump.

**Zone Control**  Heating zones in a forced hot water system can have a separate circulating pump for each zone or a single circulating pump that services all the zones. When there is a single pump, each zone is controlled by an electrically activated valve that is, in turn, controlled by a thermostat. When one of the zone thermostats calls for heat, it opens the respective zone valve, fires the burner that heats the boiler water, and starts the circulating pump. After the system is operational, if another zone thermostat calls for heat, it merely opens the zone valve. This allows the hot water to circulate through that zone.

When there are separate circulating pumps for each zone, the first thermostat calling for heat will fire the burner and activate the pump. Thereafter, as long as the system is operational, other thermostats calling for heat will merely activate their

FIGURE 14-12  Forced hot water radiant heating panels.

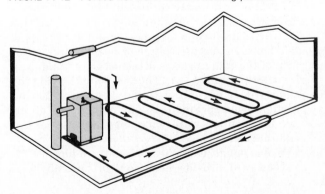

respective circulating pumps.

**Domestic Water Heater** Most boilers used in hot water heating systems can be equipped so that they will also heat the domestic water (water used for washing and bathing). This is discussed in detail in Chapter 16. When a heating system boiler produces domestic hot water, the associated burner must fire all year long and not just for the heating season. In this case, the thermostat does not control the burner. It only controls the circulating pump. The burner is activated by an aquastat that controls the boiler water temperature.

Since the boiler will have hot water during those periods when heat is not required, a flow control valve must be installed on the supply main. This valve prevents the hot water from rising up into the distribution piping and heating the house like a gravity hot water system. When heat is required, the circulating pump produces sufficient force to lift the flow control valve and circulate the hot water. In a multizoned system, if zone valves are used, then flow control valves are not needed. When the zone valves are closed, water will not circulate in the distribution piping.

**Relief Valve** Every forced hot water heating system must be equipped with an automatic pressure-relief valve as a safety control. To help ensure its effectiveness, the relief valve should be mounted directly on the boiler. Many systems have a relief valve that is mounted in the boiler feed line several feet away from the boiler. This is an improper location because over the years, the relief valve can become isolated from the boiler as a result of a lime or scale buildup in the feed line. If this should happen, the valve would be completely ineffective in the event of a pressure buildup. If the heating system that you are inspecting does not have a boiler-mounted relief valve, you should have one installed.

**Pressure/Temperature Gauge** Although not a safety or operational control, all forced hot water heating systems should have a pressure and a temperature gauge. Newer systems have a combination gauge that measures both pressure and temperature. In older systems, you will probably find a separate pressure gauge and a pencil-type thermometer attached to the boiler. The combination gauge often has two pressure scales, one in pounds per square inch (psi) and the other in altitude (feet of a column of water). The altitude scale can basically be ignored, although for your information, one psi is equivalent to a column of water measuring 2.31 feet high. The normal fill pressure of the boiler is 12 psi. This, then, is equivalent to an altitude of 27.7 feet. If the highest radiator in your house is more than 27.7 feet above the boiler, then a higher boiler water

pressure will be needed. Some pressure gauges have two points—one fixed and one movable. The fixed pointer is usually positioned over the normal altitude setting for that house. The movable pointer shows the actual working pressure of the heating system. If this pressure should exceed 30 psi, the relief valve will discharge.

## STEAM HEATING SYSTEMS

For the most part, steam heating systems are no longer used in new residential construction. You will find them, however, in older homes. In fact, in some of these homes, the boiler and its associated controls may be relatively new. The boiler used in this system is basically the same as is used in a hot water system. It will be made of either cast iron or steel. (See the discussion on boilers on pages 125–126.) You can tell whether a boiler is being used for a steam system or a hot water system by the type of controls and gauges used. A quick indication is to look for a water-level gauge. (See Figure 14-15, page 131.) If you see such a gauge, the boiler is being used to generate steam.

Unlike the hot water system that is completely filled with water, the steam boiler is only partially—about three quarters—filled with water, depending on the size and make. The remaining portion of the boiler, the distribution piping, and the radiators will be filled with air. After the system is fired, the water heats up until it actually boils, as in a tea kettle. The steam thus formed rises in the pipes of its own accord without the aid of a fan or pump, pushing the air ahead of it as it moves along. The air from the pipes and radiators is then dissipated into the rooms through air vent valves that, depending on the piping configuration, are located on the radiator or near the end of the steam main.

When the steam comes into contact with the cool radiator surface, it condenses back into water and, in the process, gives up its heat. The resulting water then flows back to the boiler for reheating. If, because of a blockage in an air vent (often the result of painting the vent), the air cannot be evacuated from a radiator, a pressure will be built up within the radiator that will prevent the steam from entering. In this case, the radiator will be ineffective, as it will not heat up. This condition can be easily corrected by replacing the air vent.

### Distribution Piping

There are two basic distribution piping configurations used with steam heating systems—one pipe and two pipe. You can easily tell which configuration is being used by the number of pipes connected to the radiator. It is as simple as counting one, two.

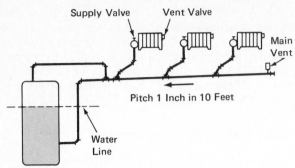

FIGURE 14-13 One-pipe distribution configuration for steam heating system.

In a one-pipe configuration, there is only one pipe connected to the radiator; in a two-pipe configuration, there are two. In a one-pipe arrangement, the steam is distributed to the various radiators through the same pipe that carries the condensate back to the boiler. (See Figure 14-13.)

The radiators used in this system must be pitched so that the condensate will flow back through the supply valve. Otherwise, the condensate can accumulate and block the steam flow. Each radiator will have a manually operated supply valve and an air vent. Some radiators are equipped with an air vent valve that has an adjustable opening. This opening can be increased or decreased in size, thus allowing the air in the radiators to be evacuated at a faster or slower rate. Adjustable air vents are often found in larger homes and are used as a means of providing a uniform steam supply to all of the radiators. Radiators closest to the boiler will receive steam before those that are farther away. In some cases, depending on the distance apart and the size of the radiator, those closest to the boiler can be fully heated before those farthest away receive any steam. By decreasing the vent opening on those radiators closest to the boiler and increasing the opening on those farthest away, it is possible for all of the radiators to receive steam at about the same time.

In a two-pipe configuration, the steam is supplied to the radiator by one pipe and the condensate returned to the boiler through another. The radiators in this system will not be equipped with individual air vent valves. They will have a steam trap on the condensate return pipe. A steam trap allows the air bound in the radiator and the condensate to flow in the return pipe, but closes on steam contact and does not allow the passage of steam. The air in the return line is then vented by a main vent. If desired, a two-pipe steam heating system can be converted to a forced hot water system. This cannot be done with a one-pipe steam system. In both one- and two-pipe systems, when the condensate is returned to the boiler, if the return line in the boiler room is above the boiler water level, it is called a "dry"

return. If the return line is below the boiler water level, it is called a "wet" return. When the system has a wet return, there should be a special piping arrangement at the boiler called a "Hartford loop." (See Figure 14-14.) The purpose of the Hartford loop is to prevent water from draining out of the boiler in the event of a leak in the wet-return piping. Should a leak occur in the return line, boiler water would drain down only until it reached the top of the Hartford loop. There would still be sufficient water to prevent damage to the boiler in the event that it continued to fire. If the heating system that you are inspecting has a wet return, look for a Hartford loop. If you do not see one, you should consider its installation.

### Controls

In addition to the thermostat, every steam heating system should have a high-pressure limit switch, a low-water cutoff, and an automatic pressure-relief valve. Also, in order to determine whether the boiler is operating properly, there should be a water-level gauge and a pressure gauge. (See Figure 14-15.) The high-pressure limit switch is connected electrically to the burner control. When the steam pressure exceeds a predetermined setting, the limit switch will shut down the burner, thereby preventing the pressure from building up further. The limit control should be physically connected to the boiler with a pipe that has a curl that looks like a pigtail. The pigtail has water in the bottom of the loop, which prevents the corrosive action of the steam from affecting the control

The low-water cutoff is a control that shuts down the burner when the level of the water in the boiler drops below the design level. There are two types

FIGURE 14-14 "Hartford loop" in the condensate return line of a steam heating system. The Hartford loop prevents water from draining out of the boiler in the event of a leak in the portion of the condensate return line that is below the boiler water level.

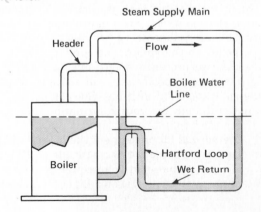

of low water controls—one that is mounted inside of the boiler and one that is externally mounted. The latter is preferred because it provides a convenient means for testing its operation. This unit has a blow-off valve that, when opened, will drop the water level in the control, causing it to operate. The manufacturer of this unit recommends that it be opened and blown down once each month to prevent a sludge accumulation that can affect its operation. All too often, homeowners neglect to perform this simple operation. I have checked many a unit that apparently had not been flushed in years; when I opened the blow-off valve, either nothing flowed out or there was a thick, dark-brown sludge oozing out. The units that are mounted in the boiler are self-cleaning and do not require any action on the part of the homeowner.

The water-level gauge provides a convenient means for determining the level of the water within the boiler. It is usually mounted on the side of the boiler; when there is an exterior-mounted low-water cutoff, it is often part of that assembly. The water level should be at the midpoint or two thirds of the way up the glass gauge. The exact position is not important. What is important is that you are able to see the water level. If the entire level gauge is filled with water, there is too much water in the system. In fact, it is possible that the system can be flooded. If too much water is introduced into the

FIGURE 14-15   Oil-fired steam boiler showing the level gauge, low-water cutoff, high-pressure limit switch, and pressure gauge. *(Courtesy Hydrotherm, Inc.)*

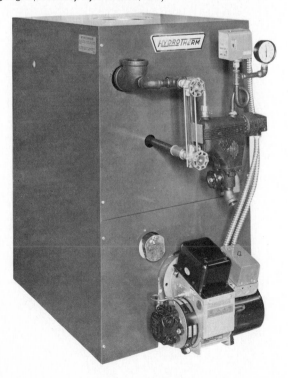

boiler, the water level will rise until it fills the entire distribution system and radiators. If any of the radiator valves or fittings are not watertight, and sometimes they are not, the water will leak out all over the room.

When there is no water visible in the gauge, water must be introduced into the boiler. This can be done by manually opening the fill valve in the water supply line. Some systems have an automatic boiler water feeder that introduces water to the required level on an as-needed basis. This is a desirable feature, but occasionally such units malfunction. Often level gauges are coated with sediment so that the water level is not visible. In this case, the glass gauge must be cleaned and all the accumulated sediment removed.

The relief valve is a safety valve that automatically discharges when the operating pressure exceeds the design pressure. For a residential steam heating system, the relief valve is set to discharge at 15 psi, although the normal operating pressure is considerably less, usually about 2 to 5 psi. Some large systems may even operate at a negative pressure (vacuum).

### Domestic Water Heater

As with hot water boilers, steam boilers can also be equipped for generating domestic hot water. When it does produce domestic hot water, the boiler must be fired all year long. During those months when heat is not required, the boiler water temperature is controlled by an aquastat. The aquastat activates the burner when the boiler water temperature drops below a preset figure and shuts off the burner when the boiler water temperature rises to about 200° F. When steam heat is required, the burner is activated by the thermostat. In this case, the thermostat overrides the aquastat control so that steam is produced.

In a forced hot water heating system that also produces domestic hot water, a flow control valve is needed in order to prevent the boiler water from circulating as a gravity system during those months when heat is not required. In a comparable steam system, no flow control valve or equivalent is necessary because the boiler water is not heated sufficiently to produce steam.

### Advantages and Disadvantages

The advantages of a steam heating system can be appreciated more in a large building than in a residential structure. It is a relatively simple system that does not require a pump or fan for circulation of the steam. Since there is no water in the pipes when the system is not operating, there is no problem of the pipes freezing and bursting. If a repair or replacement is needed to a section of pipe or a fitting, it is not necessary to drain the system. Also, if a steam leak should develop, it would result in very little water accumulation.

On the other hand, a steam system is slow in responding to an initial rapid change in heat demand because the boiler water temperature must be brought up to 212° F. before steam circulation begins. Unless the condensate is returned to the boiler by means of a pump, the boiler must be located below the radiator in the lowest rooms.

## HYBRID HEATING SYSTEMS

Depending on the extent to which the heating system has been modified or expanded, you may find a hybrid heating system in the house that you are inspecting. A hybrid system is one that is composed of two separate heating systems that are working together. As an example, I have seen the following systems.

*Steam/Hot Water.* This system functioned as a two-zoned system. The main portion of the house was heated by a steam heating system and the remaining portion of the house (the lower sections) was heated by a forced hot water system. The distribution pipe for the hot water system was tapped directly off the portion of the steam boiler that was below the water level and a pump was used to circulate the hot water. The thermostat for this zone controlled the pump and the burner. There was also an aquastat temperature control for the boiler water to keep it from generating steam when the main zone was not calling for heat.

*Hot Water/Warm Air.* In this system, the house was heated by forced warm air. The furnace, however, did not have its own burner for heating the air. The furnace was heated by distribution piping from a forced hot water heating system. The only function of this particular hot water system was to generate domestic hot water and to provide the heat source for the furnace. Since the boiler water was hot all the time because of the domestic hot water, the house thermostat only controlled the circulating pump from the hot water system. The pump, in turn, forced hot water to circulate through the furnace, heating it up, which, in turn, activated the fan. This was a very inefficient installation. Nevertheless, these types of installations do exist. If you find a hybrid heating system in the house that you are inspecting, have it analyzed by a professional.

The boilers and furnaces found in most homes today are heated with oil or gas burners or by electrical resistance coils. In many older homes, you will find a boiler or furnace that was originally designed to burn coal, but was converted to oil or gas for reasons of economics and convenience. The accessories associated with each heating element are described below.

## OIL-FIRED SYSTEMS

The most common type of oil burner used in residential heating is the high-pressure or gun-type burner. This unit has a pump that forces oil through a nozzle and produces an oil mist. It also has a fan that mixes the oil mist with a measured amount of air. The resulting flammable mixture is then ignited by an electric spark and burns in a refractory-lined firebox. If the mixture fails to ignite, a safety control will shut off the oil pump motor. This control is located either in the exhaust stack as a heat-sensitive switch or in the burner as a light-detecting photocell.

The proper draft over the firebox is very important for efficient operation of the oil burner. To ensure the proper draft, most oil burners have a draft regulator mounted in the exhaust stack near the boiler or furnace. The regulator is basically a small swinging damper that can be adjusted to open an inch or two when the burner is firing. (See Figure 16-5.) I have seen many draft regulators that have been made inoperative by someone cementing shut the opening. This can affect the efficiency of operation and result in a greater fuel consumption. Also, to ensure the proper draft, the section of the exhaust stack between the boiler or furnace and the chimney must have an upward pitch.

Another type of oil burner occasionally found in central heating systems is the pot-type vaporizing burner. It contains few moving parts and, therefore, operates quietly. Basically, the unit consists of a pot containing a pool of oil and a control for regulating the oil flow to the pot. Air needed to produce a flammable mixture is introduced by a small fan. Once the mixture starts burning, the heat produced vaporizes the oil that is mixed with the air, thus maintaining the burning operation. The initial cost for this burner is less than that for a high-pressure gun burner. However, for efficient operation, it requires a more costly high-grade oil that vaporizes easily.

Oil for the burner is stored in a tank that is either buried in the ground just outside of the house or located in the house not too far from the burner. The interior tank should be at least 7 feet from any flame and should have an outside fill connection. These tanks will generally have a 275 gallon capacity while buried tanks generally have a 550, 1,000, or 1500 gallon capacity. Most municipalities allow a maximum of two 275 gallon tanks to be stored within the structure. Oil tanks have a projected life of about twenty years. After that time, pitting and corrosion holes tend to form on the bottom of the tank. This condition is the result of an accumulation of moisture that has condensed and settled on the bottom of the tank.

All oil burners require periodic inspection, cleaning, lubrication, and adjustment to ensure an efficient soot- and odor-free operation. During the inspection, which should be performed at least once a year, the exhaust gas should be analyzed to determine whether or not the burner is operating at maximum efficiency. Preventive maintenance to the oil burner is usually provided by the company that supplies the oil. For an additional fee, oil companies usually issue a maintenance contract in which they agree to maintain and tune up the system and provide emergency service. If you take out a maintenance contract with your oil company, make sure you know exactly what will be maintained. Some companies will only inspect and maintain the oil burner and not any of the peripheral equipment or controls.

I inspected a house one summer that had an oil-fired, forced hot water heating system that also generated the domestic hot water. The burner, of course, had to fire during the summer to produce the domestic hot water. The circulating pump, however, had not operated for a few months because heat was not needed. When I turned on the heating system (by turning up the thermostat), the circulating pump started to smoke and I smelled insulation burning. The homeowner, who was with me at the time, said, "How can this be? The oil company just serviced the system two days ago." I called the oil company to find out what kind of maintenance was performed. They informed me that they maintain the oil burner only. They did not even look at the circulating pump. Do not let a maintenance contract lull you into a false sense of security by making you think that your entire heating system is being maintained. It may be. But if it is, it must state so in the contract.

## GAS-FIRED SYSTEMS

If given an option and the fixed costs are comparable, a gas burner is preferred to an oil burner. It does not require annual maintenance and is less costly to install. Gas burners have a cleaner, quieter operation and the supply of gas is not dependent on the weather. In addition, replacement costs are lower.

In this system, gas is supplied at low pressure to the burner through an automatic gas valve. The valve, in turn, is controlled by the thermostat or aquastat (if the system generates domestic hot water). At the burner, the gas that is mixed with air is ignited by a pilot light. In some homes, the pilot light is shut off during the nonheating season. This, of course, will save gas. However, if the pilot light is kept burning during the nonheating season, it will eliminate condensation within the heating unit and, thereby, reduce corrosion. Associated with the pilot light is a safety control called a "thermocouple." The thermocouple closes the gas valve when the pilot light goes out. Basically, the thermocouple converts heat (from the pilot light) into a small electric current that keeps an electrically operated valve in the main gas line open. When the pilot light goes out, the current ceases and the valve closes. If the thermocouple is faulty, the pilot will not light.

Some gas-fired systems are equipped with a self-energizing control unit (Powerpile) that enables them to operate in the event of an electrical power outage. This is a particularly desirable feature, especially for those areas that are prone to power failures. The control unit basically consists of a special pilot-thermocouple assembly, gas valve, and thermostat. It can be used on steam, hot water, and warm air systems. With a self-energizing control unit during a power failure, a steam system will operate normally and a forced hot water or warm air system will function as a gravity system.

As with an oil burner, gas burners require a small but steady draft. However, rather than using a draft regulator, gas-burning equipment uses a draft diverter hood. (See Figure 16-5.) The hood is usually located on the exhaust stack above a boiler and is often built into the sheetmetal casing of a furnace. A draft diverter hood is completely open on the underside and thus prevents air currents in the chimney (resulting from downdrafts) from blowing out the pilot light flame.

All gas-burning equipment should have the American Gas Association's seal of approval. This indicates that a similar unit has been tested for safety. Look for the seal as you inspect the equipment. It is usually located on a plate mounted on the front of the boiler or furnace.

## ELECTRICAL SYSTEMS

For the most part, electrical resistance heating is used for area heaters, such as panel or baseboard heaters. It is also used, although less often, for central heating. The heating mechanism in a boiler or furnace is very simple. Electrical resistance coils are immersed directly into the water (for a boiler) or air stream (for a furnace). As the electrical current passes through the coils, they get hot and directly transmit their heat to the air or water. Unlike oil and gas, the conversion of electrical energy to heat is 100 percent. There is no heat lost to the exhaust gas because there are no exhaust gases. There is no fuel combustion with this system. Consequently, there is no need for a chimney.

From an installation point of view, electrical resistance coils are less expensive than oil or gas burners. However, for most parts of the country, they are more expensive to operate. In order to keep the operating expense from becoming excessive, electrically heated homes must be well insulated. In evaluating the cost of heating a house, do not depend on the owner's assurance, "Oh, it only costs a few hundred dollars to heat the house." Insist upon seeing the most current year's bills. Electricity, gas, and oil rates only a few short years ago were considerably lower.

### AREA HEATERS

These units are self-contained space heaters that are used to provide warmth to a single room. Sometimes they warm up two or three adjacent rooms if the doors between the rooms are kept open. The heat distribution, in this case, is not very desirable from a comfort point of view. Other than a fireplace or stove, most area heaters of today will be gas-fired or electric.

#### Gas-Fired Units

Gas-fired space heaters are basically small, warm air furnaces and can operate either as gravity or forced air units. Some of the smaller gravity heaters have an open combustion area exposing the flames. This is a potential fire hazard and is particularly undesirable when there are small children in the house. The exhaust gases from all gas-fired space heaters must be vented to the outside. In addition, they should have the American Gas Association seal of approval. These units are controlled either automatically by a wall-mounted thermostat or manually by a calibrated knob on the gas valve. They are inexpensive to install, relatively maintenance-free, and require only periodic cleaning and adjustment.

### Electrical Units

Electrical space heaters have an advantage over central heating systems in that each room is usually individually wired so that there are as many independent heating zones as there are rooms. There are three general types of electrical area heaters:—panel, baseboard, and wall. *Panel* heating, sometimes called "radiant heating," is similar in concept to forced hot water panel (radiant) heating, as described in Chapter 14. However, instead of hot water pipes being imbedded in the walls or ceiling, electrical resistance cables are installed with each room having a separate control. Similarly, *baseboard* heaters are like baseboard convectors (see Chapter 14) except that they contain electrical resistance coils rather than circulating hot water. They are very popular because of the ease of installation and low initial cost. They also produce a uniform heat distribution. Some baseboard heaters have a thermostat mounted directly on the unit rather than on the wall. This is not a desirable thermostat location because, in many cases, it will be necessary to move furniture every time a temperature change is desired. *Wall heaters* are compact units that are mounted on or recessed into a wall. Most heaters operate in conjunction with a fan that blows the warm air into the surrounding area. They are usually used to provide heat in nonhabitable areas such as a garage or workshop and are sometimes used to supplement an existing central heating system. These heaters do not produce a uniform heat distribution but are very responsive to a call for heat. They are usually manually controlled rather than automatically controlled.

## HEATING SYSTEM INSPECTION PROCEDURE

A full heating system inspection consists of an evaluation of the operation of the boiler/furnace, the burner, the condition of the distribution system (wherever visible), and heat outlets—radiators/registers. During your interior inspection, each room

should be checked to determine whether or not there is a heat outlet and, if there is, whether or not it is properly located for maximum effectiveness. The area below the radiators should be checked for signs of leakage, and the dampers in registers should be checked for ease of operation. Distribution piping or ducts, which are often visible in the basement, crawl space, attic, and garage, should be checked for leaky joints and the need for insulation. Also, the thermostat(s) should be checked for location (should not be in a draft), condition, and type. An automatic clock-type thermostat is more convenient and, if used properly, will result in a fuel savings. A broken thermostat must be replaced, and one that is loosely mounted must be resecured.

The boiler/furnace and the associated burner are inspected after completing the interior inspection. By the time you are ready to perform this inspection, you should know whether the house is heated by warm air, hot water, or steam. You can tell by the type of heat outlets—registers for warm air or radiators for hot water and steam. A radiator with one pipe attached is a steam radiator. When there are two pipes, it may be difficult to tell whether the radiator is used for hot water or for steam. In this case, you should look at the boiler for the determination.

At first glance, two or more thermostats can lead to a false conclusion—that the house has a multizoned heating system. A house with a multizoned heating system will have more than one thermostat. However, a house with more than one thermostat need not have a multizoned heating system. The number of heating zones should be verified when you inspect the boiler/furnace. In a hot water system, the zones are controlled by either electrically operated valves, circulating pumps, or by a combination of the two. For a warm air system, the zones are controlled by electrically operated damper motors. For the most part, the number of thermostats will indicate the number of independent heating zones. However, you may find a situation in which there are more thermostats than there are zone controllers. I have inspected homes that had a one-zone heating system that was activated by two separate thermostats. When either thermostat called for heat, the entire house would be heated. Also, in older homes, you may find an old nonfunctioning thermostat on a wall.

When you are ready to inspect the boiler/furnace, stand where you can see the burner—about 3 feet away. Have someone turn up the thermostat and activate the burner. It is important to be near the unit when the burner ignites in order to determine if there is a problem condition. A puffback with an oil burner or flames licking back under the cover plate with a gas burner is an abnormal condition and a potential hazard that must be corrected. If you find this condition, record it on your worksheet. If the unit does not fire, check the master switch. If the switch is on and there is an oil burner, push the reset button once. If the burner does not fire, then a problem condition exists that must be corrected. If the gas burner does not fire and the pilot is lit, there is also a problem.

Once the unit is firing, check the overall condition. Is the boiler/furnace an aging unit? Do the burner and boiler/furnace appear to have been neglected? Are there signs of excessive corrosion (rust) dust and flakes? Are there mineral deposits indicating past or current water leakage? If there is more than one heating zone, check each zone independently. This can be done by waiting until the burner and/or circulating pump (if a forced hot water system) shuts down and then activating the thermostat that controls the zone being checked. The thermostat should activate the burner or circulating pump, depending on the system (as described in Chapter 14). Sometimes there is a time delay of about one minute or so between engaging the thermostat and activating the burner or circulating pump. This occurs because of the time that it takes to physically open the zone valve or damper. Also, some gas valves have a built-in time delay. However, if after five minutes nothing happens, then there is a problem with the controls.

Check the condition of the smoke pipe. This is the horizontal section of sheetmetal pipe that connects the boiler/furnace to the chimney. In some cases, the boiler/furnace is connected directly to a prefabricated metal chimney and there is no horizontal run. When there is, however, the pipe must have a slight upward pitch from the boiler/furnace to the chimney. If the pipe is long, it should be supported to prevent sagging sections. The pipe should not have corrosion holes, and the joints between sections should be tight. This pipe gets very hot and should not be within several inches of combustible material.

The various types of heating systems have specific items that should be checked during an inspection. Each is discussed below. At the conclusion of the heating system inspection, remember to turn the thermostat back to its original setting.

### Warm Air Systems

This system will be either gravity or forced. You can determine which system you have by whether or not there is a fan. In some of the old "octopus"-type furnaces, the fan may be difficult to locate—it may be on top of the unit 5½ feet off the ground or there may be fans in return ducts.

After the burner has fired, wait until the fan begins to operate. It should begin before the burner is shut down by the high-temperature limit control. If it begins after the burners are shut off, the fan controller is either faulty or out of adjustment. Also, if there is a canvas connection between the furnace and the main supply duct, check its condition. Torn or open sections should be patched. The canvas connection is used to isolate the supply ducts from the vibrations and sounds that develop within the furnace.

When the fan is operating, is there excessive noise or vibration? There should not be any. If there is a power humidifier, it is usually wired so that it will only operate when the fan is running. Turn the humidifier on by turning the humidity control up. If there are port holes in the unit, look to see if the fan or drum is rotating. If there are no port holes, listen to hear if the motor goes on and shuts off when the humidity control is lowered. Very often, the humidifier is in need of a tuneup. This is usually indicated by excessive mineral deposits around the humidifier and the duct to which it is attached.

When the system is operational, check the flow and temperature of the air discharging from the various heat supply registers. Put your hand in front of the register. A weak flow can be the result of air leakage in the distribution ducts, a dirty air filter, a loose fan belt, or possibly the need for rebalancing. When the temperature of the discharging air in one room is lower than in other rooms, it is probably caused by a heat loss in the branch duct leading to that room. The return register can be checked by placing a tissue on the grille. Because the return duct draws air in, the tissue should stay in place without falling down.

The item of main concern is the heat exchanger. When this portion of the heating system breaks down, the furnace must be replaced. When the furnace is aging or when excessive corrosion is noted, the condition of the heat exchanger should be suspect. Also, if the flames in a gas-fired furnace are unstable and appear to be dancing, this often indicates a crack in the heat exchanger. It is recommended that *prior* to the contract closing, the furnace and associated equipment be tuned up by a competent service organization. At that time, the serviceman can check the condition of the heat exchanger. Checking the heat exchanger usually requires the use of sprays, propane torches, mirrors, or disassembling a portion of the furnace and should be performed by a professional.

### Hot Water Systems

When inspecting a hot water heating system, you should first determine whether it is a gravity or forced system. Sometimes an open expansion tank is found in the attic during the interior inspection. This would normally indicate a gravity system. Often, however, the expansion tank is no longer functional and was replaced by a closed expansion tank when the system was converted to forced circulation. You can easily tell whether a system has forced or gravity circulation by checking the equipment associated with the boiler. A forced system will have a circulating pump in the return line near the boiler. Record the type of system on your worksheet.

Next, look at the pressure gauge and record the operating pressure. The normal operating pressure should be between 12 and 22 psi. Since the water make-up valve (pressure-reducing valve) is set to introduce water into the system when the pressure drops below 12 psi, any pressure below that value indicates either a malfunctioning valve or, at least, the need for adjustment. A low pressure reading is fairly common.

If the pressure gauge indicates an operating pressure of 30 psi, the relief valve should be discharging. Sometimes, the relief valve has already discharged and lowered the pressure to about 28 psi. In this case, the exposed end of the relief valve will have water dripping from it and there will be a pool of water on the floor. A high-pressure condition that results in the relief valve discharging will usually be caused by a waterlogged or undersized expansion tank. If domestic hot water is generated through the heating system, another possible cause for a high-pressure condition is a crack in the coils of the water heater. Regardless of the cause of the high pressure, the condition must be corrected.

Locate the relief valve. From a safety point of view, it should be boiler-mounted. If there is no boiler-mounted relief valve (and often there is not), then the installation of one should be considered. Do *not* check the valve to determine whether or not it is operational. Bits of corroded material, sediment, or mineral deposits may prevent the valve from reseating properly and shutting off. Your best bet is to check the valve after you move into the house. At that time, if it does not reseat properly, it should be replaced. A relief valve is inexpensive. These valves should be checked at least once a year by pulling the lever and allowing a small quantity of water to flow. This action flushes any sediment that tends to build up before it has a chance to clog the valve. Some relief valves do not have levers for testing the unit. If you have such a relief valve on your boiler, you should consider its replacement.

As the various zones are being checked, inspect the zone valves for dripping water and deposits. Even though the valves may be working during your inspection, if water is dripping from the valves,

they should be replaced. The dripping water will result in a mineral deposit buildup that can eventually cause the valve to "freeze" in an open or closed position. This of course may happen, as it usually does, on the coldest night of the year. Zone valves are perhaps the weakest link in the heating system chain and their occasional replacement should be anticipated.

Is the circulating pump operating properly? Just because you can hear the pump operating or feel its vibration does not mean that it is functioning properly. The coupler between the pump and the motor may be broken and the noise that you hear or the vibration that you feel may only be the motor turning, not the pump. You can be sure the pump is operating by putting your hand on the return pipe associated with that pump. After a while, the pipe will get hot, if the pump is operational. Check the gasket between the pump and the motor for signs of current or past leakage. This is a vulnerable joint for leakage.

Is the circulating pump emitting any unusual or loud sounds? If it is, the noises may indicate faulty bearings, and the condition should be checked by a service organization. If you see smoke coming from the circulating pump or smell electrical insulation burning, the entire system must be shut down immediately and the condition corrected. One last check of the circulating pump is to determine whether it operates continuously or intermittently. If the circulating pump continues to run long after the thermostat is not calling for heat, it is in the continuous-mode operation. This mode is discussed in Chapter 14 and can be modified to an intermittent operation.

If the heating system is used for generating domestic hot water, then the thermostat will not control the burner—it will only control the circulating pump. In this case, check the temperature of the boiler water (look at the temperature gauge). If the temperature drops below 150° F. and the burner does not fire, it will indicate a faulty or improperly set aquastat. In most cases, the burner will be activated when the temperature drops below 180° F.

## Steam Systems

In this system, a water line showing the level of water in the boiler should be visible in the level gauge. Look for the gauge. If it is dirty, it must be cleaned. A gauge that is completely filled with water indicates too much water in the system, and an empty gauge indicates an insufficient amount of water in the boiler. When the water level in the gauge is unsteady (rising and dropping), it reflects a problem condition that may indicate an excessive grease and dirt buildup in the boiler or, possibly, that the boiler is operating at an excessive output. In either case, it should be corrected.

Check the heating unit to determine whether or not it has all of the required safety controls. A steam system should have a low-water cutoff, a high-pressure limit switch, and a relief valve. If any of these items are missing, record the fact on your worksheet. Look for the low-water cutoff. Is it the built-in type or is it externally mounted? If it is externally mounted, you should test its operation. This is a normal procedure that the manufacturer recommends the homeowner perform periodically. If the relief valve is old, then as a precautionary measure, it should be replaced after you take possession of the house.

Look for the condensate return line to the boiler. Is it a wet or dry return? If it is a wet return, then it should be connected to the boiler by means of a special piping arrangement called a "Hartford loop." Is there one? If not, the installation of a loop should be considered.

## Oil Burners

When the heating system is oil-fired, the first thing you should note is whether or not the top portion of the chimney (as seen during your exterior inspection) is covered with soot. If it is, this is an indication that the oil burner has not been operating efficiently. When you are inspecting the heating unit, look for a card or tag near or on the unit that contains the maintenance service record. Whenever a serviceman performs any type of maintenance, even a tuneup, he records the date on this card. This will, at least, give you an idea of whether the burner has been maintained or neglected. The burner should be tuned up and checked for combustion efficiency at least once a year.

Other telltale signs also indicate the need for oil burner maintenance. Is there a smoke odor in the boiler/furnace room? When the oil burner first fired, was there a puffback of smoke and fire? At startup, while running, or at shutdown, do you feel pulsations in the boiler room? Are there particles of soot on the boiler/furnace or around the burner? Is the oil burner emitting an abnormal noise during operation? If any of the above questions are answered yes, then oil burner maintenance is needed. There are also tests that can be made, such as sampling the exhaust gas for combustion efficiency. This analysis, however, should be performed by a competent serviceman.

The proper draft over the firebox for an oil-fired system is very critical to efficient operation. Therefore, there must not be any cracks or open joints that will allow excess air to infiltrate into the combustion chamber or smoke pipe. Look for cracks and open joints at the front of the boiler near the burner, especially around the air tube, mounting plate, and front boiler doors. If you can see the flame through the cracks or open joints, the open areas should be sealed with a refractory cement. A vulnerable joint for air leakage is the joint between the smoke pipe and the chimney. If this joint is cracked, it must be sealed. Also, to ensure a proper draft, there should be a functioning draft regulator on or near the smoke pipe. Look for one. If it is missing or inoperative, record the fact on your worksheet.

Next, look inside the firebox. The refractory lining of the fire chamber should be intact. There should not be any broken sections or holes in the lining. If there are, then maintenance is needed. While looking inside of the firebox, if the heating unit is a boiler rather than a furnace, look for water dripping or seeping around the top or sides. As discussed earlier, this condition may be caused by joint movement as a result of thermal expansion. Nevertheless, as a precautionary measure, since it can also be caused by a cracked boiler, it should be checked by a professional.

The oil burner receives its oil through a feed line that runs to the oil storage tank. The feed line is usually a small-diameter copper tube that can be easily damaged and must be protected. Look for the line. It should not run exposed over the floor. (See Figure 15-1.) Someone could accidentally step on and damage the feed line, restricting the flow to the burner and possibly causing oil to leak on the floor. If the oil storage tank is the interior type, the underside of the bottom section should be checked for oil leakage. Run your hand along the underside of the tank. If your hand has a slight or heavy film of oil, then the unit may be deteriorating, in which case patching repairs would be in order. The average projected life for these tanks is about twenty years.

## Gas Burners

Gas burners do not require as much preventive maintenance as do oil burners. All that is normally needed is periodic cleaning and adjustment. Look at the gas burners. In neglected units, they are covered with an excessive amount of corrosion (rust) dust. Quite often, some of the gas ports are clogged by the rust particles and are no longer effective. This condition requires a professional cleaning. The quality of the flames on the gas burner is important. The flame should be primarily bluish in color with little or no yellow. If the flame is lifting off the burner head, it is an indication that too much air is being introduced into the mixture.

A yellow tip in the flame will result in a soot

layer building up in the flue passage of a boiler. After some years, the soot buildup can completely block the flue passage. I found this condition in a boiler that was only seven years old. A blocked flue passage is a potentially dangerous condition as it prevents the exhaust gas from rising up to the chimney. Instead, the gas, which contains poisonous carbon monoxide, seeps into the house. Fortunately, this condition can be easily corrected. All that need be done is to clean the boiler flue passages with a long, stiff brush to remove the soot buildup and to adjust the air intake to the burner.

Another safety check that should be made is to test the draft in the chimney. After the heating unit has been operational for a few minutes, put your hand near the draft diverter (located on the exhaust stack above a boiler and built into the sheetmetal casing of a furnace). There should be no outward flow of hot exhaust gas toward your hand. If you do feel a flow on your hand, a potentially dangerous condition exists that should be checked by a professional.

FIGURE 15-1 Oil-fired forced hot water boiler with an exposed oil feed line. The feed line is a small-diameter copper tube that can be easily damaged. It should be protected. Usually, the feed line is located below the floor slab and surfaces near the oil burner.

## CHECKPOINT SUMMARY

### GENERAL CONSIDERATIONS

- How old is the heating system?
- Is the boiler/furnace an obsolete unit (i.e., a converted coal-fired boiler or an "octopus" warm air furnace)?
- Check each room for heat supply registers/radiators.
- Are supply registers/radiators located on or near exterior walls (preferably under the windows or next to exterior door openings)?
- Check supply register dampers for ease of operation.
- Are there separate return grilles for each room or centrally located returns for each floor?
- Check radiators for broken shutoff valves and blocked air vents (steam systems).
- Inspect area below radiators for signs of leakage.
- Check visible portions of ductwork and piping (basement, attic, garage, etc.) for open or leaking joints and uninsulated sections.
- Are the thermostats properly located (no drafts)?
- Note whether the thermostats are manual or automatic-clock type.
- Is the clock functional?
- Check each heating zone and thermostat control independently.

### BOILER/FURNACE

- Check boiler/furnace during startup. Note any puffback with an oil burner or a licking back of flames on a gas burner.
- Is the boiler a steel or cast-iron unit? Is it aging? Is it neglected?
- Check for signs of excessive corrosion (rust), dust, flaking metal, and mineral deposits indicating past or current leakage.
- Inspect firebox, if accessible, for water seepage through joints and/or dripping water. Have this condition checked by a professional.
- Check smoke pipe for corrosion holes, open joints, sagging sections, and adequate clearance.
- Check master shutoff switches for proper operation.

### WARM AIR SYSTEMS

- Check furnace, burner area, and sheetmetal casing for excessive corrosion, rust, and flaking metal.
- Check for unstable/dancing flames (gas-fired furnace). If above conditions are noted, have the heat exchanger checked by a professional.
- If there is a canvas connection between fur-

nace and main supply duct, check it for torn and open sections.

- Check fan controller during furnace operation. If fan starts after the burners shut off, controller is either faulty or out of adjustment.
- Check fan operation for excessive noise and/or vibrations.
- If system contains a power humidifier, check for operation, signs of leakage, and excessive mineral deposits.
- During furnace operation, check air flow and temperature in room supply registers.
- Check return grilles for proper air circulation (tissue test).

## HOT WATER SYSTEMS

- Check whether system is forced or gravity circulation.
- During operation, check pressure gauge. System pressure should generally be between 12 and 22 psi.
- Inspect for relief valve, which should be boiler-mounted. *Do not* check valve operation.
- Check circulating pump(s) for proper operation (motor and pump both functioning). Note any unusual loud sounds.
- Inspect pump(s) for leaking fittings/gaskets.
- Check each zone valve independently. Inspect valves for dripping water and deposits.
- If boiler also generates domestic hot water, check temperature gauge to determine whether aquastat is faulty or improperly set.

## STEAM HEATING SYSTEMS

- Check water-level gauge for proper level, accumulated sediment, and fluctuations (rising and dropping).
- Is the water supply to the boiler a manual feed or an automatic feed?
- Check boiler for required safety controls: a low-water cutoff, a high-pressure limit switch, and an automatic relief valve.
- If low-water cutoff is an external type, check operation by flushing the unit.
- Inspect boiler relief valve. *Do not operate.* If valve is old, consider replacement.
- Inspect/check the condensate return line. Is it a wet or dry return? If a wet return, is there a Hartford loop?

## OIL BURNERS

- During exterior inspection, check top portion of the chimney for accumulated soot.
- Has oil burner been maintained or neglected? Look for a dated maintenance service card.
- During operation, note any smoke odors or soot particles in the boiler/furnace room.
- Are any abnormal noises or pulsations emitted from the oil burner during operation?
- Check for cracks and open joints near the burner, particularly around the air tube, mounting plate, and front boiler doors.
- Check for air leakage at the joint between the smoke pipe and the chimney.
- Check exhaust stack for an operational draft control.
- Check refractory lining of the fire chamber for cracked and deteriorating sections.
- Check oil burner feed lines (copper tubing). Are there kinked or exposed sections vulnerable to damage?
- Check underside of oil storage tank (interior type) for leakage.

## GAS BURNERS

- Check/inspect gas burners for corrosion dust and clogged gas ports.
- Check flame pattern for both safe and efficient operation.
- Check draft diverter on the exhaust stack for backflow of exhaust gases.

# 16. DOMESTIC WATER HEATERS

**H**ot water for bathing and washing (domestic hot water) is produced through a separate tank-type water heater or through the heating system boiler (steam or hot water) by a tankless coil. Domestic hot water is considered by manufacturers as cold water whose temperature has been raised 100° F. An important consideration in the design of water heaters is the ability of the unit to raise the temperature of 1 gallon of water 100° F. This criterion is used in evaluating the recovery rate for tank heaters and the water-flow rate for tankless coil heaters. These items will be discussed in the sections that follow.

The temperature of the domestic hot water is important from both an energy conservation and a safety point of view. The operating temperature range for most water heaters is between 120° F. and 160° F., although in some cases it is possible to achieve temperatures of 180° F. For the most part, a thermostat setting that produces a water temperature of 140° F. will be adequate for household chores including the use of automatic clothes and dishwashers. However, when dishes are to be washed by hand or when bathing, temperatures of 120° F. are more than adequate. In fact, a 120° F. water is above the tolerance level of most people and will have to be mixed with cold water. Setting the thermostat so that the water temperature exceeds 140° F. is wasteful of energy and will shorten the life of the water heater. In addition, a water temperature in excess of 160° F. is a potential hazard because of the possibility of being scalded while showering (if the mixing valve should be faulty).

## TANK WATER HEATERS

Most tank water heaters are located near the heating system or in a utility room. Sometimes, however, they are located in the kitchen or in a closet.

These heaters basically consist of a lined steel tank that is covered with an insulated sheetmetal jacket to reduce heat loss. The lining in the tank is usually vitreous enamel (glass) but can be concrete (stone) or copper. In order to minimize tank corrosion, most heaters are equipped with a "sacrificial" magnesium anode rod that is suspended inside the tank. The electrochemical action causing corrosion takes place between the water and the anode rather than between the water and the tank, thereby extending the life of the tank. Some tanks are constructed so that the magnesium anode can be inspected and replaced if necessary. Tank water heaters will be either gas- or oil-fired or will be heated electrically. (See Figure 16-1.)

### Reversed Connection

Many water heaters have at the top of the tank hot water outlet and cold water inlet fittings that are clearly marked "HOT" and "COLD" respectively. Yet, it is surprising how many times I have found heaters with a reversed water line installation. You can tell whether the installation is reversed by touching a pipe about 4 feet away from the unit and comparing it with the "HOT" outlet fitting on top of the tank. A reversed connection results in an inefficient operation of the heater. Even though there is a cold water inlet tap at the top, the cold water does not enter the tank at the top. There is a pipe (dip tube) inside the tank connected to the inlet fitting that carries the cold water to the bottom of the tank. Because the hot water tends to rise above the cold water, the hot water is normally at the top of the tank, where it flows through the outlet fitting. When the inlet-outlet connection is reversed, the cold water enters the tank at the top and mixes with the hot water as it settles to the bottom near the outlet fitting. Consequently, for the same thermostat setting, the temperature of the hot water is lower than it would otherwise have been. To compensate for the lower temperature, homeowners usually turn the thermostat to the high setting, thereby increasing the fuel cost and decreasing the life of the water heater. Some heaters have interchangeable cold and hot water fittings. In these units, the dip tube can be shifted from one side to the other.

### Relief Valve

All water heaters must have a relief valve that is both temperature- and pressure-sensitive. A relief valve that responds to pressure only will not offer adequate protection for the homeowner. An

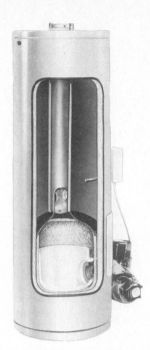

FIGURE 16-1   Tank water heaters. *Left:* Gas-fired. *Center:* Oil-fired. *Right:* Electrically heated. *(Courtesy Rheem Mfg. Corp.)*

excessively high pressure alone can cause the tank to rupture. Though this will cause water-damage problems, it is not necessarily dangerous. However, if the tank should rupture as a result of a high temperature/pressure failure, the superheated water contained therein will flash into steam, instantaneously releasing high energy in an explosion. A relief valve that is sensitive to both temperature and pressure can avoid this problem.

In order to be effective, the relief valve should be located directly on the tank or on the hot water outlet pipe near the tank. During my inspections, I have often found the relief valve located on the cold water inlet pipe. This location reduces the effectiveness of the valve. If you find a relief valve on the cold water inlet pipe of the water heater that you are inspecting, you should notify the homeowner of the potential hazard and have it relocated after you take possession of the house.

A relief valve should have an extension that will allow it to discharge into a bucket on the floor. Sometimes, a relief valve is found without this extension. (See Figure 16-2.) This is a potential hazard because a person standing near the water heater when the relief valve discharges could be scalded. On occasion, I have also found an extension on the relief valve that leads to a sink or floor drain located near the water heater or in the next room. (See Figure 16-3.) This type of a piping arrangement is usually installed to eliminate water damage in the event the relief valve discharges. Water discharging from the valve will flow directly down the

drain rather than accumulate on the floor. The disadvantage of this installation is that the homeowner may never know a discharge condition had occurred. A discharging relief valve indicates an abnormal condition of some type that should be checked out. Obviously, if the homeowner does not know that there is a problem, he will not have it corrected. By having the relief valve discharge into a bucket, water damage can be eliminated and the presence of a problem condition will be indicated.

### Rumbling Noise

Over the years, there tends to be a buildup of sediment scale and mineral deposits at the base of the tank. Manufacturers suggest that a few quarts of water be periodically drained from the water heater to help remove these deposits. However, this practice is not always effective and, if sufficient deposits accumulate, a rumbling or pounding sound can be heard when the unit is firing. If you hear a rumbling noise while inspecting the water heater, do not be alarmed. It is not a dangerous condition, although the noise can be annoying. In addition to their annoyance value, accumulated deposits at the base of the tank can act as an insulator between the water and the flame and will decrease the overall efficiency of operation.

### Exhaust Stack

All oil- and gas-fired water heaters must have an exhaust stack to vent the products of combustion to

FIGURE 16-2 If this relief valve discharges, someone standing nearby could be scalded. The relief valve should have an extension that discharges into a bucket located on the floor.

the outside. If you find an exhaust stack that is loose or broken so that the exhaust gases are discharging directly into the house (see Figure 16-4), you should notify the homeowner of this potentially dangerous condition. As with a heating system, the exhaust pipe should have an upward pitch from the heater to the chimney connection. The exhaust pipe gets quite hot and, therefore, should not be in contact with any combustible material.

### Operational Inspection

The water heater should be inspected while the burner is operational. This can be achieved by opening the hot water faucet at a nearby sink. Within a few minutes, depending on the size of the tank and the water flow at the sink, the burner should fire. (This assumes that the pilot is lit for a gas burner and that there is oil in the storage tank for an oil burner.) If the burner fails to fire, a problem condition exists that should be checked. Oil and gas burners and their controls are discussed in detail in Chapter 15.

In order to provide an adequate draft for combustion gases, oil-fired units should have a draft regulator and gas-fired units should have a draft diverter. (See Figure 16-5.) You should check the

draft in a gas-fired unit. Put your hand near the draft diverter. If you feel a flow of gases on your hand, there is a blockage in the flue passage that must be corrected.

Whenever there is a heavy draw of water, if the temperature of the inlet water is low, condensation can form on the tank. If this should occur, you might see some water beneath the heater or, in a gas-fired unit, you may hear sizzling or pinging sounds caused by water droplets falling on the burner. Consequently, if you see a little water on the floor or hear the pinging noise of droplets, do not assume that the water heater is leaking; it may be condensation. If it is, the condition will disappear after the water in the heater becomes heated. If the condition does not disappear, a leak should be suspected and the unit may require replacement.

### Water Heater Replacement

The only time a water heater requires replacement is when the tank is leaking. If there are problems with any of the controls, they can be replaced individually on an as-needed basis. You cannot tell by looking at a unit when it will start leaking. The projected life for an oil- or gas-fired water heater is from seven to ten years, although units have been known to last over fifteen years. Electrically heated units have a longer projected life than oil- and gas-fired heaters. This is because the electrical heating element is immersed in the water, imparting its heat directly to the water and not to the tank; whereas, in an oil- or gas-fired heater, the flame imparts its heat directly to the base of the tank. The

FIGURE 16-3 The relief valve has an extension that leads to a sink located in the adjacent room. This is undesirable because the effluent will go down the drain and the homeowner will not be aware of a discharge condition.

FIGURE 16-4 Disconnected exhaust stack. Exhaust gases from this gas-fired water heater discharge into the basement rather than into a chimney—a potentially dangerous condition.

intense heat results in expansion and contraction stresses that effectively shorten the life of the tank. Look at the temperature control knob (thermostat) on the tank. If it is at the maximum setting, then the unit has been operating at a high temperature and a shorter life span should be anticipated.

The age of a tank water heater can generally be determined from the serial number found on the tank's data plate. The numbering system, however, varies by manufacturer. As an example, for Rheem or Rudd water heaters, the first four numbers of the serial number indicate the month and year of production—thus 0279 would indicate that the heater was manufactured in February 1979. Usually, a water heater is installed within several months of its manufacture. With an A.O. Smith water heater, the date can also be found by checking the serial number. For example, in serial number 800-A-76-12345, the letter stands for the month of manufacture (January in this case) and the middle number (76) stands for the year of manufacture, 1976.

The letter code designation for month of manufacture is:

| | |
|---|---|
| A—January | G—July |
| B—February | H—August |
| C—March | J—September |
| D—April | K—October |
| E—May | L—November |
| F—June | M—December |

Hence, if during your inspection you determine that the water heater is over ten years old, you should not anticipate an extended life for the unit, even though it may look relatively new (shiny and clean on the outside).

I have been asked by clients whether or not it is necessary to replace a gas-fired water heater that has been in a flooded basement. No, it is not necessary to replace the unit. The tank is designed to hold water and, therefore, cannot be damaged by it. However, the burner assembly and controls (pilot, thermocouple, and thermostat) can be damaged and should be checked by a competent serviceman. If

FIGURE 16-5 *Left:* Draft regulator for oil-fired water heater (*arrow*). *Right:* Draft diverter for gas-fired water heater (*arrow*).

any of the controls are malfunctioning, they should be replaced on an as-needed basis. Also, when the insulation between the tank and the jacket gets wet to the extent that it becomes thoroughly soaked, it can sag and be less effective as an insulator. If this should occur, you will feel "hot spots" on the jacket. This condition can be easily remedied. Insulation jackets are available that fit over water heaters and can be used to reduce heat loss.

### Water Heater Capacity and Recovery

The amount of hot water that your family requires will depend on the number of people, their bathing and washing habits, and the number of tubs and showers available for simultaneous use. Do not judge whether a water heater is adequately sized by the capacity of the tank alone. Equally as important is its recovery rate—the number of gallons of water that will have its temperature raised by 100° F. in one hour. The capacity of residential water heaters typically varies between 30 and 82 gallons. The following example, although somewhat exaggerated, illustrates the point.

Let us take an average home. Assuming normal water pressure and flow, the typical faucet will deliver about 5 gallons of water per minute. Let us further assume that there will be approximately a sixty-minute demand for hot water flowing at the rate of 2 gallons per minute. This hot water will usually be mixed with cold water for washing and bathing. If the home is equipped with an electric water heater that has a 60-gallon capacity and a 10-gallon recovery rate, after about thirty minutes, there would be no more hot water. The low recovery rate of 0.17 gallons per minute is less than 10 percent of that required and would be totally ineffective in satisfying the hot water demand. On the other hand, if the home had been equipped with an oil-fired water heater that had a capacity of only 30 gallons (half the capacity of the electric heater) and a 120-gallon recovery rate, the hot water would never run out and the demand would be completely satisfied.

What is the capacity and the recovery rate of the water heater that you are inspecting? The capacity of all water heaters will usually be stamped on the data plate. Gas-fired units will also have the recovery rate on the plate. Oil-fired water heaters, however, may not indicate their recovery rate. This should be of little concern because oil-fired units have a high recovery rate—often on the order of 120 gallons per hour. Electrically heated units will not have their recovery rate on the data plate. However, the wattage of the upper heating element, the lower heating element, and the total wattage will usually be stamped on the plate. You can easily compute the approximate recovery rate for an electrically heated water heater by using the following

formula: Each 250 watts will heat about 1 gallon of water 100° F. in one hour. Thus a water heater rated at 4,500 watts will have a recovery rate of only 18 gallons per hour. This is a typical recovery rate for an electrically heated water heater and is quite low in comparison to a gas- or oil-fired unit. To compensate for the low recovery rate, electrically heated units should, and often do, have large-capacity tanks.

I have found the following rule of thumb to be effective in determining the adequacy of a water heater for a house regardless of whether the unit is gas- or oil-fired or electrically heated: For a house with one full bathroom (sink, bowl, and shower/tub), the sum of the capacity plus the recovery rate of the water heater should total about 70. For two full bathrooms, the total should be about 90; for three full bathrooms, about 105; and for four full bathrooms, about 115. This also assumes that there is a washing machine in the house that may be operating while someone is showering. Of course, your requirements may be different. If you buy a house with three full bathrooms and there are only two people in your family, you obviously do not need a water heater whose capacity and recovery rate total 105.

From an energy conservation point of view, a small tank with a high recovery rate would be better than a large tank with a low recovery rate. In addition to conserving energy, it is more costly to maintain a large tank of hot water, especially during periods when there is no hot water demand.

## TANKLESS COIL WATER HEATERS

Tankless water heaters, sometimes called "instantaneous water heaters," are used in conjunction with steam and hot water boilers. Most tankless heaters consist of a small-diameter pipe shaped in the form of a coil that is located inside of the boiler (internal generator). (See Figure 16-6.) The coil may also be located in a casing outside of, but connected to, the boiler (external generator). The coil is surrounded by hot boiler water that gives up its heat to the water flowing in the coil. Cold water enters the coil and leaves as hot water with its temperature increased by 100° F. These units are designed for a specific water-flow rate (gallons/minute) through the coil in order to achieve the desired increase in temperature.

If water flows through the coil at a greater rate, less heat will be transferred to each gallon, resulting in a lower outlet temperature. Consequently, many units have a flow-regulating valve installed in the cold water supply pipe to the tankless heater in order to limit the water flow to the capacity of the heater. The design flow through these heaters is usually on the order of 3 to 4 gallons per minute.

FIGURE 16-6 Tankless water heater. Unit (coil) is mounted inside a boiler. *(Courtesy Triangle Tube & Specialty Co., Inc.)*

Assuming a normal water supply to the house, the typical cold water flow will be between 4 to 8 gallons per minute.

In order to regulate the temperature of the hot water being distributed throughout the house, there should be a mixing valve between the cold water inlet and the hot water outlet supply pipe. (See Figure 16-7.) A mixing valve is considered a necessary feature in order to eliminate the possibility of scalding. Over the years, mineral deposits tend to build up inside of the heater coil, especially in hard-water areas. This, in turn, further reduces the water flow through the heater and, consequently, results in a higher water temperature at the outlet. The high-temperature water, which is a potential hazard, can be cooled to the design temperature by mixing it with cold water in the mixing valve. This water can then be distributed to the various plumbing fixtures throughout the house.

As mineral deposits form inside the heater coil, they restrict the water flow. It is possible for the deposits to build up to such a point that the hot water flow becomes a trickle when two or more faucets are turned on at the same time. The hot water flow should be checked during your interior inspection, as discussed in Chapter 10. A low hot water flow that is caused by a blockage within the tankless coil can often be corrected by chemically flushing the unit and dissolving the deposits. However, when the flow becomes a trickle, the heater coil should be replaced.

A tankless coil has virtually no storage capacity. Consequently, if there is a hot water demand that exceeds the design flow (and it often does), there will not be sufficient hot water. In order to provide additional hot water, some installations are equipped with a storage tank. When there is a storage tank, water heated in the tankless coil will be circulated to the tank either by gravity flow or by a pump. In this case, the pipe that distributes hot water to the various plumbing fixtures will be connected to the storage tank rather than to the tankless heater. When the hot water flow between the tankless heater and the storage tank is by gravity, the storage tank must be located above the boiler. When the flow is induced by a circulating pump, the tank can be located alongside the boiler. (See Figure 16-8.)

From an energy conservation point of view, a tankless water heater is not desirable. It is inefficient and wasteful of energy. In order to produce domestic hot water, there must be a double heat transfer. The boiler water will first be heated with oil or gas, and it will then transfer its heat to the water in the tankless coil. In order to produce domestic hot water, the boiler must be heated all year long, winter and summer. As discussed in Chapter 14, controls associated with the heating system prevent steam or hot water from being distributed throughout the house during the months when heat is not required. Nevertheless, the heated boiler water during those months does represent wasted energy. It also introduces an additional heat load on the house at a time when heat is not desired. If you should decide to replace a tankless coil with a tank-type water heater, it can be done at a reasonable cost. An oil-fired water heater, however, is more expensive than a gas-fired or an electrically heated unit.

FIGURE 16-7 Mixing valve for tankless water heater.

### Inspection Procedure

The first portion of the tankless water heater inspection is performed in the bathroom. Turn on the hot water at both the sink and the tub simultaneously and look at the flow. If the flow appears to be low, there may be a mineral deposit buildup in the tankless coil and maintenance may be needed. On the other hand, the low flow may reflect a constriction within the distribution piping. Record the fact that there is a low flow on your worksheet as a reminder that the condition must be corrected regardless of the cause.

At the boiler, look at the joints around the tankless heater mounting plate. This is a vulnerable area for leakage. If there are water stains and deposits around the joint, even if you do not see water dripping, maintenance is needed. The deposits tend to self-seal the leak, but this is not a permanent fix. Any movement or vibration of the boiler can cause the deposits to loosen, reactivating the leak. Often, all that is needed is tightening of the mounting bolts around the joint or replacing the gasket around the joint. Look at the inlet and outlet water pipes to the heater and the mixing valve (if there is one) for signs of past or current leakage.

The temperature of the boiler water that heats the domestic hot water is controlled by an aquastat. You can check the operation of the aquastat by opening one of the hot water faucets. After a while, the temperature of the boiler water will drop to a point where the aquastat will cause the oil or gas burner to fire. Tankless coils are designed to operate with a boiler water temperature of about 200° F. Look at the boiler-mounted thermometer when the burner fires. If the boiler water temperature is less than 180° F., the aquastat may be in need of adjustment. In some homes, the aquastat is intentionally set lower. This, of course, will result in a lower hot water temperature.

Look for a temperature/pressure-relief valve on the hot water outlet line of the tankless coil. If there is a storage tank associated with the tankless coil, the relief valve can be located on the tank. A temperature-sensitive relief valve is a necessary safety control and is normally factory-set to discharge when the domestic hot water reaches a scalding temperature. If you do not find a relief valve, record the fact on your worksheet as a reminder to have one installed after you move in.

### CHECKPOINT SUMMARY

- Is hot water supplied by a separate tank-type water heater or by a tankless coil?
- If you have a tank-type heater, record the

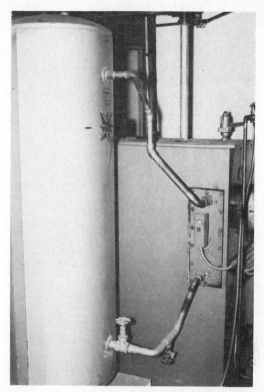

FIGURE 16-8  Storage tank connected to tankless water heater. The hot water circulates between the tank and the coil to maintain the high temperature. The tank increases the overall amount of available hot water.

capacity (gallons), the recovery rate (gallons per hour), and the age (from serial number).
- Is tank-type heater adequately sized for house? See table.

| Number of Full Bathrooms | Sum of Tank Capacity plus Recovery Rate |
|---|---|
| 1 | 70 |
| 2 | 90 |
| 3 | 105 |
| 4 | 115 |

- Is hot water flow adequate when two fixtures are turned on?
- Are hot and cold water supply lines incorrectly installed (reversed)?
- Does water heater contain a properly installed temperature/pressure-relief valve?
- Look for signs of corrosion or past leakage.
  Tank type (gas-fired unit): corrosion dust and flaking metal in burner area.
  Tankless coil: rust and deposits around fittings and gasket.

# 17. AIR CONDITIONING

**B**efore outlining the procedure to use for inspecting a central air-conditioning system, let us discuss the components found in a typical residential system and their function. Central air-conditioning systems provide comfort cooling by lowering the air temperature and also removing excess moisture. This is achieved by recirculating air from the house across a cooling coil. As the air flows across the coil, its temperature drops, causing some of the moisture in the air to condense out on the coil. The cool, dehumidified air is then distributed throughout the house, and the moisture is disposed of through a drain.

The basic components of an air-conditioning system are the compressor, condenser, expansion device, and evaporator. The evaporator is the cooling coil mentioned above. The other components simply provide the means so that the evaporator coil can cool the circulating air. This is done using a cooling medium, commonly called a "refrigerant," which cycles between the components. (See Figure 17-1.) The refrigerant normally exists as a gas at atmospheric pressure and temperature. By applying pressure to the refrigerant (1) and removing absorbed heat (2), the refrigerant will change from a gas to a liquid. At this point, the refrigerant exists as a high-pressure liquid. When the pressure on the liquid refrigerant is released, the refrigerant expands (3) and changes back to a gas. In the process of changing from a liquid to a gas, the refrigerant absorbs heat (4) from its surroundings, thus cooling the circulating air passing over the coil.

An air-conditioning system is a closed system, and, theoretically, there should never be a need for additional refrigerant. However, in practice, the various fittings on the connecting pipes can loosen or develop hairline cracks that can allow some of the refrigerant gas to escape. Usually, when a system is low in refrigerant, the practice is to introduce additional refrigerant and not to look for the openings within the system that allowed the refrigerant to escape. If, however, the air-conditioning system cannot hold a refrigerant charge for at least one season, then the leaks in the pipes or fittings should be located and corrected.

## AIR-CONDITIONING CAPACITY

The overall cooling capacity of an air-conditioning system is usually measured in BTUs (British thermal units) or tonnage. One BTU is the amount of heat that is required to raise the temperature of 1 pound of water 1 degree Fahrenheit. When an air-conditioning system is rated in BTU per hour, it indicates the amount of heat that the unit will remove in that time. A ton of air conditioning, historically, represented the cooling effect achieved by melting 1 ton of ice in twenty-four hours. An air-conditioning system that is rated at 1 ton will provide 12,000 BTUs of cooling in an hour.

The amount of cooling needed for a specific house depends on several variables, such as size of the rooms, whether or not there are cathedral ceilings, the number and type of windows, the amount of insulation in the walls and ceilings, and whether or not shading is provided by trees. The following rule of thumb can be used to determine the size of the air-conditioning system needed to cool the house that you are inspecting. One ton of cooling capacity (12,000 BTU) is needed for every 550 square feet within the structure. Therefore, if you are inspecting a house with 1,800 square feet, you will require an air-conditioning system that is rated at 3 tons. The exact requirement can be determined by a professional. However, the rule of thumb is quite effective in determining whether or not the unit servicing the house is grossly oversized or undersized. Calculate your cooling requirements and then ask the homeowner the capacity of the air-conditioning system.

You can check the capacity yourself by looking at the data plate on the compressor/condenser. Even though most manufacturers do not put the system's capacity on the data plate, it can be approximated. The model number of the compressor on most air-conditioning systems contains digits that represent the approximate number of thousands of BTU of cooling capacity. As an example:

| Manufacturer | Model Number | BTU/hour | Tons |
|---|---|---|---|
| General Electric | BTB930A | 30,000 | 2½ |
| Bryant | 567CO36RCU | 36,000 | 3 |
| Carrier | 38CC042-1 | 42,000 | 3½ |
| Tappan Company | CM48-42C | 48,000 | 4 |

Another figure located on the data plate that can be used for determining the cooling capacity is the full load amperage (FLA) or rated load amps (RLA). There are approximately 7 amps per ton of cooling. The FLA for the Tappan compressor mentioned above is 27.1. When this figure is divided by 7, you get approximately 4 tons, which verifies the figure indicated by the model number.

An air-conditioning system should be properly sized or slightly undersized, but it should not be oversized. A unit that is too large operates intermittently. It quickly chills the air and then shuts down. During the period that the system is shut off, moisture in the air does not condense and the system does not dehumidify the air. In order for the system to remove enough moisture to make the air comfortably dry, the evaporator coil must be kept cold. This means that the compressor should run almost continuously for maximum comfort. Even though a system that is too small will also run continuously, its cooling capacity is not adequate to remove enough heat to cool the room to a comfortable level.

## AIR-CONDITIONING SYSTEMS

There are basically two types of central air-conditioning systems used in residential structures. They are the integral system and the split system.

### Integral System

This system, sometimes referred to as the "single-package unit," is self-contained. That is, all of the components mentioned above (compressor, condenser, expansion device, and evaporator) plus the electrical controls and fans are contained in a single housing. This system, which must be vibration-mounted, is often installed in the attic or a crawl space with ducts projecting through the exterior wall or roof to provide air for cooling the condenser. The integral system is less expensive than the split system. However, the noise level from the compressor makes an interior installation less desirable.

### Split System

In this system, the compressor/condenser is physically apart from the evaporator coil. In order to eliminate the interior noise and to provide outside air for cooling the condenser, the compressor and condenser are housed in a unit located outside of the structure, usually at the rear or side. The evaporator coil, on the other hand, is located in the house, either in the attic or inside the heating system. The specific location often depends on the type of heating system. When the house is heated by forced warm air, the evaporator coil is usually located in the furnace plenum and utilizes the furnace blower to move the air through the coil. When

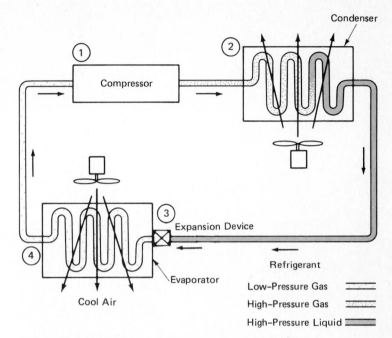

FIGURE 17-1 Basic air-conditioning cycle. Normally the compressor and condenser are contained in a single housing. (See Figure 17-3.)

the house is heated by steam or hot water, the evaporator coil is usually located in the attic with a separate blower (fan) to move the air through the coil and distribute it throughout the house. When there is no attic, the evaporator unit can be located in a closet or the basement.

The compressor/condenser is connected to the evaporator coil by means of two copper pipes that contain the refrigerant that cycles between the two units. (See Figure 17-2.) The diameters of the two pipes are different. One pipe is the size of a pencil and the other is the size of a broom handle. The small pipe (pencil size) is the liquid line; it carries the high-pressure liquid refrigerant from the condenser to the expansion valve. The larger pipe (broom-handle size) is the suction line; it carries low-pressure refrigerant gas from the evaporator coil to the compressor. The suction line should be insulated. Usually it is covered with black foam-rubber-type of insulation.

#### Inspection Procedure

Whether or not the air-conditioning system can be checked operationally will depend on the outside air temperature. Most manufacturers do not recommend turning on the system at temperatures below 60° F. because of the possibility of damage to the compressor. If the outside temperature is below 60° F. during your inspection, do not start up the air conditioner. If the system cannot be checked prior to purchasing the house, the seller should provide you with a guarantee of its operational integrity. If

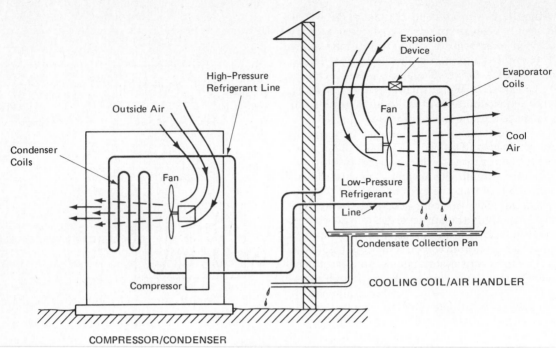

FIGURE 17-2  Schematic diagram of a split air-conditioning system. The compressor/condenser is located outside the house and the cooling coil is inside the house (usually in the furnace or attic).

the temperature is above 60° F. during your inspection, walk over to the compressor and have someone turn down the thermostat that controls the air conditioner so that the system will begin to operate.

**Compressor**  The compressor is the most important part of any air-conditioning system and the most costly to replace. Its projected life is about eight to ten years, although units have been known to last over fifteen years. In areas of the "Sun Belt" with long air-conditioning seasons, the projected life will be somewhat less. After the system has been turned on, listen for any unusual sounds. The compressor should start up smoothly. If there is a straining, grunting, groaning, or squealing noise, it indicates a problem condition that should be checked and corrected by a competent service organization. Shut the unit off and indicate the condition on your worksheet. Once the compressor starts up smoothly, it should then operate continuously without any noise (except a low hum) or squeaks. The compressor should not operate in short cycles (shut down and start up repeatedly). If this should occur, it indicates a problem condition and the unit should be shut down.

When the air-conditioning system is turned on, the fan associated with the condenser should begin to operate at the same time as the compressor. Look inside the unit to see if the fan is turning. If the interior portion is not visible and you cannot see whether the fan is operating, place your hand over the unit. Air rushing over your hand is an indication that it is operating. After the system has been

operational for about fifteen minutes, the air being discharged through the condensing coil should be warm. This air is removing the heat that has been generated during the compression of the refrigerant. If the air is not warm, it is usually an indication that the compressor is not operating properly, a condition that should also be checked by a competent service organization.

After the system has been operational for about fifteen minutes, also look at the low-pressure refrigerant line (the pipe that is about the size of a broom handle). Usually the pipe is covered with insulation. If a section of the pipe is exposed, grab it with your hand. If the compressor is working properly and if there is an adequate refrigerant charge, the pipe will be quite cool to the touch. On many occasions, the pipe and end fittings will be "sweating" as a result of condensation of the moisture in the air. This is a normal operating condition. However, when the low-pressure line is covered with frost, it usually indicates a deficiency in refrigerant. Even though cooling can be obtained with an air-conditioning system that is deficient in refrigerant, the efficiency of the system is greatly reduced.

Occasionally, you will find a sight glass on the small-diameter refrigerant line. A sight glass is a small device that is installed directly into the high-pressure liquid refrigerant line and allows the homeowner to see whether or not there is a problem with the flow of the liquid refrigerant. The refrigerant is colorless and, if the system is operating properly, nothing unusual will be noted when looking at the sight glass. However, when the system is low in refrigerant, bubbles will show up in the liquid as it passes under the glass. If you see a stream of bubbles under the glass, record it on your worksheet.

The location of the compressor/condenser is important for efficient operation. (See Figure 17-3.) The compressor should be located where it will receive a minimum of direct sunlight since the cooler the air flowing across the condenser, the more efficient the cycle. Look to see if the compressor is positioned so that the condenser air intake is at least 12 inches away from any obstruction or dense shrubbery. If it isn't, there will not be an adequate amount of air flow for condenser cooling.

The compressor/condenser can be a noisy piece of equipment and, as such, should be vibration-mounted on a concrete slab or precast concrete blocks that will not settle. The unit should be level. Excessive uneven settlement can cause fractures in refrigerant line fittings and thereby allow the refrigerant to escape.

Look for an electrical disconnect switch on the exterior wall near the compressor. The purpose of this switch is to allow the maintenance man to disconnect the unit so that if someone in the house unknowingly turns the thermostat down, the unit will not be activated while he is making repairs. If there is no electrical disconnect switch, it should be recorded on your worksheet. The overall compressor/condenser unit should be checked to see whether it is in need of a cleaning. These units require periodic cleaning as leaves, seed pods, twigs, and dust tend to clog the condenser, thus restricting the air flow. The condenser has fins like an automobile radiator, which can clog easily.

The condenser discussed above is air-cooled. On occasion, you may see a condenser that is water-cooled. A water-cooled unit can be located inside the structure since it does not require outside air. These condensers are generally not used for residential structures as they are quite wasteful and costly to operate. In order to adequately cool the condenser, cold water flows through a jacket around the coils absorbing heat and is then directed into a sink or floor drain. If the central air conditioning system operates for twelve hours a day, this type of system can waste several thousand gallons of water a day. If you find this type of condenser in the air-conditioning system that you are inspecting, you should consider its replacement.

In large air-conditioning systems such as those found in apartment buildings, water-cooled condensers are not wasteful or costly to operate because the cooling water is recirculated. After the water absorbs heat in the condenser, it is pumped up to a cooling tower, often located on the roof, where it loses its heat, and is then recirculated to the condenser.

**Evaporator**   After checking the compressor/condenser, you should inspect the evaporator unit, commonly called the "cooling coil." The evaporator will usually be located in the attic or the basement. When the unit is located in the attic, you will often find the refrigerant lines from the compressor running up along the outside of the structure and entering the building at the attic level. When the evaporator coil is located in the basement either as a separate unit or in the furnace plenum, the refrigerant lines from the compressor are short and run directly into the structure. If possible, the evaporator coil should be observed after the unit has been operational for about thirty minutes. The coil may not always be accessible because it may be covered with a sheetmetal casing that cannot be easily disassembled. If the evaporator is accessible, look at the coil and the associated refrigerant tubing. The evaporator is used to cool and dehumidify the circulating air. If you notice a frosting condition (a buildup of ice) on portions of the coil and refrigerant tubing rather than dripping water, the system is not operating properly. The frosting is usually the result of an insufficient air flow through the evaporator coil or an inadequate amount of refrigerant in the system. If you see this condition, it should be indicated on your worksheet.

### Furnace-mounted Evaporator

When the house is heated by forced warm air, the most common location for the evaporator is in the furnace plenum. A furnace-mounted unit takes advantage of the ducts that have been installed for heating the house and also uses the heating system blower to circulate the cool air.

You can tell if the evaporator coil is located inside the furnace plenum by whether or not there are refrigerant lines entering the sheetmetal casing of the plenum. The refrigerant lines inside of the sheetmetal casing are connected directly to the

FIGURE 17-3   Typical compressor/condenser for a split air-conditioning system. Air flow through unit must be unobstructed.

FIGURE 17-4  Evaporator (cooling) coil mounted within furnace plenum.

evaporator coil. The most common type of coil found inside a furnace plenum is a two-section design called an "A-coil" because of its shape. Sometimes an inclined or horizontal coil is used. (See Figure 17-4.)

Below the evaporator coil is a pan that collects the water that condenses out of the circulating air. The water is then removed by means of a plastic drain line that will be visible when looking at the furnace plenum. Look for it. Depending on the location of the furnace, the condensate drain line will run to a nearby sink, where the condensate drips down the drain, or will run through the foundation wall, where the condensate drips on the outside. When the condensate drain line is extended through the foundation wall, there should be a

FIGURE 17-5  Attic-mounted blower coil. Unit is resting on a styrofoam pad to minimize vibrations. Below the unit is an auxiliary condensate drain pan and associated drain line. Note that the main condensate drain line does not have a U-shaped trap.

splash plate below the end of the pipe so that the dripping water can be directed away from the foundation.

Sometimes the condensate drain line runs from the furnace down to a small hole in the floor slab. The condensate trickling out of the drain line accumulates below the slab. This method of removing the condensate is not very desirable in those areas where the water will not readily drain because of a high water table or a high clay content in the soil. Even though the amount of water discharging from the condensate drain is small, the introduction of additional water could aggravate a condition that makes the lower level of the structure vulnerable to water seepage.

The condensate drain line should terminate at the plenum with a U-shaped trap. Since the condensate drain line is an open pipe leading directly into the cooling coil, the trap (which is partially filled with water) will prevent any of the cool air from escaping through the pipe. Look for a trap. If it is missing, record it on your worksheet.

Occasionally, the condensate drain discharges into a small rectangular box located near the furnace. This box is the reservoir for a lift pump. The purpose of the pump is to lift the condensate to a level where it can then flow to any desired location. Without a pump, it is often necessary to position the drain line so that it blocks a portion of the room or interferes with foot traffic. Check the pump's operation. These pumps have a float control that is activated when the water reaches a preset level. If there is only a small amount of water in the reservoir, the pump can be checked by pouring water from a glass into the reservoir. A malfunctioning pump should be recorded on your worksheet.

Now look at the overall furnace plenum around the evaporator coil. Rust and mineral deposits indicate a past or present problem in condensate removal. Water overflowing the condensate drain pan can damage the heat exchanger below. If you see this condition, you should have the furnace heat exchanger checked by a heating contractor for signs of deterioration. (See Chapter 14.)

When the evaporator coil is located inside the furnace plenum, the blower for the heating system is also used as the blower for circulating the cool air. Because cool air is heavier than warm air, when the blower is used for air conditioning, it should operate at a higher speed. Most often, however, the furnace is equipped with a one-speed motor. Consequently, the air-conditioning system is often not as effective as it might be. A pair of double- or triple-sheaved hubs can be installed to allow multispeed operation. When the blower is turned off by the master switch, check the tension in the fan belt. There should not be any excessive slack. Press the belt midway between the pulleys. If the belt gives more than ¾ of an inch to an inch, it is too loose, and adjustment is needed. When the blower is operating, listen for any unusual noises or vibrations. If any are noted, they should be recorded on your worksheet. You might also ask the owner when the unit was last serviced, for there is no substitute for periodic maintenance.

*Blower Coil*

When the evaporator coil is housed in a separate casing that contains a blower for circulating the cool air, the coil is commonly referred to as a "blower coil." Most often, the blower coil is located in the attic. However, it can also be located in a closet or in the basement. The blower coil should be vibration-mounted to prevent the noise of the blower unit from being transmitted into the living area. Vibration mounting can be achieved by placing the unit on rubber, cork, or styrofoam pads. (See Figure 17-5.) The vibrations may also be isolated in the attic by suspending the unit from the roof rafters.

The base of the blower coil is basically a condensate collection pan. The accumulated condensate is removed by means of a drain line that, depending on the structure, will extend through the exterior wall, terminating on the outside, or will extend through the lower portion of the roof, terminating in the gutter. Sometimes, the condensate drain line terminates in the plumbing vent stack located in the attic. (See Figure 17-6.) In many communities, this type of termination is not permitted, as it is not in compliance with the plumbing code. If you see the drain terminate in the vent stack, record it on your worksheet. The legality of this type of connection should then be verified with the local Building Department.

The purpose of the vent stack is to channel sewer gases that are within the plumbing system to the outside. If the condensate drain line is connected to the vent stack and there is no trap on the drain line, then the possibility exists that the sewer gases will back up into the condensate drain line, enter the blower coil, and be circulated throughout the house. The condensate drain line should have a U-shaped trap near its connection to the blower coil housing. On many installations, this trap is omitted. Look for it. If it is missing, one should be installed.

When the blower coil is located in the attic, certain steps must be taken to prevent cosmetic damage to the ceiling below in the event of a blockage in the main condensate drain line. Some blower coil housings have a fitting for an auxiliary drain line that is located just above the main condensate drain fitting. The purpose of the auxiliary drain is that if the main drain becomes clogged, the level of

FIGURE 17-6 Air-conditioning condensate drain line (*arrow*) terminating in plumbing vent stack. In many communities, this type of termination does not comply with the plumbing code.

the condensate will rise and be drawn off by the auxiliary drain.

For those blower coils that do not have a fitting in the housing for an auxiliary drain line, there should be an auxiliary drain pan below the unit. The auxiliary pan will collect any condensate that overflows from the main pan when there is a blockage in the main drain line. Look for an auxiliary drain pan. If you don't see one, record it on your worksheet. Unfortunately, many air-conditioning contractors do not install the auxiliary drain or drain pan. Because the rising costs make it difficult to remain competitive, they cut costs wherever they can.

The auxiliary drain pan must have a separate drain line that discharges to the outside. It should not be connected to the main drain line. (See Figure 17-7.) If it is, it reflects poor-quality workmanship because if the main drain line becomes clogged near the discharge end, then the auxiliary drain line will also not function.

If the evaporator coil is accessible, it should be inspected for frost buildup. From an efficiency point of view, the attic is the least desirable area for locating the blower coil because of the high temperatures—easily reaching 140° F. to 150° F.—that normally occur during the summer months. Even though the blower coil is insulated, there will be a heat gain because of this high temperature. The overall attic temperature, however, can be lowered by increasing the number or size of the attic vent openings. A ridge vent is quite effective, as is a thermostatically controlled power ventilator.

**Ducts** After the air-conditioning system has been operational for about fifteen minutes, the air

FIGURE 17-7 Auxiliary condensate drain line connected to main condensate line. This negates the use of an auxiliary drain and reflects poor-quality workmanship. If the main drain becomes clogged near the discharge end, the auxiliary drain will not function. Note that the U-shaped trap is missing.

discharging from the registers should be felt to determine whether it is relatively cool. The temperature of the air discharging from the supply registers should be about fifteen degrees lower than the temperature in the room. If the air does not have a slight chill, it may be because there is a heat gain along the duct leading to that register as a result of inadequate insulation, or the system may be undersized or low in refrigerant.

While checking the temperature of the air leaving the supply registers, also check the air flow. If the air discharging from the registers has a low flow and appears to be sluggish, it may indicate that there is an obstruction within the system caused by dirty filters or possibly icing on the evaporator coils. Sometimes the condition is caused by an undersized fan or possibly the need for balancing the air flow between the registers. In any case, the condition is abnormal and should be recorded on your worksheet.

As with a heating system, the location of the supply registers is important for effective air conditioning. Since cool air is heavier than warm air, the cool air will tend to accumulate near the lower portion of the room and the warm air near the top. As a result, there usually is a temperature difference between the ceiling and floor. This stratification of heat layers can be minimized by adequate circulation within the room. Adequate circulation can be achieved by locating the supply register(s) on the opposite side of the room from the return grille. When the return grille is near the supply register, the air discharging from the supply is drawn in by the return grille and does not have a chance to adequately circulate around the room. In many

houses, the rooms do not have individual return grilles. Instead there may be a large central return located in the hall. In these cases, the supply registers should be located on a wall that will allow the supply air to completely circulate prior to being drawn off and returned to the central grille. Also, the doors to the individual rooms must be undercut so that when they are closed, the supply air will be able to flow to the return grille.

Ideally, air-conditioning supply registers should be located in or near the ceiling. In order to minimize the air-conditioning installation cost, rather than install new ducts, many new homes use the ducts and registers provided with a forced air heating system. These registers are usually located near or at the floor level and are quite effective for heating purposes. However, when they are used for air conditioning, they are less effective and tend to increase the stratification effect. Some houses that have forced warm air heating have what are called "high-low registers." The duct supplying the heat register is extended vertically to a point near the ceiling level, where it terminates at another register. When the system is used for heating, the damper controlling the upper register is manually closed and the lower register is opened. When the system is used for cooling, the damper controlling the lower register is closed and the upper register is opened. This type of arrangement is very desirable and is often found in high-quality construction.

Even though there is a central air-conditioning system, it does not mean that the entire house is air conditioned. Look specifically for registers as you walk through the house. In many raised ranches, I have found that the upper level is air conditioned and the lower level is not. If there is any question, check each room while the air-conditioning system is operating.

There are two basic types of ducts used in residential structures—sheetmetal and glass fiber. While checking the distribution portion of the air-conditioning system, look for exposed ducts. The glass-fiber-type of duct is by its very nature insulated. However, the metal duct may or may not be insulated. The fact that there is exposed metal on the outside does not mean that the duct is not insulated. The insulation may be located inside of the duct. Whether or not the metal duct is insulated can be determined by feeling the duct when the system is operating (if no insulation, the duct will be quite cool) or by striking the duct with your fingernail. If there is no insulation, there will be a ringing sound to the duct, and if there is insulation, there will be a dull thud. All ducts that lead through unfinished areas such as crawl spaces and attics must be insulated so that the cool air flowing through the ducts will not absorb heat from its surroundings. Pay particular attention to the joints for indications of air leakage. If there are any open joints, they should be sealed with inexpensive duct tape. Also, regardless of whether the evaporator coil is located inside the furnace plenum or in the attic, check the joints around the housing for air leakage. Very often, there are open joints that must be sealed.

## Heat Pump

A heat pump is a year-round air-conditioning system that provides warm air during the winter months and cool air during the summer months. It is basically a compressor-cycle air-conditioning system (similar to the one described previously) that can operate in reverse. During the reverse operation, the condenser functions as an evaporator and the evaporator functions as the condenser. The overall refrigerant cycle, however, remains the same. (See page 148 and Figure 17-1 for the operational flow details.)

When the system is operating, the condenser (which is now located in the house) is cooled by the air that is circulated around the house. As this air passes over the condenser, it absorbs heat which, in turn, is used for heating the house. In order for the cycle to operate properly, the evaporator (which is now located on the outside) must absorb heat from the outside air. Even when the outside temperature drops to as low as 20° F., the evaporator can absorb heat because the refrigerant within the evaporator is at a lower temperature. However, as the temperature of the outside air drops, the ability of the evaporator to absorb heat decreases, decreasing the effectiveness of the heat pump. Even though a heat pump may be operational at temperatures as low as 20° F., the BTU output is sufficiently reduced so that auxiliary heaters are usually required.

A heat pump should be sized for the air-conditioning load and not the heating load. Otherwise, the air conditioner will be oversized. Except for a small section of the deep South, the heating load on a house will always be greater than the cooling load. A heat pump will produce approximately 20 percent more BTUs per hour for heating than it does for cooling. Consequently, in most parts of the country, when a house is heated by means of a heat pump, auxiliary heat will also be needed. As an example: In the New York area, a typical eight-room house would require a furnace that could produce about 100,000 BTUs per hour for winter heating and also a 3½ ton (42,000 BTU/hour) air-conditioning unit for summer cooling. If a properly sized heat pump were used for heating, it would only produce 50,400 BTU/hour. The remaining 49,600 BTU/hour that is needed would have to be provided by auxiliary heat-

ers, which are usually electrical resistance heaters.

The auxiliary heaters in heat pumps are automatically activated when the pump cannot supply sufficient heat to keep up with the heat loss of the structure during the winter months. In northern communities, where there is a considerable amount of moisture and low temperatures during the winter months, there is a tendency toward an ice buildup on the metal fins of the outdoor evaporator coil. An excessive ice buildup could cut off air circulation across the coil and result in a loss of heating capacity. With some heat pumps, this icing condition is automatically controlled by a defrost cycle that reverses the flow of the refrigerant for a short time. The hot refrigerant, in turn, heats the outdoor coil and melts the ice. During the defrost cycle, the auxiliary heaters are usually energized to offset the cycle's cooling effect on the indoor circulating air.

A heat pump can operate in either the heating or air-conditioning mode. Most manufacturers suggest that the unit be operated in the air-conditioning mode when the outdoor air temperature is above 65° F. (unlike a regular air conditioner where the recommended temperature is 60° F.) and in the heating mode when the temperature is below 65° F. Operating a heat pump in the wrong mode can result in damage to the compressor.

The components and problems of heat pumps are basically similar to those of air-conditioning systems. Consequently, the overall inspection procedure outlined earlier in this chapter for air conditioners should be used when inspecting heat pumps. However, during an inspection, you should not check both modes of operation. As long as the unit is functioning properly in the mode tested, it is an indication that the major and most costly components (compressor, fans, and coils) are operational. The system then should also function in the opposite mode. If it doesn't, this usually indicates a faulty reversing valve.

## Evaporative Cooler

One of the benefits of air conditioning is the dehumidification of the circulating air. This benefit is not without cost. Cooling and dehumidifying the air is more costly than cooling alone. In the southwestern part of the United States, the outdoor air is relatively dry, and dehumidification is not necessary. In this area, cooling can be achieved by means of an evaporative cooler. Because of the low humidity, water readily evaporates. In the evaporation process, the water absorbs heat from its surroundings and thus lowers the temperature.

The typical evaporative cooler consists of a sheetmetal and plastic casing containing a fan, pads, filter, and a water source. The pads, which hold the water, can be wetted by means of a spray, a trickling stream, or by passing through a reservoir on a rotating drum. In some units, the wetted pads also function as air filters. As the air passes over or through the pads, it is cooled by the evaporating water and then distributed throughout the house.

When inspecting an evaporative cooler, turn the unit on and listen for any unusual sounds or vibrations in the blower compartment. Also look for signs of water leaks and check the pads for deposits and crusting. For efficient operation, the pads may require cleaning or possibly replacement.

## CHECKPOINT SUMMARY

### GENERAL CONSIDERATIONS

- How old is the air-conditioning system?
- When was the unit last serviced?
- Do not turn system on if the outside air temperature is below 60° F.

### COMPRESSOR/CONDENSER

- Check compressor during startup. Listen for any unusual sounds, such as straining, groaning, or squealing.
- Does compressor operate smoothly without short-cycling (repeated startup and shutdown)?
- Is condenser fan operating properly?
- Does compressor appear to be functioning properly? (Warm air should be discharging from unit.)
- Are there indications that the system is low in refrigerant (frosting on low pressure refrigerant line and/or air bubbles in sight glass)?
- Is compressor/condenser located properly for maximum effectiveness (minimum sun exposure and unrestricted air flow)?
- Is unit in need of a cleaning (clogged with leaves, twigs, dust, etc.)?
- Check that unit is level and adequately supported by a concrete pad or blocks.
- For safety/maintenance, check for a main electrical disconnect for the compressor located near the unit.

### EVAPORATOR (COOLING COIL)

- During operation, if possible, check cooling coil for frosting (ice buildup), usually the result of an insufficient air flow and/or lack of refrigerant.

**Furnace-mounted Evaporators** *(installed in the furnace plenum)*

- Check for signs of leakage, mineral deposits, and areas of rust and corrosion.
- Note method of condensate discharge. Is it
    to a nearby sink?
    to the exterior?
    to a floor drain?
    to a hole in the floor slab? (less desirable)
- If condensate discharges into a reservoir lift pump (small rectangular box), check operation of pump.
- Check blower/motor for unusual noises and/or vibrations. Is blower a single- or two-speed unit?

**Blower Coil** *(housed in a separate casing and most often located in the attic)*

- Is unit vibration-mounted?
- If access is available, inspect evaporator coil for frost buildup.
- Check for a condensate drain line.
- Does this drain line discharge the condensate to a nearby roof gutter or directly into a plumbing vent stack? (The latter type of connection is usually not permitted and should be verified with the local Building Department.)
- Check blower coil casing for auxiliary drain line fitting; if not present, check for auxiliary drain pan below the unit. The auxiliary pan should contain an independent drain line that is *not* connected to the main drain line.
- If blower coil is located in attic, is the attic adequately ventilated?
- Is ventilation provided by ridge vent or thermostatically controlled power ventilator?

### DUCTS—REGISTERS

- Check air flow and temperature after fifteen minutes of operation.
- Note type of supply registers—that is, ceiling units, combined type (heating and air conditioning), or high/low registers.
- Check whether *all* rooms are air conditioned.
- Are supply registers and return grilles efficiently located?
- If rooms do not have individual return grilles, check for a large central return grille (often located in the hall).
- Are doors to the rooms undercut to permit proper air circulation?
- Check ductwork for open joints, signs of air leakage, and uninsulated ducts (particularly in the attic and crawl spaces).

Energy Audit
Insulation
Attic Ventilation
Storm Windows
Caulking and Weatherstripping
Fireplaces and Wood-Burning Stoves
Heating and Air-Conditioning System

**M**any states have enacted an "Energy Conservation Construction Code" to supplement their existing Building Codes. The purpose of the energy conservation code is to provide a construction standard that will help minimize energy consumption in a building while still maintaining the necessary human comfort factors. The conservation code applies to new construction, renovations, and additions to existing buildings. The code is *not* retroactive and, therefore, does not apply to buildings that were constructed prior to its enactment. You can check with the local Building Department to determine whether or not there is an energy conservation construction code in your state and, if so, whether it was in effect prior to the construction of the house that you are planning to buy.

If you are considering the purchase of an existing building, there is a high probability that the house is not as energy-efficient as it could be. Although the energy-deficient items are usually found during a prepurchase home inspection, they are often not upgraded until after the buyer takes possession of the house. Consequently, after you move into the house, you should perform an energy audit to help bring back into focus those items that are needed for conservation improvements.

Having an energy-efficient house is not only good citizenship but is also good for your pocketbook. It will result in reduced utlilty bills. The actual dollar savings will, of course, depend on the gas, oil, and electricity rates in your area, the climate, and the extent to which your house is already energy-efficient. You can often find out the projected savings and payback period for the costs involved in making your home energy-efficient by contacting your local utility company. For a nominal fee, many utility companies have a service that will analyze your energy-conserving improvements taking into account current and projected energy costs and will estimate your dollar savings per year.

## ENERGY AUDIT

An energy audit is an inspection of the house to determine the extent to which there are deficiencies that will result in energy being wasted. The decision on whether or not to upgrade deficiencies is usually based on economics. Are the dollars spent in making energy conservation improvements a wise investment? Will the improvements save you enough money on heating and cooling to pay for themselves? For most homes, the answer is *yes*, especially with ever-increasing costs for fuel.

One cause for wasted energy in a house, especially an older one, is the lack of adequate insulation. Insulation is a basic energy saver and should be used in all houses, regardless of their location. In colder climates, it will reduce heat loss and, thereby, reduce fuel costs. In warmer climates, the insulation will reduce heat gain and, consequently, will reduce the cooling costs (electricity is used for running most residential air-conditioning units). During your energy audit, you should determine whether or not your house is adequately insulated.

## INSULATION

Insulation is available in a variety of forms and materials. The three most common forms are flexible insulation, loose-fill insulation, and rigid insulation. *Flexible* insulation is manufactured in two types, batts and blankets. Both are made of fibrous materials such as glass fibers, rock wool, wood fibers, or cotton. Organic fibers are treated chemically to make them resistant to fire and decay. Batts are precut in 4- or 8-foot lengths and are available in thicknesses that range between 2 and 6 inches. Blankets are furnished in continuous rolls and are available in thicknesses that range between 1½ and 3 inches. Both batts and blankets are manufactured in 15- and 23-inch widths so that they can be readily used in homes that have been constructed with joist and stud spacing of either 16 or 24 inches.

*Loose-fill* insulation is generally made from rock wool, glass fibers, vermiculite, pearlite, cellulose, granulated cork, shredded redwood bark, sawdust, or wood shavings. It is normally supplied in bags or bales and can be poured, blown, or placed by hand. Loose-fill insulation is suited for use in the sidewalls of existing homes that were not insulated during construction or for use between the floor joists of unheated attics. However, if there is no floor covering, it is not recommended for use between the floor joists when there is an attic fan that could blow the loose material around.

*Rigid* insulation is generally made from extruded polystyrene, polystyrene bead board, urethane, fiberglass, or wood fiberboard. It is often used to insulate masonry walls and comes in widths of 24 and 48 inches. Most rigid insulation boards are not fire-resistant and should be covered with at least ½-inch gypsum wallboard to assure fire safety. Rigid insulation boards are also used as backer boards for aluminum and vinyl exterior siding.

Another type of insulation is the *"foamed-in-place"* insulation. It is usually made from urea formaldehyde. This insulation should only be installed by a skilled, manufacturer-certified operator. According to the U.S. Consumer Product Safety Commission, urea formaldehyde foam should not be used in attics and ceilings because of its tendency to degrade at high temperatures and high humidity. Also, if it is not properly installed, formaldehyde vapors could be released, which can irritate the eyes, nose, or throat.

One measure of the effectiveness of insulation is its resistance to heat flow, commonly called the "R-number." The higher the R-number, the greater the resistance to winter heat loss or summer heat gain. The table below shows typical R-numbers for various types and thicknesses of insulation.

| Insulation type | R-number | | | | | |
| --- | --- | --- | --- | --- | --- | --- |
| | 11 | 13 | 19 | 22 | 30 | 38 |
| BATTS/BLANKETS | | | | | | |
| Fiberglass | 3½" | 4" | 6" | 7" | 9½" | 12" |
| Rock Wool | 3" | 4" | 5½" | 6" | 8½" | 11" |
| LOOSE-FILL | | | | | | |
| Fiberglass | 5" | 5½" | 8½" | 10" | 13½" | 17" |
| Rock Wool | 4" | 4½" | 6½" | 8" | 10½" | 13" |
| Cellulose | 3" | 3½" | 5½" | 6" | 8½" | 11" |
| Vermiculite | 5" | 6" | 9" | 10" | 14" | 18" |
| RIGID BOARD | | | | | | |
| Polystyrene (extruded) | 3" | 3½" | 5" | 5½" | 7½" | 9½" |
| Polystyrene (bead board) | 3" | 3½" | 5½" | 6" | 8½" | 10½" |
| Urethane | 2" | 2" | 3" | 3½" | 5" | 6" |
| Fiberglass | 3" | 3½" | 5" | 5½" | 7½" | 9½" |

R-numbers are additive. You can add an insulation rated at R-11 to one that is rated at R-19 to achieve a resistance value of R-30. The thermal resistance of an area covered with loose-fill or flexible-type insulation can change over the years. The insulation value depends not only on the material, but also on the amount of trapped air contained within the material. If the loose-fill is disturbed or the flexible insulation crushed (because of items being stored on top of it), it will no longer be as thick as when it was installed. Consequently, its effective R-number will be reduced. In order to determine the current R-number of the insulation in your home, you should measure its thickness.

The amount of insulation that is recommended for your house can be determined from the map in Figure 18-1. You may be surprised to learn how much insulation is recommended. The R-numbers, however, are based on current and projected fuel costs. If your house is already insulated, once you determine the amount of existing insulation, you can add the difference. Remember, the R-numbers are additive. In some homes, it may not be economically justifiable to increase the insulation to the recommended value.

In determining whether or not your house is adequately insulated, you should check the exterior walls and the ceilings and floors that face unheated areas, such as the attic and crawl space. (See Figure 18-2.) In unfinished areas where the insulation is exposed (often found in the floor of an attic or ceiling of a crawl space), the thickness can easily be measured. If the attic floor is covered, you can pry up one board and look for insulation. Determining the amount of insulation in a finished exterior wall is a bit more difficult. However, you can make a quick determination as to whether the wall is inadequately insulated or has no insulation at all by feeling the inside surface during the heating season. If the wall feels cold to the touch, insulation is needed.

Sometimes, you can tell the amount of insulation by removing the cover to a light switch and peeking into the wall space using a flashlight. If you do this, caution should be observed as the light switch is electrically hot. Because of the small amount of open space between the wall and switch box, this method is usually not effective. Also, it is possible that the electrician who installed the wiring in the house may have pulled the insulation away from the switch and outlet boxes to facilitate the installation. In this case, you might think that there is no insulation in the wall. The only way to positively determine how much insulation there is in a finished exterior wall is to make a small hole in the wall (in a nonobvious location such as a closet) and measure it. The hole can then be patched.

While you are determining the amount of insulation, you should also determine whether or not there is a *vapor barrier* associated with the insulation. A vapor barrier is a thin sheet material such as polyethylene film, aluminum foil, or an asphalt-impregnated kraft paper through which water vapor cannot readily pass. Many of the insulation materials are produced with a vapor barrier applied on one side. If the insulation does not have a vapor barrier, a separate one can be installed. The purpose of a vapor barrier is to prevent moisture problems in exterior walls and ceilings and floors that face unheated areas due to condensation of water vapor (normally existing in a house) that passes through those surfaces. In order to be effective, the vapor barrier *must* be facing the heated room rather than the cool, unheated area. (See Figure 18-3.)

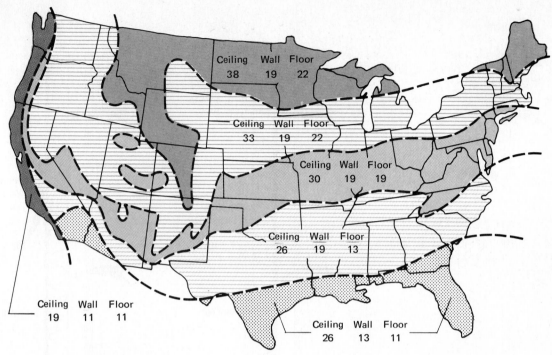

FIGURE 18-1  Recommended R-numbers for insulation in the ceilings, wall, and floors facing unheated areas. *(Courtesy Owens-Corning Fiberglas Corp.)*

In addition to the need for insulation of the building shell (exterior walls, ceilings, and floors), all hot water pipes and heating and cooling ducts that pass through unheated portions of the house (such as a crawl space, garage, or unfinished attic) must be insulated. Most houses usually have no more than 1 or 2 inches of insulation wrapped around ducts in unheated areas. Because of increasing fuel costs, this is considered minimal for most areas, and additional insulation can usually be justified. Check the condition of the insulation. Are there any loose, torn, or missing sections? Also, if there are any exposed duct joints, check them to see if they are sealed tightly. When the ducts are used exclusively for air conditioning or when they serve a dual function (such as for heating and air conditioning), the outside of the insulation should be covered with a vapor barrier to prevent condensation. A vapor barrier, however, is not needed on ducts used only for heating purposes. If there is a vapor barrier on the ducts, check its condition. Look for torn and missing sections. All vapor barrier joints must be tightly sealed.

If the domestic hot water is produced in a tank-type water heater that is located in an unheated area, then the tank should be covered with an insulation jacket. These jackets are readily available and can be purchased in most building supply or hardware stores. Although tank-type water heaters are normally insulated by the manufacturer, by installing an outer insulation jacket, you will fur-

ther reduce heat loss and, thereby, minimize the amount of energy needed to maintain the desired water temperature. The temperature of the hot water should not exceed 140° F. (See Chapter 16.) Temperatures in excess of 140° F. are not only wasteful of energy, but will also shorten the life of the water heater.

FIGURE 18-2  Where to insulate.

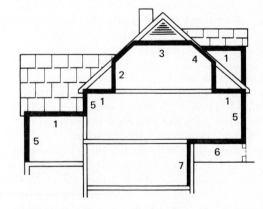

1. Ceilings below an unheated area.
2. "Knee" walls of a finished attic level room.
3. Floor of a crawl attic.
4. The sloping portion of the roof in a finished attic. Leave an air space between insulation and roof.
5. Exterior walls.
6. Floors above cold crawl spaces. Floors above a porch or an unheated garage.
7. Walls of a heated basement.

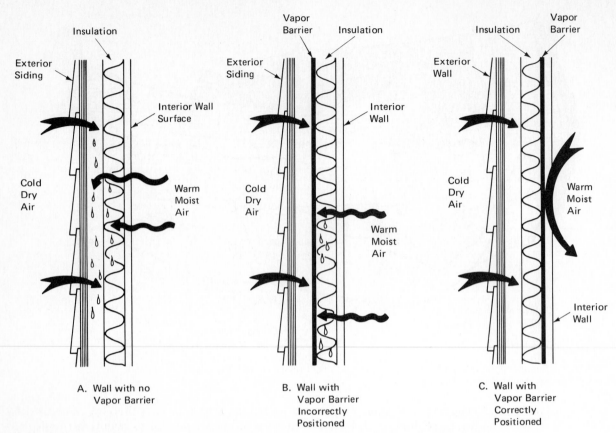

FIGURE 18-3   How a vapor barrier, if correctly positioned, prevents condensation in the exterior wall.

## ATTIC VENTILATION

While in the attic checking the insulation, look to see if the area is adequately ventilated. As discussed in Chapter 9, attic ventilation is necessary not only to prevent condensation problems during the winter months, but also, from an energy conservation point of view, to reduce the heat load on the structure during the summer months. Because of trapped air, attic areas can become excessively hot during the summer, reaching temperatures of about 150° F. If there is an air-conditioning blower coil located in the attic, the high temperature will tend to lessen the efficiency of operation.

Ventilation in an attic should be provided by *at least* two vent openings, located so that air can flow in one opening and out of the other. Vents in the eaves and also at the gable ends are better than gable vents alone. One of the most effective methods for ventilating the attic is a combination of vents in the eaves and a continuous ridge vent. Remember, the attic must also be adequately ventilated during the winter months. As long as the attic is adequately insulated, the benefits of ventilation greatly exceed any fuel savings that might result from blocking the vent openings.

## STORM WINDOWS

In addition to insulation, most homes with single-pane windows will benefit by the installation of storm windows. (See Chapter 5.) A storm window, whether it be a storm sash, panel, or combination unit, will reduce the heat loss through a single-glazed window by about 50 percent. In cold climates, it will also add to physical comfort by reducing an apparent draft. Body heat radiates toward a cold surface. Also, warm air hitting a cold surface will lose its heat, become dense, and fall to the floor. This combined effect creates what appears to be a draft to someone sitting or standing near the cold surface (window). If the storm window is a sash or combination unit (both of which cover the window frame), it will also help reduce cold air infiltration through the movable and fixed joints around the window.

Basically, a storm window is effective because it traps a layer of air between itself and the window. This dead air space acts as an insulator and thus reduces heat loss. If installing storm windows is not economically justified because you are planning to move, or if your budget does not presently permit the purchase of storm windows, you can still make your windows energy-efficient. Simply cover them with plastic sheets and secure the edges with tacks, molding strips, and caulking. Although temporary, these inexpensive, homemade storm windows are an effective approach to reducing heat loss. They will more than pay for themselves in fuel savings in the first year.

## CAULKING AND WEATHERSTRIPPING

In a well-insulated house with thermal-pane or storm windows, air leakage is the greatest source of heat loss. In order to further conserve energy by reducing the cold air infiltration during the winter and the loss of air-conditioned air in the summer, the movable joints (such as those around windows and doors) should be weatherstripped and the fixed exterior joints should be caulked. (See Chapter 5 for discussion on types of caulking compounds.)

Check windows and doors for weatherstripping and tightness of fit. Loose-fitting windows and doors not only lose heat, but also result in uncomfortable drafts. All window sashes, exterior doors, and interior doors or hatches leading to unheated areas (such as an attic, basement, or crawl space) should be weatherstripped on their sides, tops, and bottoms. Check the condition of the weatherstripping. Over the years, some types of weatherstripping will wear, tear, crack, and generally deteriorate to the point where replacement is required.

The condition of the caulking on the exterior joints should be checked during your energy audit. Specifically, look at the joints (1) between the exterior siding and the window and door frames, (2) at the inside and outside corners formed by the exterior siding, (3) just under the bottom side of the exterior siding and the foundation wall, (4) between dissimilar siding materials (such as a masonry and shingle wall), (5) where the chimney meets the siding, and (6) where storm windows meet the window frame (except for drain holes at the window sill). If the caulking is old, brittle, broken, or missing altogether, the joints should be recaulked. Good home maintenance includes an annual check of *all* exterior joints, particularly in view of rising fuel costs.

## FIREPLACES AND WOOD-BURNING STOVES

Most fireplaces are used for creating a relaxed, cozy atmosphere rather than for heating purposes. Usually, their use as an auxiliary source of heat cannot be economically justified as they are very inefficient. A fireplace requires a large volume of air for combustion. Normally, this air is drawn from the heated air in the house. Since the combustion air flows up the chimney, all the fuel that had been used in heating the air is wasted. To minimize this problem, a fireplace should have dampered air vents that provide combustion air from the outdoors. Most existing fireplaces, however, do not have this feature and, as such, waste more heat than they generate. In fact, in terms of the total heating value of the wood being burned, a fireplace does not generate much heat at all. Only about 10 to 15 percent of the available BTUs actually find their way out into the room, while much more warm air disappears up the chimney.

Even when a fireplace is not being used, it is a potential source for heat loss. If the flue is not blocked, heat from within the house will be drawn up the chimney. This condition can normally be minimized by closing the damper. Check the fireplace(s) to see whether or not there is a damper and, if so, whether it properly seals the flue opening. Fireplaces in many older houses do not have dampers. If a movable damper is too costly to install, you can always block the flue with a piece of sheetmetal that is supported by guides on the sidewalls. It can be inserted and removed on an as-needed basis.

Some fireplaces have built-in convection ducts around the firebox that function as a heat exchanger. Cool air entering the bottom of the ducts is heated as it circulates around the firebox. The warm air rises and flows out into the room through openings in the upper section of the ducts. This type of fireplace has a greater heating efficiency than the conventional open-faced masonry fireplace. Nevertheless, a much more efficient way to heat the house is by using a wood-burning stove rather than a fireplace. A good-quality stove will allow only the amount of air needed for combustion into the unit. Consequently, heated room air is not lost up the chimney. By controlling the air flow through the stove, a log will produce more heat by burning for a longer period of time. In addition, since the stove is physically located in the room that it is intended to heat, the entire surface of the unit will heat up and warm the room by convection and radiation.

The cost effectiveness of a wood-burning stove for heating will depend on the cost of the wood that is being burned. In those areas where wood is inexpensive, a stove is an economically viable method for providing auxiliary heat and reducing your overall heating bill. Even in those areas where wood is more costly, as the utility rates increase, the use of a wood-burning stove becomes more attractive. Different woods have different burning characteristics. As an example, wood from conifer trees (softwood) such as pine, spruce, and poplar burn more quickly and give less heat than wood from deciduous trees (hardwood) such as maple, oak, and beech. To aid you in making a proper selection for your fireplace or stove, the following table shows the various characteristics of wood. It was prepared by the Maine Bureau of Forestry.

### Characteristics of Woods for Use in a Fireplace or Stove

| Species | Ease of Starting | Ember Generation | Sparks | Fragrance | Heating Value |
|---|---|---|---|---|---|
| Apple | Poor | Excellent | Few | Excellent | Good |
| Ash | Fair | Good | Few | Slight | Good |
| Beech | Poor | Good | Few | Slight | Excellent |
| Birch (white) | Good | Good | Moderate | Slight | Good |
| Cherry | Poor | Excellent | Few | Excellent | Good |
| Cedar | Excellent | Poor | Many | Good | Fair |
| Elm | Fair | Good | Very few | Fair | Good |
| Hemlock | Good | Low | Many | Good | Fair |
| Hickory | Fair | Excellent | Moderate | Slight | Excellent |
| Locust (black) | Poor | Excellent | Very few | Slight | Excellent |
| Maple (sugar) | Poor | Excellent | Few | Good | Excellent |
| Oak (red) | Poor | Excellent | Few | Fair | Excellent |
| Pine (white) | Excellent | Poor | Moderate | Good | Fair |

## HEATING AND AIR-CONDITIONING SYSTEM

During your energy audit, you have been mainly concerned with those items needed to reduce heat loss. Another item of concern is maximizing the BTU output of your heating system. As you walk around the house, check the radiators and/or heat registers to see that they are unobstructed. If your house is heated with a warm air furnace, check the filter to see if it needs replacement. If the oil or gas burner for the heating system was not cleaned and tuned up prior to your energy audit, it should be done as soon as possible. A heating system out of adjustment will result in a greater fuel consumption, which can be quite costly. Heating systems require a periodic tuneup for efficient operation.

Various devices on the market to be fitted on or around the chimney flue are supposed to cut fuel consumption and conserve heat. Many of these furnace attachments, however, do not live up to the manufacturers' claims of saving a significant amount of energy. One device of concern from a safety point of view is the automatic flue damper. This device is designed to close the furnace chimney after the burner turns off. The intention is to conserve heat by preventing room air from being drawn up the chimney. However, if the automatic flue damper fails to open when the burner fires, poisonous carbon monoxide fumes will vent into the house. If your furnace has such a device, you should find out whether it has been approved by a nationally recognized testing agency and also by your local utility company. If it has not been approved, you should consider its removal or replacement as a precautionary measure.

By lowering the thermostat setting five to ten degrees each night before going to sleep and raising it in the morning, you will reduce fuel consumption and save dollars. The amount of the savings will depend on the duration of the setback, the climate, and the fuel costs in your area. See the following table.

| | Percent of Energy Savings for an 8-Hour Temperature Setback of: | |
|---|---|---|
| Degree Days | 5° F. | 10° F. |
| 5,000 | 8.1 | 12.1 |
| 6,000 | 7.2 | 10.8 |
| 7,000 | 6.1 | 9.6 |
| 8,000 | 5.2 | 8.5 |
| 8,500 | 4.6 | 7.8 |

The degree day is a unit that is used to express the severity of the climate in a given area. The reference temperature for evaluating degree days is 65° F. Degree days are the number of degrees that the average (of the high and low temperatures for a twenty-four-hour period) is less than 65° F. As an example, if for a given twenty-four-hour period (during the heating season), the high and low temperatures are 50° F. and 30° F. respectively, the average temperature would be 40° F. The degree day number for that day is then 65 − 40, or 25. The total number of degree days for an area, therefore, is simply the sum of the degree day numbers during the heating season. You can check with the local utility company to find out the total number of degree days for your area.

From a convenience point of view, if your heating system is controlled by a manual thermostat, you should consider replacing it with an automatic-clock thermostat. With this type of thermostat, you can regulate the amount of the setback and its duration. Depending on your requirements, thermostats with double setbacks are also available.

If there is a central air-conditioning system in your house, then it must also be cleaned and tuned up to maximize the efficiency of operation. Prior to the cooling season, have the system checked to see if it needs a refrigerant charge. The system will cool even if it is low in refrigerant. However, it will operate inefficiently. Check the location of the compressor to see if it is in the shade and whether the air flow into and out of the unit is unobstructed. If the compressor is in the midday and afternoon sun, it will not perform efficiently. You should build a sun screen to shade the unit, if necessary. Be careful, however, not to obstruct the air flow.

For most families, the purchase of a home is an emotionally charged event filled with anxiety, hopeful dreams and, sometimes, disappointments after moving in. The disappointment, however, can be avoided or, at least, minimized if you know the true condition of the house that you are buying. Prior to purchasing the house, you or a professional should perform a home inspection.

## PROFESSIONAL HOME INSPECTION

The purpose of this book is to provide a sufficient amount of background material and an overall procedure so that you can perform a technical inspection of the house that you are considering buying or the one that you are currently living in. However, as previously pointed out, there are times when the services of a professional home inspector are necessary. A professional inspector, however, will not inspect in as detailed a fashion as is suggested in this book. He will normally not operate every window, check every light switch, check the temperature of every radiator, indicate every cracked wall, floor, or ceiling (unless the crack represents a structural problem), check the caulking at every joint, and so on.

The main concerns of an inspector are the major problems or deficiencies—ones that will be costly to correct and ones that pose a health, safety, or fire hazard. Because of the inspector's training and experience, he is better able than a lay person to pick up problems through a more cursory inspection and relate problem conditions in one area to difficulties in another (if such should be the case).

When selecting a professional home inspector, choose one whose sole endeavor is inspection. It is advisable not to use an inspector who is affiliated with an exterminating company, a real estate broker, or a contractor (plumber, electrician, roofer, and so on). The inspector must be completely unbiased, and the inspector must not have a vested interest in finding problem conditions. Licensed professional engineers who specialize in home inspections have an advantage (because of their educational training) in that they can evaluate certain problems in depth.

## HOME INSPECTION LIMITATIONS

A home inspection is not perfect and will not necessarily reveal *every* problem that exists, but it is the best thing available. A home inspection is basically a visual inspection as well as an operational check of the various visible elements and components of the house. If performed in the manner suggested herein, you should have a fairly good picture as to the condition of the house at the time of the inspection. By taking into account the age and present condition of the various items, predictions can usually be made about future problems.

However, a home inspection cannot reveal a deficiency or problem if the conditions causing it are not visible. The following are just a few examples of such possible situations. (1) A house with a concrete block foundation may have termite infestation within the voids of the foundation walls. This condition would not be visible during an inspection. Nevertheless, a week later, there may be visible termite shelter tubes or a swarm. (2) A basement or crawl space can be "bone dry" for the first three years and then flood in the fourth year because of a new building development nearby. (3) The operation of a septic system will depend on the condition (porosity and degree of saturation) of the subsoil in the leaching field—an item that is not readily apparent during an inspection. Depending on the weather, the level of the water table, and the amount of usage prior to the inspection, it is possible for a malfunctioning septic system to appear to operate properly during the period of time that it takes to perform an inspection. (4) If there is an inadequately insulated water pipe in an exterior wall, it can freeze and burst during a severe cold spell. Since the pipe would not be visible during an inspection, the condition would not be detected.

Even with such limitations, a home inspection, if properly performed, will reveal a considerable amount of information about the house that, very often, even the owner does not know.

## REAL ESTATE WARRANTY PROGRAM

Many homes throughout the United States are being sold with a warranty protection plan for the buyer. The warranty usually covers the following components:

Electrical system
Heating system

Water heater
Plumbing system
Central air-conditioning system
Built-in appliances

and is in effect for the first year that the buyer owns the house. The warranties are usually made available to the buyer through the real estate broker. Not all brokers, however, are affiliated with companies that offer home warranties.

The home warranties that are currently available when you buy a house are very limited in scope and *should not* be considered as a replacement for a home inspection. The warranty is basically an insurance plan that will protect the new homeowner against defects or malfunctions in the covered components and nothing more. When you are planning on buying a house, there are many questions about the house that should be answered so that you can make an intelligent decision. These questions concern items that are not covered by the warranty, and their answers can have a significant impact on the true cost of buying the house. Remember, the true cost of a house is the purchase price plus the costs for upgrading substandard, deteriorated, or malfunctioning components.

As an example, the electrical system is covered against defects under the warranty. The fact that the electrical service in the house may be totally inadequate (i.e., 110 volts at 30 amps) and would have to be upgraded, at a considerable expense, is not covered by the warranty. Also not covered by the warranty, but costly to correct are basements that are subjected to periodic water penetration, structural damage to the foundation and/or wood-framing, termite infestation and deterioration, roof replacement, and improvements needed for energy conservation. In addition, items of concern are general and latent defects, such as an inadequately ventilated attic. A home warranty is definitely of value—as long as you realize that it is not the answer to all of your questions or potential problems.

## PRIVATE HOME INSPECTION WARRANTY PROGRAMS

For an additional fee, some private home inspection companies offer a warranty protection plan after they inspect the house. The warranty applies for a twelve-month period and is usually effective from the day of the inspection or the transfer of title. The warranty plan is basically an insurance program. In fact, in some states, inspection companies have been forced to drop their warranty program because they were not licensed by the State Insurance Commission to sell insurance.

As with all types of insurance, you should know exactly what you are buying before you put your money down. The warranty plan will protect the buyer against defects in most of the major housing components, providing that the components are in reasonably good condition to begin with. If, during the inspection, any "covered" component is judged to be in less-than-satisfactory condition, it is excluded from coverage, although this is not reflected in the warranty fee. Also, for an item such as the roof, there is usually a prorated repair schedule that is a function of age. As an example, in one plan, if the roof is nine years old (which is not considered old or even aging), only 30 percent of the repair or replacement costs are covered. If the deductible (which may be $100 or $250) is subtracted, there may not even be any coverage.

The warranty agreement should be read very carefully. In addition to items excluded because of condition or age, many components that are costly to correct are often not even included in the plan. As with the real estate warranty plans, these warranties can also be of value, as long as you know exactly what you are buying and understand the limitations.

## MANUFACTURERS' WARRANTIES

Many of the components and items in a house have the manufacturer's guarantee or warranty against defects for a specific number of years. Items that are usually covered are the furnace, water heater, roof shingles, well pump, air-conditioning compressor, and the electrical appliances. If you are purchasing a relatively new house or, if in an older house, any of the above components are relatively new (because of replacement), you should obtain their warranties or bills of sale. Depending on the manufacturer, many warranties are transferrable to a new owner. Also, if the house had been termite-proofed, do not forget to get a copy of the guarantee, if it is still in effect.

## CONTRACT

Many lawyers indicate that the best time to inspect the house that you are considering buying is before, rather than after, the contract signing. This avoids the problems that can develop if the contract has already been signed and the subsequent inspection reveals major deficiencies in the house. Often in this case, the buyer either wants a price adjustment or he wants to back out of the deal. By inspecting the house before the contract signing, the correction of problems and deficiencies can be written into the contract. In a seller's market, however, the buyer may feel pressured into signing the contract prior to the inspection in fear of having the house sold to another buyer before the inspection has been performed.

If you do sign a contract before the house has been inspected, then for your protection, the contract should include an inspection contingency clause.

It is important that the clause be broad enough to include all of the major problems that can occur in a house. Otherwise, there may be legal problems in "backing out" of the deal because of a major defect that was not covered in the contract. As an example, a few years ago, I received a telephone call from a buyer for whom I had done a home inspection. The buyer indicated that his contract had an inspection clause that provided him with the option of declaring the contract null and void if there were structural deficiencies. That was basically the extent of the clause; it was very limited. My inspection had revealed that the electrical service was inadequate, the heating system had to be replaced, and there was evidence of water penetration into the basement. After the inspection, the buyer decided that he no longer wanted to buy the house. He called to find out if the problem items were considered structural deficiencies. No, they were not and, unfortunately, because of the wording in the contract, the buyer lost part of his deposit.

One contingency clause that has been used states that the sales agreement is contingent upon having a home inspection within $X$ days of the signing. The inspection is defined to include a physical check of the exterior and interior components of the house (including the structural integrity of the building) and the condition of the electrical and mechanical equipment. If the inspection reveals any defects for which the cost exceeds $X$ dollars, the buyer should have the following options: Have defects corrected by the seller, negotiate the cost of the correction(s) with the seller, or declare the sales agreement null and void. The limitation of this clause is in defining the means by which the costs for correcting the defects are determined.

In order to avoid this type of problem, one attorney I know uses the following clause:

> This contract is contingent upon the Purchaser's making, or having made on his behalf by another, a physical inspection of the entire premises. If such inspection reveals any condition or state of facts unsatisfactory to the Purchaser, in his sole discretion, the Purchaser shall receive back all monies paid hereunder. Upon receipt of said monies, this agreement shall be null and void, and neither party under any obligation whatsoever to the other.

This clause may not be applicable to your state. In order to avoid any legal entanglement, your best bet is to consult an attorney.

As mentioned in Chapter 1, just prior to the contract closing, you should perform a final "walk-through" inspection of the house. Although most sellers will not deny you the right to make this inspection, it is not assured. Consequently, the right to a final walk-through inspection should be made part of the contract.

No two houses are alike. Just as a person changes with age, so does a house. Regardless of whether you are a home buyer or a homeowner, it is important to know the true condition of the house. Hopefully, with this book, you are now prepared to find out. Try doing the inspection yourself. It's really a lot of fun. Worksheets are provided on which you can record your observations. Good luck!

# GLOSSARY

**Alligatoring.** Extensive surface cracking in a pattern, which resembles the hide of an alligator.

**Areaway.** An open subsurface space around a basement window or doorway. Provides light, ventilation, access.

**Backfill.** The gravel or earth replaced in the space around a building wall after the foundation is in place.

**Bottom plate.** The bottom horizontal member of a frame wall.

**Cantilever.** A structural member which projects beyond its supporting wall or column.

**Control joint.** A groove which is formed, sawed, or tooled in a concrete or masonry structure to regulate the location and amount of cracking.

**Cornice.** Horizontal projection at the top of a wall or under the overhanging portion of the roof.

**Cupping.** An inward curling distortion at the exposed corners of asphalt shingles.

**Downdraft.** A downward current of air in a chimney, often carrying smoke with it.

**Dry well.** A covered pit, either with open-jointed lining or filled with coarse aggregate, through which drainage from downspouts or foundation footing drains may seep into the surrounding soil.

**Eaves.** The lower edge of a roof which projects beyond the building wall.

**Efflorescence.** A white powdery substance appearing on masonry wall surfaces. It is composed of soluble salts which have been brought to the surface by water or moisture movement.

**Fascia (or facia).** A horizontal board that is nailed vertically to the ends of roof rafters; sometimes supports a gutter.

**Feathering.** The tapering of one surface into another.

**Flashing.** Sheetmetal or other thin, impervious material used around roof and wall junctions to protect the joints from water penetration.

**Flue.** A passageway in a chimney for conveying smoke, gases, or fumes to the outside air.

**Frost line.** The depth of frost penetration in soil. This depth varies in different parts of the country.

**Gable roof.** A double-sloped roof from the ridge to the eaves; the end section appears as an inverted V.

**Girder.** The main structural support beam in a wood-framed floor. The girder supports one end of each joist.

**Grade.** The ground level existing at the outside walls of a building or elsewhere on a building site.

**Header.** A framing member which crosses and supports the ends of joists.

**Hip roof.** A roof which slopes upward from all four sides of a building.

**Joist.** One of a series of parallel beams used to support floor and ceiling loads, and supported in turn by larger beams (girders) or bearing walls.

**Knee wall.** A wall that acts as a brace by supporting roof rafters at an intermediate position along their length.

**Lally column.** A steel tube, sometimes filled with concrete, used to support girders and other floor beams.

**Lath.** A building material of wood, metal, gypsum, or insulating board that is fastened to the frame of a building to act as a plaster base.

**Lintel.** A horizontal structural member that supports the load over an opening such as a door or window.

**Nosing.** The rounded edge of a stair tread that projects over the riser.

**Parapet wall.** That part of a wall which extends above the roof line.

**Pier.** A masonry column, usually rectangular in horizontal cross-section, used to support other structural members.

**Pigtail.** (1) A flexible conductor attached to a light fixture which provides a means of connecting the fixture to a circuit. (2) A short length of copper conductor that is attached to the end of an aluminum branch circuit by a special fastener. The copper conductor is then fastened to the terminal of a switch or outlet.

**Pilaster.** A pier-type projection of the foundation wall that is used to support a floor girder or stiffen the wall.

**Plenum.** A chamber or large duct above a furnace that serves as a distribution area.

**Ply.** A term to denote the number of sheets in a layered construction, such as plywood, roofing, etc.

**Pointing (repointing).** The filling of open mortar joints. Removal of deteriorated mortar from between joints of masonry units and replacement of it with new mortar.

**Rafter.** One of a series of inclined structural roof members spanning from an exterior wall to a center ridge beam or ridge board.

**Relay.** An electromechanical switch. A device in which changes in the current flow in one circuit are used to open or close electrical contacts in a second circuit.

**Refractory.** A material, usually nonmetallic, used to withstand high temperatures, as in the combustion chamber of an oil-fired heating system.

**Resilient tile.** A manufactured interior floor covering that is resilient, such as vinyl or vinyl-asbestos tile.

**Ridge beam.** The beam or board placed on edge at the ridge (top) of the roof into which the upper ends of the rafters are fastened.

**Riser.** The vertical height of a stair step. Also used as the name of the vertical boards that close the space between the treads of a stairway.

**Sheathing.** The structural covering, usually wood boards or plywood, over a building's exterior studs or rafters.

**Sheave.** A wheel with a grooved rim (pulley).

**Shelter tube.** Mud-type tube (tunnel) built by termites as a passageway between the ground and the source of food (wood).

**Sill plate.** The lowest member of the house framing resting on top of the foundation wall. Also called mud sill.

**Soffit.** The visible underside of a roof overhang or eave.

**Stringer (step).** One of the enclosed sides of a stair supporting the treads and risers.

**Stud.** One of a series of slender wood or metal vertical structural members placed as supporting elements in walls and partitions.

**Subfloor.** Boards or plywood laid on joists over which a finished floor is to be laid.

**Swale.** A shallow depression in the ground to form a channel for storm water drainage.

**Thermocouple.** A device consisting of two junctions of dissimilar metals. When the two junctions are at different temperatures, a voltage is generated. Used in controlling gas valves.

**Toenail.** Driving a nail at an angle into the corner of one wood-frame member in order for the nail to penetrate into a second member.

**Tread.** The horizontal board in a stairway on which the foot is placed.

**Weep hole.** A small opening at the bottom of a retaining wall or the lower section of a masonry veneer facing on a wood-frame exterior wall, which permits water to drain.

# INSPECTION WORKSHEETS

Address:_____

## EXTERIOR

Front Exposure: N E S W                                                                 Condition

1. **Sidewalks:** none_____ concrete_____ asphalt_____ stone_____cracked_____ uneven                    _____

2. **Exterior walls:** brick_____ stucco_____ stone_____ wood siding_____

   wood/asbestos shingle_____ aluminum/vinyl siding_____ other_____ vines growing_____          _____

3. **Trim:** cracked_____ rotting_____ broken_____ loose_____ needs paint touch-up_____          _____

4. **Paths:** concrete_____ stone_____ brick_____ asphalt_____ cracked_____ settled_____

   overgrown_____                                                                          _____

5. **Steps:** concrete_____ stone_____ brick_____ wood_____ needs repair_____

   Handrail:_____                                                                          _____

6. **Porch:** front/rear/left/right: cracked_____ rotting_____ chipped_____ loose_____          _____

7. **Windows:** wood_____ aluminum_____ cracked_____ broken_____ reputty_____

   broken cords_____ needs lubrication/adjustment_____ do not close properly_____

   corroding/rotting frames_____ Thermal panes_____                                        _____

8. **Storms/screens:** none_____ partial_____ full_____ cracked_____ broken_____

   torn screens_____                                                                        _____

9. **Roof:** asphalt_____ wood_____ slate_____ tile_____ roll roofing_____ other_____

   Shingles: missing_____ loose_____ cracked_____ aging_____ eroded_____            _____

10. **Gutters/downspouts:** none_____ partial_____ full_____ built-in_____ aluminum_____

    copper_____ galvanized_____ wood_____ loose/sagging_____ open joints_____

    need splash plates/elbows_____ need cleaning_____                                      _____

11. **Chimney:** brick_____ masonry_____ prefabricated_____ needs repair_____          _____

12. **Garage:** none_____ attached_____ detached_____ car occupancy_____

    Doors: operational_____ need lubrication/adjustment_____ automatic opener_____        _____

13. **Driveway:** cracked_____ uneven_____ broken_____ heaving_____ drain_____        _____

14. **Patio:** yes_____ no_____ concrete_____ stone_____ brick_____ needs repair_____

    cracked_____ settled_____                                                              _____

15. **Deck:** cracked_____ rotting_____ broken_____ needs additional bracing_____

    loose railings/handrails_____ loose steps_____ loose posts_____                      _____

16. **Landscaping:** grass needs recultivation_____ shrubs need pruning_____

    Trees:_____ overhanging roof_____ need pruning_____ dead/dying_____                _____

17. **Retaining walls:** brick_____ stone_____ concrete/block_____ wood_____ need repair_____    _____

18. **Fencing:** wood/metal_____ broken_____ rotting/rusting_____ needs painting_____    _____

19. **Drainage/grading:** satisfactory_____ poor_____ low spots_____ needs regrading_____

    stairwell_____ window well_____                                                        _____

20. **Termites:** no visible evidence_____ visible evidence_____ where_____               _____

21. **Caulking:** needed around exterior joints: yes_____ no_____                           _____

## ATTIC AREA

**Type:** full_____ crawl_____ finished_____ unfinished_____

**Accessible:** yes_____ no_____ Evidence of condensation: yes_____ no_____

**Insulation:** floor_____ roof_____ walls_____ partial_____ adequate_____ inadequate_____

   none visible_____ loose sections_____ improperly installed_____ Vapor barrier: yes_____ no_____

**Ventilation:** adequate_____ inadequate_____ none_____ need roof/gable vents_____ ridge vent_____

   power ventilator_____ Attic fan:_____ operational: yes_____ no_____

**Past leakage:** chimney_____ plumbing vent stacks_____ rafters_____ other_____

**Firestopping:** needed around chimney and attic floor: yes_____ no_____

## CRAWL SPACE (BASEMENT LEVEL)

**None:**_____ Accessible: yes_____ no_____

**Floor:** dirt_____ concrete_____ cement_____ asphalt_____ other_____

    Vapor barrier needed for floor: yes_____ no_____

    Past water seepage: yes_____ no_____

**Insulation needed:** yes_____ no_____ loose section(s)_____

**Ventilation:** adequate_____ inadequate_____ Dehumidifier needed: yes_____ no_____

## ELECTROMECHANICALS

**Electricity:** _____ amps     110–220 volts     circuit breakers_____ fuses_____

    Service: adequate_____ marginal_____ inadequate_____

    Wiring/outlets: adequate_____ marginal_____ inadequate_____

    Aluminum branch circuits_____

**Heating system:** forced_____ gravity_____; hot water_____ hot air_____ steam_____

    oil_____ gas_____ electric_____; zones_____

    Condition: good_____ fair_____ aging_____ poor_____

    Thermostat(s): manual_____ automatic clock_____

    Furnace room ventilation: adequate_____ inadequate_____

    Fire-code Sheetrock needed: yes_____ no_____

**Domestic hot water:** tankless coil thru heating system_____

    separate tank unit_____ capacity_____ recovery_____ age_____

    oil_____ gas_____ electric_____

    Capacity: adequate_____ marginal_____ inadequate_____

    Condition: good_____ fair_____ aging_____ poor_____

**Plumbing:** Pipes and fittings: copper_____ brass_____ iron_____ other_____

    Water flow: adequate_____ low_____

    Drainlines: cast iron_____ galvanized_____ copper_____ lead_____ plastic_____

    Condition: good_____ fair_____ aging_____ poor_____; leakage_____ corrosion_____

    Water inlet: copper_____ iron_____ lead_____ inaccessible_____

    Septic system: yes_____ no_____

**Well pump:** none_____ jet_____ submersible_____ other_____

    Storage tank: yes_____ no_____ Insulation needed: yes_____ no_____

    Relief valve needed: yes_____ no_____

    Condition: good_____ fair_____ aging_____ poor_____

## BASEMENT AND/OR UTILITY ROOM(S)

**Evidence of water seepage:** yes_____ no_____

    water stains_____ Efflorescence: on walls_____ on floor_____

    swelled floor tiles/joints_____

    peeling and flaking paint on walls_____ corrosion below radiators_____

    Seepage condition extensive: yes_____ no_____

    Sump pump: yes_____ no_____ Dehumidifier needed: yes_____ no_____

                                                                      **Condition**

1. **Foundation walls:** concrete_____ block_____ stone_____ brick_____ other_____;

    cracked_____ reseal_____ cracked and loose mortar joints_____

    repoint_____                       _____

2. **Girders:** wood_____ steel_____ none_____ not visible_____     _____

3. **Joists:** (partially) covered_____ sagging_____     _____

4. **Columns:** wood_____ steel_____ screw jack type_____     _____

5. **Termites:** evidence of_____ no visible evidence_____ conditions conducive to activity_____

ROOM:_____                                                                 **Condition**

  1. **Ceiling/walls:** Cracked: yes_____ no_____ Broken: yes_____ no_____

      Evidence of past leakage: wall_____ ceiling_____ peeling and flaking paint/paper_____

      old layers of paint_____                                                  _____

  2. **Floor:** wood_____ tile_____ concrete_____ carpet_____ other_____

      squeaks_____ slopes_____ sagging_____ refinish_____ torn/chipped_____ loose_____   _____

  3. **Trim:** cracked_____ chipped_____ missing_____                              _____

  4. **Electric outlets:** not observable_____ number_____ should have_____       _____

  5. **Doors:** Exterior:_____ weatherstripped: yes_____ no_____ sliding glass_____   _____

      Interior:_____ cracked_____ chipped_____ broken_____                   _____

  6. **Hardware** (locks, hinges, knobs, handles): missing_____ needs repair_____       _____

  7. **Closets:** yes_____ no_____ number_____                                    _____

  8. **Heating:** radiators_____ baseboard_____ air registers_____ convectors_____   _____

      radiation panels_____ none_____

  9. **Fireplace:** yes_____ no_____ cracked/chipped mortar joints_____ needs cleaning_____

      Damper: missing: yes_____ no_____ needs repair: yes_____ no_____

      indication of backsmoking_____                                             _____

10. **Cabinets/counter:** none_____ kitchen_____ medicine/vanity_____

      cracked_____ chipped_____ loose_____                                  _____

11. **Plumbing fixtures:** yes_____ no_____ leaks_____ Operational: yes_____ no_____

      Water flow: adequate_____ low_____ Drainage: adequate_____ blockage_____

      Regrouting/caulking needed at tub/shower joints: yes_____ no_____         _____

12. **Exhaust fan:** yes_____ no_____ operational_____                           _____

      Comments: _____

ROOM:_____                                                                 **Condition**

  1. **Ceiling/walls:** Cracked: yes_____ no_____ Broken: yes_____ no_____

      Evidence of past leakage: wall_____ ceiling_____ peeling and flaking paint/paper_____

      old layers of paint_____                                                  _____

  2. **Floor:** wood_____ tile_____ concrete_____ carpet_____ other_____

      squeaks_____ slopes_____ sagging_____ refinish_____ torn/chipped_____ loose_____   _____

  3. **Trim:** cracked_____ chipped_____ missing_____                              _____

  4. **Electrical outlets:** not observable_____ number_____ should have_____       _____

  5. **Doors:** Exterior:_____ weatherstripped: yes_____ no_____ sliding glass_____   _____

      Interior:_____ cracked_____ chipped_____ broken_____                   _____

  6. **Hardware** (locks, hinges, knobs, handles): missing_____ needs repair_____       _____

  7. **Closets:** yes_____ no_____ number_____                                    _____

  8. **Heating:** radiators_____ baseboard_____ air registers_____ convectors_____   _____

      radiation panels_____ none_____

  9. **Fireplace:** yes_____ no_____ cracked/chipped mortar joints_____ needs cleaning_____

      Damper: missing: yes_____ no_____ needs repair: yes_____ no_____

      indication of backsmoking_____                                             _____

10. **Cabinets/counter:** none_____ kitchen_____ medicine/vanity_____

      cracked_____ chipped_____ loose_____                                  _____

11. **Plumbing fixtures:** yes_____ no_____ leaks_____ Operational: yes_____ no_____

      Water flow: adequate_____ low_____ Drainage: adequate_____ blockage_____

      Regrouting/caulking needed at tub/shower joints: yes_____ no_____         _____

12. **Exhaust fan:** yes_____ no_____ operational_____                           _____

      Comments: _____

**ROOM:**_____                                                      **Condition**

  1. **Ceiling/walls:** Cracked: yes_____ no_____ Broken: yes_____ no_____

      Evidence of past leakage: wall_____ ceiling_____ peeling and flaking paint/paper_____

      old layers of paint_____                                                      _____

  2. **Floor:** wood_____ tile_____ concrete_____ carpet_____ other_____

      squeaks_____ slopes_____ sagging_____ refinish_____ torn/chipped_____ loose_____   _____

  3. **Trim:** cracked_____ chipped_____ missing_____                         _____

  4. **Electric outlets:** not observable_____ number_____ should have_____   _____

  5. **Doors:** Exterior:_____ weatherstripped: yes_____ no_____ sliding glass_____   _____

      Interior:_____ cracked_____ chipped_____ broken_____         _____

  6. **Hardware** (locks, hinges, knobs, handles): missing_____ needs repair_____   _____

  7. **Closets:** yes_____ no_____ number_____                           _____

  8. **Heating:** radiators_____ baseboard_____ air registers_____ convectors_____

      radiation panels_____ none_____                                    _____

  9. **Fireplace:** yes_____ no_____ cracked/chipped mortar joints_____ needs cleaning_____

      Damper: missing: yes_____ no_____ needs repair: yes_____ no_____

      indication of backsmoking_____                                          _____

10. **Cabinets/counter:** none_____ kitchen_____ medicine/vanity_____

      cracked_____ chipped_____ loose_____                          _____

11. **Plumbing fixtures:** yes_____ no_____ leaks_____ Operational: yes_____ no_____

      Water flow: adequate_____ low_____ Drainage: adequate_____ blockage_____

      Regrouting/caulking needed at tub/shower joints: yes_____ no_____   _____

12. **Exhaust fan:** yes_____ no_____ operational_____                   _____

      **Comments:** _____

**ROOM:**_____                                                      **Condition**

  1. **Ceiling/walls:** Cracked: yes_____ no_____ Broken: yes_____ no_____

      Evidence of past leakage: wall_____ ceiling_____ peeling and flaking paint/paper_____

      old layers of paint_____                                                      _____

  2. **Floor:** wood_____ tile_____ concrete_____ carpet_____ other_____

      squeaks_____ slopes_____ sagging_____ refinish_____ torn/chipped_____ loose_____   _____

  3. **Trim:** cracked_____ chipped_____ missing_____                         _____

  4. **Electrical outlets:** not observable_____ number_____ should have_____   _____

  5. **Doors:** Exterior:_____ weatherstripped: yes_____ no_____ sliding glass_____   _____

      Interior:_____ cracked_____ chipped_____ broken_____         _____

  6. **Hardware** (locks, hinges, knobs, handles): missing_____ needs repair_____   _____

  7. **Closets:** yes_____ no_____ number_____                           _____

  8. **Heating:** radiators_____ baseboard_____ air registers_____ convectors_____

      radiation panels_____ none_____                                    _____

  9. **Fireplace:** yes_____ no_____ cracked/chipped mortar joints_____ needs cleaning_____

      Damper: missing: yes_____ no_____ needs repair: yes_____ no_____

      indication of backsmoking_____                                          _____

10. **Cabinets/counter:** none_____ kitchen_____ medicine/vanity_____

      cracked_____ chipped_____ loose_____                          _____

11. **Plumbing fixtures:** yes_____ no_____ leaks_____ Operational: yes_____ no_____

      Water flow: adequate_____ low_____ Drainage: adequate_____ blockage_____

      Regrouting/caulking needed at tub/shower joints: yes_____ no_____   _____

12. **Exhaust fan:** yes_____ no_____ operational_____                   _____

      **Comments:** _____